PERNICIOUS TOLERANCE

PERNICIOUS TOLERANCE

how teaching to "accept differences" undermines civil society

Robert Weissberg

Transaction Publishers

New Brunswick (U.S.A.) and London (U.K.)

Copyright © 2008 by Transaction Publishers, New Brunswick, New Jersey.

All rights reserved under International and Pan-American Copyright Conventions. No part of this book may be reproduced or transmitted in any form or by any means, electronic or mechanical, including photocopy, recording, or any information storage and retrieval system, without prior permission in writing from the publisher. All inquiries should be addressed to Transaction Publishers, Rutgers—The State University of New Jersey, 35 Berrue Circle, Piscataway, New Jersey 08854-8042. www.transactionpub.com

This book is printed on acid-free paper that meets the American National Standard for Permanence of Paper for Printed Library Materials.

Library of Congress Catalog Number: 2007031976
ISBN: 978-1-4128-0695-4
Printed in the United States of America

Library of Congress Cataloging-in-Publication Data

Weissberg, Robert, 1941
Pernicious tolerance: how teaching to "accept differences" undermines civil society/ Robert Weissberg.
      p. cm.
  Includes bibliographical references and index.
  ISBN 978-1-4128-0695-4 (alk. paper)
  1. Toleration. 2. Toleration—Study and teaching. 3. Pluralism (Social sciences) 4. Difference (Psychology)—Social aspects. 5. Civil society. I. Title.

HM1271.W462007
179'.9—dc22
                                            2007031976

Dedicated to N., the Perfect Child
1977-2004

Contents

Preface

After completing *Political Tolerance: Balancing Community and Diversity* a decade ago, I reasonably assumed that I had exhausted what I might have to say about tolerance. Matters, obviously, have turned out differently. Returning to this topic was almost accidental—a request to contribute a chapter to an anthology, *Tolerance in the Twenty-First Century,* edited by Gerson Moreno-Riaño. In undertaking this task I began noticing a "literature" barely existing years back, namely a steady parade of heartfelt pleas and alleged accomplishments to instruct children about "appreciating differences," all in the name of "tolerance," so as to quell burgeoning "hate." Curiosity aroused, and thanks to modern Web-based technology, I soon uncovered dozens upon dozens of examples of this enterprise, many of which appeared in small-town newspapers or obscure journals directed at classroom teachers. As these accounts multiplied, my reaction was akin to that of savvy New Yorkers (like me) who, upon encountering an occasional cockroach scurrying behind the refrigerator, would rightfully assume that the one or two visible critters indicated hundreds in hiding.

This campaign was evidently part of a much larger, ongoing radical ideological ("culture war") quest to transform America by first capturing education. Endless obsession with homophobia, sexism, racism, and other alleged "hateful" disorders made that conclusion indisputable. What most instigated my ire was not that ideologues were infiltrating schools to gain their ends. Though I reject their aims, politicizing education is certainly permissible (though ultimately unwise) in a democracy. Rather, in pursuing their objectives, radical pedagogues were substituting an incredibly worthy idea—tolerance as enduring the odious—with a fantasy—tolerance as blank-check appreciation of diversity—guaranteed to promote civil strife. This is the equivalent of fighting fire with gasoline, all the while rejecting a proven formula that will bring tranquility at lower costs without creating totalitarian-like Thoughtcrimes.

This oddity, I argue, is explainable only by the primacy of a truly subversive ideological agenda. Put bluntly, today's professional educators risk civic disaster in the hope of achieving legitimacy for those they believe are unfairly marginalized, stigmatized, under-appreciated, or otherwise disdained. That such people are never persecuted by the state, and enjoy ample police protection from harm, all the while often receiving special state-mandated favors, hardly matters to these ideologues. This is a utopian campaign of leveling human accomplishment, a plea to make everything just as worthy as anything else. A "medical" flavor also often infuses this enterprise when putative experts advise grade-school teachers how to help pupils overcome "psychologically damaging" aversions to what is different (e.g., homosexuality). Chalk up another example of twisting learning into misguided therapy.

Despite divergences in subject matter, this book continues from insights initially proposed by Paul Gottfried in his *Multiculturalism and the Politics of Guilt* (2002). Gottfried recognized that today's ever-expanding welfare state is not only concerned with our material being, but, critically, also with our "mental health," defined as beliefs about the vulnerable, i.e., women, various ethnic/racial minorities, homosexuals, and other officially certified "victims" in waiting. This therapeutic state does not stop at imploring "good thinking" as one might tell youngsters to show kindness toward the elderly. It goes much further and *criminalizes* evil thoughts as if thinking poorly of those at-risk is tantamount to inflicting bodily harm. My chapter 5, "Bringing Tolerance by Criminalizing Hate" sadly shows that Gottfried's unease is more than justified—today's criminal code makes "hate" a serious offense. Not even George Orwell would have predicted the relentless legal efforts to probe a mugger's hidden bigotry when he or she actually stole a pocketbook. And, uncovering evidence of "bad thinking" can add years to a criminal sentence totally apart from the crime itself.

There is also substantial collateral damage in this quest for ersatz tolerance: facilitating intellectual sloth while raising anti-intellectualism up to an honored professional norm. Sad to say, teaching this "accept everything" as "tolerance" is the perfect escape for lazy teachers. It certainly outshines imposing classroom discipline or teaching students how to write. That this enterprise comes at a time when American education can ill afford wasting classroom time chasing feel-good ephemera only exacerbates the damage, and mis-education is especially debilitating for the poor unable to escape public education.

At the outset, let me acknowledge the unscientific nature of the data collection underlying my inquiry. I rely on published outcroppings that appear in newspapers, websites, professional journals, and even daily syndicated opinion columns. I have not conducted systematic surveys to assess the prevalence of this new tolerance in schools, nor personally calibrated lesson impact. As I confess in the epilogue, my exposé may be much ado about nothing, though my arguments often rest on solid empirical research conducted by others. Still, possible exaggeration and selection bias aside, I am absolutely convinced that an alarm is worth sounding. The potential hurt is enormous, and to draw a parallel with the introduction of rabbits into Australia, little exists to stop these pernicious ideas from gaining ascendancy. Such empty-calorie "doing good" feasting is all too irresistible in a world where innocuous slights are now "dangerous hate." If recent ideological battles prove anything, it is that foolish, counterproductive nostrums sweeping education often begin life as a bizarre silliness easily dismissed as "too dumb to be taken seriously." Who, fifty years ago, would have predicted flourishing academic fashions such as Queer Studies, Whiteness Studies, Critical Race Theory, and Post-Modernism—let alone the cult of anti-Americanism, and other now academically "respectable" intellectual endeavors whose bizarre messages often filter into classrooms. Unworried skeptics should read chapter 6 to see how kindergarten students now learn about gay marriage. Better to be apprehensive before these views become the entrenched orthodoxy.

Professional pedagogues will not welcome *Pernicious Tolerance*. Their predictable response is that it is a mean-spirited, right-wing polemic endorsing hatefulness. A few will detect half-hidden racism, homophobia, and similar perilous ideas. Surely, they will insist, how could any upstanding, supposedly educated person oppose teaching children to appreciate the world's wondrous diversity? Can't people see the evil of American society, and why should young-sters be shielded from these defects? My assessment of a negative reaction from today's education experts is hardly hypothetical. I have periodically sent draft chapters to scholars and professional educators, and the reaction has been almost complete stone silence save, in one instance, a perfunctory journal form letter rejection. My heresies, obviously, are not worth debating: "everybody" knows that you can never have enough tolerance, so to counsel caution in extending welcomes is even more ludicrous than insisting that the earth is flat. Moreover, to recall Oscar Wilde's quip that socialism will never work because it takes too many evenings, the traditional tolerance that I celebrate—carefully deciding which specific odium deserves suffering—is undoubtedly too arduous for many contemporary educators. Better to just say "yes" to everything demanding respect save, of course, intolerance itself. Why tackle tough intellectual quandaries when there are so many multi-cultural potluck dinners to organize?

Hopefully, *Pernicious Tolerance* will be read by parents and teachers who suspect that something is amiss with endless homilies—like "diversity is our strength" and "we are all the same but different"—infusing today's classrooms. Unfortunately, those uneasy about these clichés are seldom intellectually equipped to discern the underlying ideological agenda and can be easily silenced by reassuring "experts." Only intuitively do they sense the truly subversive (and bogus) nature of the message that, for example, America is seething in hatefulness toward people whose only sin is that they are "different." Optimistically, this exposé will finally permit outraged parents to confront disingenuous ideologues hoping to transform America under the guise of preaching "tolerance." Given the marketplace's need for attention-getting sensationalism, this book could have been titled *An Idiot's Guide to Fighting Today's Radical School-Takeover.*

Book writing is an inherently solitary endeavor, but I would like to thank Nino Languilli and Paul Gottfried for their helpful comments and encouragement. Most of all, as is now becoming an honored custom, I would like to acknowledge the love and forebearance of Erika Gilbert. Those who know what cannot be uttered will understand the full meaning of this thankfulness.

1

Two Tolerance Visions:
From John Locke to PBS

"We strive to include all persons without regard to sexual orientation, race, nationality, gender, family configuration, ethnic background, economic circumstances, difference in ability, culture or age."—Trinity Episcopal Church's Statement of Affirmation, Boston (cited in Ross Mackenzie, "On neckties, race, religion, NFL pat-downs, 24/7 sex, etc." Townhall.com. November 26, 2005).

Every era has its best and worst of times, but for religious souls in Europe during the sixteenth and seventeenth centuries, it was indisputably the worst of times. In contemporary society, where only well-schooled theologians might accurately depict theological quarrels among Christian sects, it is virtually unimaginable that seemingly arcane doctrinal divisions could inspire wholesale slaughter. The Protestant Reformation and the subsequent Catholic Counter-Reformation instigated a parade of bloodbaths, and the viciousness was hardly one-sided or confined to a few villages. Zealots took turns persecuting each other, and when that strife was occasionally inopportune, or religious antagonists were all vanquished, violent attention turned to sectarian cousins. Particularly as denominations proliferated following the Reformation, even miniscule disputes invited suppression. Some denominations compelled Bible reading as the path to heaven; elsewhere Bible possession was a crime, and owners were, with great fanfare, gruesomely dispatched to the hereafter.

A modest sampling might prove enlightening, given that this mayhem has largely receded from memory. Beginning on August 24, 1572, at the instigation of Catherine de Medici, the Catholic queen mother of Henry of Navarre, political intrigue coupled with avarice prompted what is now called the St. Bartholomew's Day Massacre. From August to October of 1572, Catholics, often spontaneously but also directed from above, enthusiastically murdered Huguenots (French Protestants, many of whom were wealthy) by the thousands, including entire families. Estimates range from 30,000 to 70,000 killed, and contemporary accounts describe rivers so overflowing with rotting corpses that fish became inedible. Countless Huguenots fled France, many never to return. Pope Gregory XIII, so enraptured by this bloody religious fervor, ordered Rome's church bells rung for an entire day while special commemorative medals honored the occasion. Huguenots meanwhile returned the barbarism and cruelly butchered thousands of Catholics. Peace eventually returned, but only as a truce—in 1685 violent prosecution of the Huguenots began anew, and with similarly brutal carnage.

The St. Bartholomew's Day Massacre was, however, just a prelude. The Thirty Years' War (1618-1648) involved nearly every continental country, punctuated by shifting alliances, generally pitting Catholics against Protestants, though multiple other quarrels intruded. Battles occurred largely on German soil, and the death toll from both the war itself and subsequent diseases (notably bubonic plague and typhus) and famine was devastating. Estimates of the German population loss range from 15 percent to 30 percent, and these figures are in addition to widespread rape, killing of animals, pillaging, and the destruction of schools and churches. The state of Württemberg's population declined from 400,000 to 48,000, and such desolation was commonplace. This religiously inspired chaos probably set German civilization back 200 years. Hostilities ceased in 1648 with the Treaty of Westphalia (though France and Spain battled on for another decade) which stipulated that princes could determine their subjects' religion, whether Catholic or Protestant.

England, too, experienced continuous religious discord during this era, periodically erupting into full-fledged civil war, and the twists and turns virtually guaranteed that today's pious souls would be tomorrow's persecuted heretics. Matters began in 1531 when Henry VIII, personally a faithful Catholic, abrogated the pope's religious authority in England so as to dissolve his union with Catherine of Aragon to marry Anne Boleyn. With Henry's Church of England formally established in 1534, religious opposition was outlawed, and dissidents were often burnt at the stake side by side: Catholics on one side, Lutherans on the other. Subsequent monarchs, whether Protestant or Catholic, imposed their spiritual orthodoxy and, in varying degrees, forcefully insisted on national uniformity. Religion soon resembled quick-changing fashion, but who could foretell the latest monarch's creed, so inattention literally risked life and limb. Queen Mary (who reigned from 1553-1558) was especially energetic in executing Protestants (hence the nickname, "Bloody Mary"); under Queen Elizabeth I who followed Mary, it was the Catholics who lived in fear. In this tumultuous context, holding a "generous" view of religious difference might mean permitting a chosen handful of not-too-different dissenters to worship freely, but only if they first obtained a license, took oaths of allegiances, all the while being barred from public office. The Toleration Act of May 27, 1689 did, in fact, permit this guarded acceptance, and was celebrated for calming civil discord.

John Locke and Religious Toleration

In the winter of 1685, the English doctor and philosopher, John Locke, then exiled in Amsterdam, hiding under an assumed name to avoid persecution in England for endorsing greater religious freedom, wrote *Epistola de Tolerantia*

("A Letter Concerning Toleration") to his friend, Philip von Limborch. Composed in Latin, with authorship only hinted at by obscure cryptic letters, the missive was so controversial by the era's standards that Locke never fully acknowledged his authorship, though this paternity was eventually recognized. Published anonymously in the Dutch city of Gouda four years after its completion, and translated into English by William Popple, it was smuggled into England in 1689. By today's hyper-generous standards of permissibility, it is, as we shall see, incredibly mild-mannered, but in its day it was widely denounced as extreme, opening the door to religious anarchy. A few fervent Protestants denounced the "Letter" as a Jesuit plot to restore papal domination, though Locke himself was a devoted Church of England follower.

Locke, to be sure, was not the period's sole champion of religious tolerance, and this single appeal scarcely exhausted his views—he published two additional tolerance letters, portions of a fourth (unfinished due to his death in 1704), plus countless rejoinders to critics. And, admittedly, his earlier pronouncements were quite different. Still, this first "Letter" ranks among *the* classic defenses of tolerance, and to this day remains a compelling, and still relevant, benchmark for those hoping to quell civil discord. What is important for our purposes is how this justification, authored by a refugee from religious persecution, who personally risked his life for a modicum of religious freedom, differs from many of today's more spirited, far more encompassing admonitions. To compare Locke's pleas to today's tolerance admonitions demonstrates just how far this undertaking has shifted and, as we shall see, this change is deceptively momentous, and new may not be "new and improved." Perhaps writing under the imminent threat of death in exile, versus enjoying the luxury of unchallenged permissiveness encourages sensible thinking.

Locke was principally concerned with reducing, but not eliminating, the Crown's (or Parliament's) religious meddling. Officialdom, with its power to punish, even kill those who disagreed, required hobbling. By contrast, the religious fanatic intent on mayhem was less troublesome for he or she was subject to the criminal code. Nor was this a plea for some sweeping abstract religious equality, or a separation of Church and State (Locke to a degree accepted an official religion); the aim was merely to end vigorous state repression of Quakers, Presbyterians, Baptists, and other "non-conforming" Protestant religious bodies. And this assault was serious: sect members—about 10 percent of England's population—often paid fines, had property confiscated, and so lost their livelihoods while thousands rotted in hellholes solely because they rejected the official Church of England faith. This war on heresy had even instigated political rebellion in 1661, 1663, and 1685, and the prospect of future bloody civil wars over doctrinal disputes was ever present.

Locke's solution rested on civil government disregarding the outward signs of religious devotion, including matters of theology and internal church administration where the state lacked a compelling interest. A division of labor would bring calm: government would decide lawful behavior, even public morality, so as to promote its principle purpose—peace and security—while churches, with their own particular ceremonies and conventions, attended to their principle purpose—saving souls. For the Sovereign or Parliament to agree with every noxious religion in every aspect was unnecessary; Locke only argued that at least some dissenting dogmas and practices must be stomached since the alternative—perpetual civil chaos—was far worse. Why should the king fulminate about trifling details of ritual provided adherents heeded the law? Surely God had not granted the king or any other civil official power to adjudicate theological veracity, and the people themselves had not ceded this authority to rulers. Nor could king or Parliament discover the one true pathway to salvation and thereby justify imposing a single faith. Let church officials or congregants wrestle with such mysterious disputes, and if the religiously observant insisted upon disobeying the law, they should be willing to suffer the punishment. Furthermore, if these unorthodox rituals and customs displease divine authority, it is He, not the magistrate, who will punish miscreants in the hereafter. At most, admonitions and advice by fellow congregants might sway errant churchgoers, but legal punishment could only rile civil society.

Establishing tolerance was a practical matter. Locke held that it was futile for the king or Parliament to try and discern what people genuinely believed, and this inner faith was all that ultimately mattered in the eyes of God. Lying about one's true faith had existed since time immemorial, hypocrisy was everywhere, and not even torture could be trusted to expose true conviction. Religion could only be voluntary, and while the state might encourage conversion, even rightly ban abhorrent church practices (e.g., human sacrifice) as inimical to civil decorum, pushing further went nowhere. Moreover, since history clearly showed that a proclivity towards proliferating faiths was quintessentially human, and that fracturing was not subject to reasoned argument, no single "true" faith could triumph except by brute force. Even then, this triumph would be only momentary, schisms were irrepressible regardless of repression. To repeat, religious toleration was a *practical* tactic involving putting up with certain noxious religious practices, to avoid endless carnage, save where such exercises contradicted civil society.

By today's standards, Locke's appeal is quite limited, almost feeble. Tolerance narrowly concerned faith, not all matters about which people disagreed. This kindness was, moreover, less a sign of one's virtue than a concession to harsh reality: one suffered the disagreeable since the alternative—violence—was even worse. Its agenda was equally modest: only matters of dogma. Passionate racial and ethnic animosities certainly existed in Locke's day. Homosexuals were prosecuted, a few were even killed, but these antagonisms paled in comparison to religious strife. And, as we shall eventually see, even on religious matters Locke was stingy—some, like the Roman Catholics, *deserved* suppression in light of their untrustworthy political allegiances. Jews and atheists were likewise abhorrent. Tolerance was also essentially negative—rulers must resist despotic urges, not accommodate, let alone praise, deviants, and even then, acquiescence was not carte blanche. Constructing some grand social utopia was absolutely not on the agenda.

Tolerance Three Hundred Years Later: PBS Extols Tolerance

Fast-forwarding to the beginning of the twenty-first century, we find, happily, that the kind of religious atrocities that left millions dead no longer plague Western civilization. Militant Islam is the notable exception, but even here, casualties pall by comparison. Virtually no one can accurately recall what the Spanish Inquisition sought, let alone the very idea of torturing religious heretics so as to please God. Holy wars still exist, as one can witness from Middle East news report, but at least in the United States, Europe, and much of the rest of the world, heretics no longer face immolation, and unorthodox sects hardly require licenses to practice their faith. Nor, blissfully, has any other division replaced religion as the source of deadly civil strife. Racial and ethnic disputes are largely peacefully fought politically though, admittedly, violent eruptions do occur. Losers now lose lawsuits or legislative battles, not their lives. There is nothing, absolutely nothing, in today's society that even remotely compares to Europe's sixteenth- and seventeenth-century carnage. Even the kookiest sects reside in peace unless they violate the criminal code.

Alas, 9/11 would again push religious tolerance to the forefront. The possibility that a handful of American Muslims might give their political allegiance to those seeking America's destruction, and are secretly plotting to overthrow the constitution and replace it with a Muslim theocracy oddly echoes Locke's seventeenth-century unease with Roman Catholics. Catholics, Locke argued, were subversive agents of the pope, of the French and Spanish kings scheming to topple England's Protestant regime, not just another sect deserving admission to civic life. Sedition justified exclusion, and this went to the heart of Catholicism given obligatory Catholic fidelity to an Italian pope.

Without reawakening the bloodshed of past centuries, how, then, should Americans confront this alleged Muslim enemy in our midst? Do we resurrect Locke and draw a sharp line between theological issues in which government has no compelling interest (e.g., which Muslim splinter sects best honor the Prophet's message) and instead confront only those plotting terrorism? Or, might Washington intrude further into the Muslim faith on the grounds that it is the theology itself, (e.g., the Koran's embrace of *jihad* and forced conversion) that comprises the true threat? If plunging into Islam itself is necessary to protect the peace, then toleration must be cautiously selective, a situation reminiscent of how the federal government wrestled with the Mormon faith in the nineteenth century: prohibiting polygamy while ignoring religious tenets antithetical to mainstream Christianity. Navigating these tolerance perplexities is, obviously, exceedingly demanding and quandaries are almost endless.

Into this thicket of possibilities comes a tolerance lesson plan ("Tolerance in Times of Trial") developed by the Public Broadcasting Service (PBS) aimed at middle and high school students. This is not a tightly argued philosophical treatise akin to Locke's "Letter." This plea is sufficiently simple for middle and high school students and their teachers. As such, no responsibility extents to confronting complicated disputes or offering sophisticated nostrums. Still, like Locke's missive, it is, despite its brevity, a far-ranging solution to a palpable problem, i.e., how to confront, if at all, a religion in which many adherents preach a violent hatred of America both at home and worldwide. More is involved here than just acknowledging the "current events" that relate to the post-9/11 world. Chapter 3 will show, this PBS design is emblematic of dozens of similar ventures comprising a vast "tolerance industry" permeating America's schools and thus illustrates a more pervasive transformation of "tolerance."

To appreciate this particular remedy's character, consider other potential menu items for post-9/11 pedagogy. For example, teachers could instruct students that abstract Islam, like other major world religions, warrants unqualified toleration but, that conceded, any anti-Americanism requires stern reprobation. Or, lessons could carefully separate "good" from "bad" Islamic theology, to wit, espousing Islam's roots in the Judeo-Christian ethos is commendable, but the Koran's message about killing polytheistic heretics deserves rejection. Or the Muslim threat could be skipped altogether as inappropriate for classroom discussion, a predicament better taken up by elected leaders, not ignorant teenagers or untrained educators. Conceivably, lessons could be practical anti-terrorism training: how to spot suspicious activity and what government agencies to contact. Finally, teachers might simply remind students that personal anger aside, vigilantism is illegal—leave fighting subversion to the police.

Compared to Locke's modest admonitions, this PBS lesson plan is far more ambitious, if not revolutionary, in its sweep. Most plainly, the PBS framework envisions tolerance as centrally pertaining to individuals themselves, even at a tender age, not to a potentially repressive government. Whereas Locke (realistically) agonized over preventing kings from ordering heretics burnt at the stake, here the apprehension is over millions of youngsters, most of whom lack any contact with practicing Muslims, possibly abusing Muslims. This is a huge endeavor. The emphasis, and again diametrically opposed to Locke's counsel, is *exclusively* on refashioning private attitudes and feelings (hate), not learning to control impulsive, possibly illegal behavior. Instilling tolerance is thus preventive, and is rooted in a particular psychological theory regarding the centrality of attitudes in foretelling actions. Simply put, tens of millions must exhibit "good thinking" if the world is to escape the religious carnage of yesteryear.

Since inner thoughts are the chief culprits of civil discord, lessons naturally demand expelling any, no matter how slight, aversion towards Muslims. This is not merely an admonition to "stop scheming to harm them." Rather, the tolerance message is "don't even think unkindly about them." Students thus are counseled against glibly associating the label "terrorist" with "Arab" or "Muslim." Students further learn that blood-boiling TV footage following 9/11, that is, Palestinians publicly cheering the twin towers collapse, were atypical Middle Eastern reactions. Meanwhile, teachers are encouraged to explain how movies like *The Siege* or *True Lies* falsely link Arabs to terrorism. Also advised are field trips to places of worship, art exhibitions, and similar educational exposures that help breakdown negative ethnic stereotypes. A website link to an MSNBC story recounting how Arabs felt threatened post-9/11 further reiterates the point that Muslims require protection from awaiting mayhem. That humdrum criminal sanction, laws against assault, for example, not reshaped attitudes, might better inhibit aggressive behavior (as well as less violent discrimination, harassment and the like) passes totally unnoticed.

That government, not ordinary citizens, plausibly poses the greatest danger to those expressing heretical views receives short shrift. Conceivably, instruction could have celebrated America's traditional commitment to limited government, rule of law, the sanctity of private religious beliefs, the potential troubles associated with expanded emergency police power, and strategies for curtailing unwelcome state intrusion. In this alternative tolerance pedagogical vision, ordinary people, perhaps by resisting media-hyped hysteria or voting against hate-mongering demagogues, serve as a bulwark against officially sponsored repression since, as we have already said, impromptu, bottom-up tyranny (e.g., torching mosques) is already legally prohibited (and there is little doubt that these protective laws will be enforced).

Significantly, when the specter of government-led repression does surface, it has zero to do with checking any impending, officially sanctioned threats to Muslims. Instead, PBS supplies this threat of imminent harm by resurrecting a dimly remembered, sixty-year-old event, specifically the federal government's World War II treatment of people of Japanese and German ancestry—internment camps, xenophobic war effort propaganda, and the like. Teachers even "personalize" this internment by asking students to write diaries as if they were imprisoned in these camps. One can only assume that this history excursion intends to alert—even frighten—students that without a tolerance-loving citizenry America might slide into tyranny, that is ship innocent, demonized Muslims to internment camps.

What is revealing about this brief historical foray is its total historical irrelevance and, to anticipate a point we shall make repeatedly, its resurrection demonstrates how tolerance devotees consciously twist reality to advance an ideological agenda. This is, to be frank, factually incorrect mis-education, if not propaganda, albeit for what seems a high-minded purpose. Some simple fact checking will show that this internment did not arise from outside-the-law popular hysteria as is suggested in this PBS account. It was absolutely legal. Roosevelt's Executive Order 9066 ordering the internment was issued pursuant to the Alien Enemies Act, and was signed after carefully considering other options. The U.S. Supreme Court upheld his action in 1944 as a wartime necessity.

Equally relevant, though historians disagree on evaluating the evidence, little question exists that sabotage and spying by west coast residents of Japanese ancestry *was* a genuine threat, if not an actuality in light of captured documents and confessions. Japanese submarines had shelled California oil refineries, and other attacks were expected. Many of those relocated held dual U.S.-Japanese citizenship (which demanded loyalty to Japan in wartime). Meanwhile, military intelligence had tracked extensive Japanese efforts to recruit spies among those of Japanese ancestry, several west coast Japanese newspapers were adamantly pro-Japanese and the U.S. was relatively defenseless against internal threats when internment was implemented. That this serious threat was not publicized had more to do with protecting counter-intelligence success in cracking Japanese codes than a lack of proof (see Malkin 2004 for additional justifications). If this is not convincing, recall that events in Europe had clearly showed the dangers of a "Fifth Column."

What this incomplete, lopsided PBS account offers is group victimization, not a balanced argument that, perhaps, these measures were just too heavy-handed and ineffectual. In a peculiar non-sequitur, this PBS tale announces that employment discrimination against those of German and Japanese ancestry—not potential as enemy spies or saboteurs—set the stage for mistreatment (actually, it was the employment of Japanese Americans in sensitive areas that made internment especially pressing). In the eyes of these PBS "historians," wartime policies receive condemnation since they harmed distinctive ethnic/racial minorities; that they unnecessarily over-extended state authority apart from the victims' identities is probably inconceivable. That is, since those who differ on race or ethnicity (assumedly) enjoy extra-special protection, these wartime actions were inherently odious. That internments and propaganda efforts were legal, implemented by democratically accountable officials, and based upon reasonable military intelligence, remains beyond discussion—victim ethnic traits are what counts in navigating tolerance quandaries.

Further infusing the lesson plan is the unchallenged assumption that the group today deserving tolerance, that is, Muslims, is totally blameless (just as those of Japanese or German ancestry were complete innocents during World War II). To be sure, establishing culpability would be an arduous quest, and may well be beyond what is possible in classrooms. Nevertheless, such complexity hardly warrants an unqualified "not guilty" verdict, and the PBS staff is certainly capable of doing the required research. Surely it would not be mean-spirited to admit that perhaps some Muslims are guilty, or that certain elements of Muslim dogma deserve reprimand.

Equally noteworthy is the unsupported supposition that ordinary Muslims residing in the U.S. are sufficiently seriously at risk that allocating considerable classroom time to heading off this catastrophe is justified. At most, a diligent teacher might recount to a small scattering of minor incidents whose veracity remains legally unproven, if not murky (chapter 5 will in fact show that many of these initial claims were bogus). Of the utmost importance, these anxiety-generating attacks are certainly a far cry from past religious persecution, let alone state repression, in which thousands died daily. In fact, according to the FBI, for all of 2001 there were only 481 anti-Muslim hate incidents versus some 1,374 anti-religious incidents directed against Jews ("FBI: Racial prejudice top factor in hate crime" http://msnbc.msn.com/id/10042601/). These PBS experts just assumed that since the terrorists responsible for 9/11 were Muslims, Muslims would shortly be persecuted en mass, and educators (not police) must to guard against this forthcoming mob-led reign of terror—a modern-day St. Bartholomew's Day Massacre in the making, so to speak, to be thwarted by public radio and TV.

Where the Lockean and PBS versions sharply diverge is the scope of tolerance. Recall that Locke was solely concerned with permitting specific Protestants religious liberty to espouse a limited menu of heretical views, and this graciousness would *not* include full civil freedom. Nor was Locke upset over repressing homosexuals, foreigners, the disabled, etc. etc, who suffered society's forceful displeasure. By contrast, the PBS lesson is generous to the point of eschewing boundaries altogether. An infatuation with "diversity" and calls to banish stereotypes make graciousness indisputable—the welcome mat is out for everyone, no questions asked. Though "diversity" is mentioned eight times, diversity of what (e.g., ideological? theological? racial? socio-economic?) is unspecified. Vagueness also applies when identifying those groups, beyond Muslims, who might be at-risk from intolerance. Those potentially in jeopardy are merely "minority groups" or just "some groups." One could reasonably surmise that all human variations deserve tolerance, even if proclivities entail risky behavior (e.g., the obese, smokers). When all is said and done, students learn that different groups and minorities require acceptance sans any details, a graciousness light years distant from Locke's cautious, narrow plea.

Competing Appeals

These two visions are poles apart, and it is pointless to insist that one is "better" or "worse" than the other in some grand beauty pageant. Nonetheless, it is indisputable that when it comes to attracting modern-day tolerance crusaders, PBS-style pleas far outdraw Locke's more restrained prescription. At least to pedagogues devising classroom messages, broadening probably appears as a natural evolution, a sign of progress akin to the advancement of modern medicine. This contemporary embrace coupled with the total abandonment of the Lockean view should come as no surprise in today's cultural milieu where openness to "differences" seems the ultimate virtue. The PBS vision is a universal one, equally applicable to gays, the disabled, the destitute, those with controversial lifestyles, eccentrics, screwballs, or just about any group or person demanding acceptance. It further avoids all the opprobrium associated with being judgmental, let alone practicing discrimination against those who are disadvantaged, unfortunate, or might superficially appear unsavory. This across-the-board agreeableness is no small virtue in a society where banishing the disagreeable can bring contentious litigation. Overall, the PBS pedagogy (and countless similar prescriptions) invokes the upbeat image of one big non-antagonistic family, each member unique but still a valuable part of the human race, and who could argue with that alluring picture?

The stress on welcoming, not rejecting, would also appear to be a practical recipe for tranquility, if not for ending hate, at least in today's zeitgeist. The legal code with its anti-discrimination strictures plus countless accommodation requirements certainly reflects this inclusion-will-mitigate-conflict framework. Even apart from legal requirements, everyday terms like "marginalizing," "ostracizing," or "prohibiting" now possess an unsavory flavor and are clearly outshone by, say, "appreciating" or "being hospitable." This is a momentous, though rarely recognized shift in thinking from past eras when "differences" of almost any stripe—religion, language, ethnicity—were generally perceived as provoking civil dissension. In today's moral atmosphere, then, Locke's restrictive standards, his willingness to exclude dozens of prominent sects, let alone condemn those of unconventional sexuality and morality, seems almost mean-spirited, a narrow-mined recipe for making untold people feel undeservedly scorned. And, such scorned people cause trouble, and who wants trouble? Put generally, Locke saw divisions as troublesome but inescapable so there must be some limited tolerance; according to PBS, on the other hand, differences are not only inevitable, but they deserve a robust welcome, and the more the merrier.

These visions also differ in their intellectual demands. PBS's lesson plan—just celebrate diversity, banish stereotypes—is uncomplicated, readily grasped advice. Its inexactitude if not its total lack of boundaries regarding exactly who deserves welcoming further simplifies. Indeed, in this gracious perspective those insisting upon imposing distinctions regarding potentially unwelcome diversity (e.g., interrogating people of Japanese ancestry during World War II to uncover possible treason) only adds arduousness in addition to raising the specter of wicked intolerance. By contrast, following Locke demands assembling evidence, case by case, will surely overburden hurried students and teachers. And who wants to make schooling any more tedious, especially when lessons elsewhere are so burdensome? One can only imagine students and teachers wrestling with distinctions between abstract Islamic doctrine and its violence-laden interpretation by radical offshoots. Or the entire issue of collective guilt. In any case, delving into these quandaries is tough work, and tomorrow's events could change everything, so it is just easier to say, "always cherish differences."

The upshot in this "battle of visions" is that, thanks to countless professional educators and likeminded advocates, this easy-to-embrace PBS tolerance plan (and dozens of equivalent versions) quickly and invisibly triumphs. This achievement is consequential far beyond scholarly debates: tens of thousands of students yearly learn to celebrate tolerance, and that this newly interpreted virtue now means appreciating freshly discovered diversity, banishing innumerable dangerous stereotypes, and otherwise thinking "good thoughts" about those who might pose dangers. It is difficult to challenge this message, even raise modest objections, since expelling all the antagonisms plaguing American society is doubtless a praiseworthy aim. At worst, idealistic educators are only squandering a few hours per week to improve the world, and such instruction, it would seem, certainly cannot hurt. No wonder that these tolerance advocates confidently march onward, one classroom after another, with only a handful of Christian fundamentalists far beyond the educational mainstream resisting.

A Different View

The analysis presented here sternly rejects this burgeoning "tolerance means celebrating diversity" perspective and instead advises returning to the more modest Lockean vision though, obviously, Locke's views can only be adapted to contemporary issues, not mechanically applied to quarrels unimaginable centuries back. Rejection is largely practical: intentions aside, this facile "embrace differences" tolerance update cannot achieve tranquility nor cool any antagonisms. It is, moreover, a deceptively bogus, pernicious solution to problems better addressed by other means. It will probably exacerbate strife, and those who loathe America or want to stir the pot of racial animosities will not mend their ways if only we respect their cultures. Nor will schools become more peaceful by instructing students that there is no good or bad, just enviable differences.

The cost of PBS-like projects far outweigh squandering untold hours of classroom time when many students remain illiterate. Students absorbing these intellectually shallow lessons will lose their capacity for navigating tough moral dilemmas. Whatever the character of the latest arrival, whether virtuous or noxious, there will be a lazy proclivity to accept unconditionally since to exclude is to display the dreaded intolerance. There are also costs to schools over and above neglecting more important academic subjects. At least some parents alarmed at what arrives with this easy embrace will withdraw their children from schools rather than permit indoctrination of the underlying moral relativism. School administrators must also defend these divisive embraces at a time when support for public education is receding. The venerable adage that the road to hell is paved with good intentions indisputably applies here.

Challenging this contemporary tolerance enterprise is, we admit, no easy task given that contemporary educators seem totally infatuated by it while countless parents are easily seduced by any scheme that promises to "do good." More is required than just disagreeing—the entire enterprise must be attacked assumption by assumption, datum by datum, while faulty arguments and their shoddy intellectual underpinnings are brought to light. Chapter 2 begins our sacrilegious endeavor by addressing complicated issues blithely evaded by those preaching glib accept differences tolerance. We begin by explicating varied conceptions of "tolerance" to show that what today's educator-led embrace proposes is but one of many conceptual possibilities. This is not tolerance; it is only one of several different understandings of the term, and hardly the most useful. We then move on to dilemmas afflicting any tolerance promotion effort, for example, dealing with thin-skinned people who chronically feel unappreciated regardless of welcoming efforts. Does this hypersensitivity to alleged slights guarantee permanent intolerance? Similarly, how much coercion, and of what type, is permissible in a democracy to achieve tolerance? And who decides *precisely* what deserves tolerance? Are, for example, education experts authorized to determine that militant black civil rights organizations, but not the Ku Klux Klan, warrant appreciation? Such quandaries are conveniently slighted when extolling the benefits of tolerance to ninth graders, but such avoidance hardly resolves these perplexities.

Chapter 3 samples in detail what professional educators advance under the "promoting tolerance" banner. Our PBS example is but one outcropping in an energetic enterprise of lesson plans, workshops, and freely distributed reading materials that have already deeply penetrated classrooms. Sadly, this pedagogy often offers a highly unrealistic, if not bizarre, view of the world in the name of "promoting tolerance." "Mis-education" is a more accurate depiction of this hectoring.

The quest to achieve tranquility is doomed at the onset, though this does not mean that the enterprise is without consequences. Chapter 4 argues that the project's intrinsic nature, its need to refurbish millions of attitudes, invites failure. Youngsters may lack the intellectual maturity necessary to grasp the complexity of tolerance and, of the utmost importance, "appreciate differences" messages can easily be resisted by both parents and the children themselves. These messages are also so muddled and mired in contradictions that they will be unfathomable to those peeking below glib generalities. Moreover, to be effective, this instruction must be all-encompassing, and it is beyond belief to suppose that the hateful will mend their loathsome ways if only sufficiently admonished by public school teachers. There are better ways to constrain the dangerous fanatic.

Chapter 5 singles out one particularly prominent feature of this instruction, namely battling hate via the criminal code. Insofar as hatefulness toward differences is deeply ingrained in human nature, this quest for "hate free" humans is truly revolutionary. Not even the Soviet Union could refurbish human nature, and democratic societies are far more constrained when embracing social engineering as the pathway to betterment. It is also, we argue, an unnecessary campaign—comparable benefits are achievable at far less cost simply by focusing on outward behavior, not inner thought.

The futility of this expensive pursuit raises questions about whether achieving tolerance is the endeavor's authentic aim. Chapter 6 argues that the quest has multiple agendas, including legitimizing plain old-fashioned sloth. More important, a radical ideological agenda likely often lurks behind all high-sounding "appreciating diversity brings peace" rhetoric. Scanning lesson plan specifics shows that graciousness is selective—only those residing on the political spectrum's left side appear to deserve tolerance. Even those in primary school learn, for example, that they should appreciate gays and civil rights groups but there is silence when it comes to fundamentalist Christians or the military. Liberal proselytizing need not, however, bring the hoped for tranquility and often engenders the very divisiveness it is supposed to eliminate.

A brief epilogue observes that the quest to eliminate alleged harm via promoting the acceptance of "differences" is futile. People will always feel slighted, demeaned, or stigmatized. More important, this brand of tolerance is a flight from drawing communal boundaries at time when the very idea of a United States, defined by common values, is under assault. Students taught that nothing is better than anything else, only "different" are rendered incapable of defending *any* value, and this stance can only create mayhem. The stakes here are momentous—in the name of inculcating tolerance, millions of impressionable children are indoctrinated into a multicultural flavored moral relativism that will eventually render them incapable of resisting truly subversive ideas. Refusing to make choices only guarantees weakness in defending against what is dangerous. If it is mean-spirited and "exclusionary" to condemn clearly dangerous drug addiction, how can we argue with those who insist that liberal democracy itself deserve extermination? Defending a democratic civil society requires certain habits of mind, a willingness to make distinctions, and a refusal to separate good from evil is not part of any sturdy defense. In the final analysis, this bogus "new and improved" tolerance can only weaken our communal ties, and such weakness will produce the very opposite of what its devotees desire.

2

Some Arduous Choices
on the Road to Social Harmony

"I don't think we know what tolerance is."—Carol Quillen, director of the Boniuk Center for Study and Advancement of Religious Tolerance at Rice University (cited in the Houston Chronicle, May 22, 2004).

Achieving tolerance requires more than heartfelt admonitions. This quest is an enormous undertaking, and if there is a guaranteed blueprint for success, it remains undiscovered. Even when universally endorsed, and immense resources are marshaled, daunting choices remain. Surprisingly little consensus exists on what precisely tolerance entails, how clashes with other equally worthy values are to be resolved, or who decides these and countless other disputes. Impediments are hardly hidden. An immense body of scholarship wrestles with these problems, and while precise agreement is rare, impasses are plain to see. Unfortunately, today's tolerance-infatuated educators blithely ignore tribulations, perhaps believing that everything is settled or that they are just too time consuming in a world in turmoil. Such obliviousness, intellectual shallowness to be blunt, invites yet one more educational fiasco, the blind leading the blind into bewilderment and worse.

Here we delve into uncertainties that require resolution *before* launching any tolerance crusade. We begin by exploring the multiple meanings "tolerance" has acquired over centuries and show that far-reaching definitional disputes still remain. We also show that promoting peacefulness does not necessarily demand sizable educational investments. Alternatives exist to quelling unrest by refurbishing attitudes, and other options deserve careful attention. Tolerance and intolerance are, moreover, loosely used concepts, and what stands behind these terms can vary by historic circumstances and personal inclination, so that what once passed as "tolerance" may now be construed as "hate." We then consider the coercive element that inevitably surfaces when instructing forbearance, a predicament particularly relevant for educators since students can scarcely resist indoctrination. Can we force students, or anybody for that matter, to bestow tolerance on people or ideas they dimly grasp? An especially troubling tolerance-related theme concerns limits. It is preposterous to accept *everything*. Where should lines be drawn, and equally germane, who possesses this authority? While this predicament is undoubtedly beyond a permanent resolution, as a practical matter it *will* be settled, somebody has to decide. The only question is who actually wields this power. We conclude with an overview of questions that must be tackled before launching any tolerance crusade.

Defining "Tolerance"

What does one do, precisely, when displaying tolerance? This is a deceptively complicated question, but not a surprising one given centuries of contentious use. Yet it deserves scrutiny lest, like the proverbial blind men describing the elephant, we talk past one another. More is involved here than comparing dictionary entries to certify proper usage. Competing definitions all arrive with implicit ideological baggage and, as we shall see when examining how educators concretely apply this term, "capturing" tolerance is a great prize in today's political battles.

Combing historical scholarship hardly offers a single, authoritative answer. As Ingrid Creppell's (2003, *x*) historical overview concluded, "A language of toleration is a collection of ideas, terms, conceptions, reasons, examples, stories, theories and linkages that have been elaborated to address problems of conflict, differences and disagreement." A scholarly review drawn from modern sociology (where definitional precision might be assumed) lamented that "The concept of tolerance is in a state of disarray.... The tolerance label is typically pasted over conglomerate indices of attitudes, opinions, behaviors and beliefs which assume some unspecified definition of tolerance" (Ferrar 1976, 63).

Variety acknowledged, we certainly cannot fault educators (or anyone else) for selecting the "wrong" understanding. Consequences must guide choices—having elected one alternative framework over rivals, where does one wind up? To appreciate this outcome, briefly consider what we call "classic tolerance," roughly Locke's view depicted in chapter 1, with today's educator-devised pathway exemplified by what the PBS lesson plan extolled. Again, this is not a beauty contest or a search for a Platonic reality; inquiry concerns effectively pursuing an assumed worthy aim—a more accommodating society—within distinct conceptual contexts.

"Classic tolerance" derives from the term's Latin roots—*tolerare* or *tolerantia*—the first the verb meaning, "to forbear" the second the noun denoting "forbearance." One "puts up with" the objectionable—one extends acceptance, but only grudgingly. An ability to live with pain (assumed to be distasteful) reflects this understanding. This cosmology thus consists of (1) what is appreciated; (2) what is insufferably loathed (the intolerable); and, falling between these; (3) what is disdained *but* not so strongly as to be beyond acquiescence (the tolerated). One now half-century old tract put it nicely: "...Tolerance is a Halfway House between bigotry and brotherhood" (Wise, nd). Nothing here implies that bearing the objectionable (tolerance) is somehow morally inferior to unqualified appreciation; indeed, it is arguable that stomaching the despicable helps sustain civil society, and embracing the cherished is effortless, and therefore hardly praiseworthy.

An even less-demanding version of classically understood tolerance is what Oberdiek (2001, 29-30) calls "mere toleration." This is encapsulated by commonplace slogans such as "live and let live," or "you go your way, I'll go mine." Adherents of this view tolerate the disagreeable to the extent that it is personally irrelevant, if not out of sight, a trifling sideshow, and comes close to indifference. Even if the disliked person engaged in self-destructive behavior (e.g., drug abuse), the merely tolerant would say, "It's their funeral." Needless to say, this "weak" version is unlikely to draw heartfelt appreciation from today's ardent tolerance champions ("it's just too easy"), but as a remedy to cool bitter antagonisms it has undoubtedly saved millions of lives.

This tripartite framework by its nature requires navigating specific, complicated circumstances. Locke's "Letter" certainly reflected the particular disputes of his day when he distinguished certain (but not all) politically troublesome dissenting Protestant sects worthy of tolerance versus, most plainly, Roman Catholics who deserved banishment given their alleged disloyalty to England. It would thus be pointless to speak of Locke tolerating his beloved Anglican Church. J.S. Mill (1947) similarly embraced this tripartite division and, for example, deemed a loathsome opinion as something that deserved tolerance versus inflaming a mob with provocative language, an intolerable act.

Of the utmost importance, classic tolerance inescapably connects "tolerance" to a *negative* judgment. The tolerant eschews neutrality. Philosophers routinely acknowledged this with the terse, "the paradox of tolerance." T. M. Scanlon (1996) put it succinctly: "Tolerance requires us to accept people and permit their practices even when we strongly disapprove of them." John Gray is even more forceful: "…our tolerance for our friends' vices makes them no less vices in our eyes; rather, our tolerance *presupposes* that they are vices" (Gray 1992, italics in original). Joshua Halberstam (1982-83) further adds that the stronger the disagreement, the greater the tolerance if the disagreeable is suffered. Refusing to pronounce regarding vices may or may not be commendable, but this is *not* tolerance. Bestowing tolerance on, say, homosexuality means that the tolerant person believes that something insalubrious attends homosexuality. Nor is indifference synonymous with tolerance and scholars who specifically evaluate indifferences as tolerance-like soundly reject this equivalence (for example, Fletcher 1996; Williams 1996; Horton and Nicholson 1992).

Because boundaries separating categories are usually unclear, and reasonable people can readily disagree on where lines are crossed, applying this classic understanding invites arduous work. A sweeping tolerance cannot be commanded, as one might, for instance, plead for everlasting honesty. Factual details are essential, and these can shift, and the evidence necessary for a judgment is seldom indisputable. Much may come down to iffy interpretation. For Locke, one might suppose, banishing Roman Catholics was straightforward, given the plain-to-see English-French conflict. Putting Unitarians into the "not to be tolerated" category was probably a more taxing call since their defect—the rejection of the Trinity and thus the untrustworthiness of their oaths—was relatively minor compared to supporting foreign enemies. But some of Locke's contemporaries could disagree and insist that Catholics were, after all, bearable unless legally found to be treasonous.

Judgments require adaptation and are always finely grained. The permanently unacceptable category is certainly miniscule; murder might occasionally be virtuous (e.g., assassinating Hitler). Recall that Locke suffered certain dissenting Protestant sects such as Baptists but would deny them public office. A twenty-first-century Locke would judge differently. Now, one might suppose, all Christians, including the once excluded Roman Catholics and Unitarians, even the once distrusted Jews, are fully welcomed, conceivably even admired. Locke today would more likely draw careful distinctions regarding militant Islam. A twenty-first-century Locke might also decide with wholly new criteria, for example, now weighing a penchant for terror more heavily than, say, the untrustworthiness of oaths that came with rejecting a deity.

Decisions may vary among the generally likeminded, depending on idiosyncratic circumstances. Two Christian fundamentalists sharing an overall Bible-based abhorrence of homosexuality may, for example, still disagree on specifics—one accepts a beloved lesbian daughter while the other tries to rescue promiscuous male gay friends from impending HIV infection by frequent condemnation. Similarly with regard to "tolerating homosexuality," a person might treasure a few gay mannerisms as entertaining, grudgingly allow specific sexual behaviors despite their unsavory nature but insist on criminalizing pedophilia (and pedophilia itself invites interpretation). The philosopher Hans Oberdiek (2001, 58) further adds that we may tolerate something if done occasionally but not repeatedly or tolerate those who refrain from further pushing the limits.

Choices may even reflect new-found scientific research—second-hand smoke was once abided as a nuisance but it now may be intolerable in light of its recently discovered carcinogenic impact. Marriage between cousins was once acceptable, even promoted; today it is usually illegal thanks to greater understanding of its harmful genetic impact. Certain normal peacetime behaviors such as challenging authority may be judged treasonable in wartime. Moreover, as all experienced travelers realize, personal behavior such as loud belching may be barely noticed in one place but deemed absolutely abhorrent elsewhere. "Being tolerant," then, cannot be akin to some enduring, general personality disposition such as being optimistic.

Such fluidity does not, however, mean that everything is arbitrary, and one choice is just as good as another, so why not tolerate everything. Oberdiek (2001, 63) correctly argues that solid reasons exist for agreed upon limits though these invariably vary by time and place. Civil society would be impossible without such concurrence even if a consensus is debatable (for example, driving on the left versus the right). Visualize a society if, for example, people differed sharply on how they judged dishonesty, violence, open sexuality, and all else defining conventions. While some societies may tolerate rampant thievery, exporting that standard to a more law-abiding nation would be disastrous though the thief could rightly insist that such behavior was "perfectly fine back home."

The concept's meaning shifts drastically, however, among contemporary educators. Recall the PBS lesson plan, and this version is ubiquitous among educators: tolerance means unqualified appreciation, and everything denied approval becomes intolerance, so the tripartite "classic" vision with its multiple shades of gray and ambivalences is condensed into a black/white dichotomy. Now, finely distinguishing among degrees of abhorrence, some bearable, others not, is totally unnecessary. Everything is (at least conceptually) greatly simplified—one appreciates or one dislikes.

A few go even further in expunging the tolerance category of the slightest negative connotations. To be tolerant now requires affirmation. Crista Martinez, director of Cambridge's Families First Parenting program, announced, "I don't even like the word 'tolerance.' 'Embrace' is a better expression for the kind of respect and acceptance 'tolerance' implies" (cited in Furi-Perry 2004). Nor will passive forbearance suffice in this new conceptualization. Tolerance now requires active outreach. Sharon Nichols writing in the *Elementary School Journal* typifies modern educators when arguing that achieving tolerance for homosexuals requires schools to address the unique needs of homosexual students, and this might include having a "diversity room" with a "diversity specialist" (1999). Totally gone is the older notion that the tolerated draws acceptance *despite* certain unpleasantness or that tolerance is possible passively (bearing the noxious). To acquiesce to something and simultaneously detest it is now, *by definition*, impossible.

This distinction is consequential in today's atmosphere were "being tolerant" signifies righteousness while intolerance is, at least according to a gathering at New York's Interfaith Center, a synonym for racism, anti-Semitism, sexism, ageism, and every other malicious ism (Schmemann 2002). According to this framework, then, countless once-tolerant people might now be reclassified as "intolerant" given the rarity of unabashed appreciation of everything. A virtual "one drop" rule applies: the smallest distaste now signifies intolerance. Somebody confessing, "I generally put up with homosexuality, but am repulsed by certain homoerotic practices," is now certifiably homophobic. The absence of a middle ground imposes a tough, unforgiving standard. We shall elaborate this point when exploring why imposing this black/white approach often fails.

To be fair, the simplified vision favored by educators hardly lacks respectability. The *American Heritage Dictionary of the English Language,* Fourth Edition (2000, on-line version) defines tolerance as, "The capacity for or the practice of recognizing and respecting the beliefs or practices of others." In 1995, UNESCO offered much the same: "Tolerance is respect, acceptance and appreciation of the rich diversity of our world's cultures, our forms of expression and ways of being human" (http://unesco.org/tolerance/declaeng.htm). These respect/acceptance=tolerance definition examples can be multiplied, so those embracing this dichotomous framework can legitimately cite chapter and verse.[1] Nor can we hold common usage-based definitions accountable for promoting lofty goals—there is nothing about definitions that necessitate them to ameliorate hostility. Whether this theoretical roadmap assists in delivering the promised benefits is, of course, another matter.

This definitional shift brings a vocational, make-work dividend for educators. The embrace of the dichotomous conceptualization means, naturally, that the world abruptly overflows with antipathy since qualms exist about anything. In an instant, then, tolerance apostles gain immense responsibilities while educational resources are justifiably conscripted in a never-ending war. Who wants to live where bigotry and prejudice flourish? This assignment is light years distant from how a classically oriented educator might view his or her mission. He or she would argue that repugnance is inescapable, unquestionably hard-wired into human nature, and so campaigns to banish it are futile. Better to allocate classroom time elsewhere and, if one must address odious behavior, just hand the miscreant over to the disciplinary process.

Achieving Tranquility without Tolerance?

All those advancing tolerance, regardless differing definitions, seek a more peaceful, harmonious society, a world free of racism, sexism, and similarly contentious tribulations. But, it does not automatically follow, as many educators implicitly argue, that the primary pathway is to refurbish inner dispositions. It is, admittedly, hard to visualize a gracious acceptance of human variety among bigots and hate-mongers, and education does instinctively seem a powerful cure for hatefulness. Nevertheless, viewed from another angle, a "tolerant society" can be comprised of intolerant people, and no reason exists why private convictions must be the sole element, or even the most essential one, in a peacefulness formula. A plausible case exists that countless reasonably harmonious societies were, paradoxically, composed of intolerant people. It is a mistake to conflate overall traits with separate individual characteristics. The Japanese as people may be meek, strenuously avoiding conflict, yet Japan as a nation had been exceptionally warlike in the first half of the twentieth century.

Abandoning an inner attitude focus and seeking solutions elsewhere offers considerable practical benefits as well. Most clearly, even if this approach is successful, and chapter 4 challenges this claim, to insist that overall tolerance is *best* achievable by converting the intolerant launches a hugely expensive effort. Now millions of students must be convinced while hundreds of thousands of teachers need special training. Imposing commitment is no small accomplishment in our fragmented, fractious educational system. Whether the quest itself will be welcomed is also unclear since this aim falls outside the schools' historic mission, and idealistic administrators (and parents) might still prefer traditional instruction. Since the menu of those denied welcome is forever in flux (yesterday Catholics, today homosexuals, tomorrow who knows what), this enterprise demands constant updating.

These obstacles acknowledged, what other investment options are available? Treating tolerance as something concerning society, apart from people collectively, suggests entirely different and, critically, proven recipes. The aim now shifts from convincing millions to abandon their errant ways to preventing harm to those who differ. Whereas educators ask, "How can we inculcate tolerance so as to alleviate hatefulness?" the latter perspective steps backwards and inquires, "How can we prevent hurtfulness?" No assumption is made that refashioning inner thoughts is fundamental or even a first step. This shift is immensely far-reaching—just protecting the unpopular requires far less effort than reeducating millions. Elaborate inculcation programs may not even be necessary or, conceivably, divisive if pursued.

Hostilities can be cooled simply by separating potential antagonists and this may occur as a matter of policy or just result from fortuitous physical barriers. It is always easier to feel good about those one never encounters. This may be entirely voluntary insofar as people who share a common trait may prefer to reside among those sharing ethnic or racial identities. Colonial America as a whole displayed ample religious liberty insofar as colonies, even small towns, trended to attract co-religionists. It was "easy" for New England Calvinists to put up with Maryland Catholics given almost insurmountable physical separation. The ethnic-based urban neighborhoods of yesteryear further illustrate this possibility. Here the Irish, Germans, Jews, and Italians of New York during the late nineteenth century seldom esteemed one another, but New York as a city certainly appeared "tolerant," superficially even a melting pot, provided each hostile faction minded its own business (and this was occasionally assisted by the police or ethnic-based gangs protecting turf). What is important is that everybody freely indulges his or her aversions but not necessarily in close proximity, so hostility usually came to naught. Again, tolerance admonitions are irrelevant. Colonial-era Boston Quakers did not plead for acceptance among those who despised them, even occasionally hanging them; persecuted Quakers instead migrated to Pennsylvania to practice their faith freely. Colonial intolerance would be imposing an orthodoxy while forbidding migration.

Even where antagonistic groups mingle, people may grit their teeth despite social tensions. It may be a matter of priorities, not transforming aversion into appreciation. Agreeableness may be utilitarian. Voltaire (1765 and 2000) centuries ago observed that marketplaces readily quell religious hatreds if making a buck (or shilling, or euro) ranks supreme. Jewish merchants need not treasure their Muslim customers as human beings (and vice versa) if the two can profitably co-exist. Some Americans today may exhibit scant admiration for Hispanic culture, or even individual Hispanics, yet it is obvious that Hispanics are generally—but not entirely—accepted given their economic contributions. The xenophobic bigot may loathe Mexicans, want to deport or jail them all, but he or she places a higher priority on enjoying cheap labor, and so decides to live and let live. As a human urge, avarice may be a far more powerful nostrum to lessen strife than just pleading for mutual respect, let alone admiration.

Crass symbiosis of all sorts can ameliorate loathing—just subordinate hostilities to other values. Blacks and whites may dislike each other regardless of endless admonitions to the contrary, but they still can cooperate in sports, the military, at work and in entertainment. Aversion may exist but mere existence does not certify that this view is paramount. To wit, countless openly gay celebrities enjoy successful careers, so a person's unconventional sexual identity is hardly career-ending. People who might otherwise be appalled by open homosexuality may still enjoy a hearty laugh at particularly "campy" gay behavior. Ironically, if sexuality were elevated to be person's core identity (along with race and class), as at least some educators advocate, this might marginalize those rejecting the culture's dominant values, hardly what this consciousness-raising enterprise intends.

The sheer propagation of proclivities, whether religious, ethnic, racial, or whatever, can alleviate hostilities. It is not that each new arrival rushes to appreciate all others though this may be true. Rather, as Voltaire observed, "The more sects there are, the less dangerous each one becomes; as they multiply, so they weaken...." (24). In other words, it is far easier for an overwhelming majority to repress a minority and less likely when everybody is but a minority in a sea of differences. Such proliferation may be a natural outcome, for example, the result of fresh waves of immigrants, or a matter of conscious policy or minimal legal requirements for creating a church. Try imagining hundreds of different sects agreeing on a common enemy. In any case, "intolerance gridlock" can exist outside of some educationally instilled appreciation for those who differ. Such variety cannot, admittedly, eliminate occasional friction but, more importantly, it can greatly moderate seventeenth-century-style carnage.

Greater self-control in the face of threats can similarly supply peacefulness. Again, instilling respect for multiple endangered groups and views among students becomes unnecessary. As has been true since the beginning of time, children learn to repress anger when it erupts. Civil society has long depended on politeness and etiquette to survive inescapable friction, far less on actually appreciating the loathsome. Notable stratagems might include learning to avoid potentially contentious situations, cultivating stoicism, or the venerable technique of counting to ten before reacting. Imparting "good manners" among people may likewise be effective, though this fuddy-duddy subject will unlikely draw appreciation among today's educators favoring avant-garde pedagogy.

Moreover, as history certainly demonstrates, divisions provoking intolerance can, unintentionally or by design, be made less important. The violent religious hatreds of the sixteenth and seventeenth centuries are now almost unimaginable since church affiliation (though not necessarily faith) is often more a practical than theological choice. Building location or daycare facilities, not defend-to-the-death doctrines, is now decisive. Similarly, assimilation and endless inter-marriage have generally cooled once contentious ethnic rivalries. Though some may bemoan growing indifference to historic religious and ethnic identities, lack of concern can promote easy acceptance. As Stanley Fish (1994, 217) so aptly put it, "My General Law of Tolerance is that tolerance is exercised in an inverse relationship to there being anything at stake. The more there is something generally at stake, the less likely tolerance."

Nor can we dismiss state coercion to impose tranquility in the face of pervasive hatefulness. The emphasis could shift to overt behavior, not impos-sible-to-discern inner thoughts, so an accepting atmosphere arrives by simply imposing civility. This approach, recall, is Locke's prescription for handling provocations. The familiar adage, voiced by countless generations of children, comes to mind: "sticks and stones can break my bones but names can never hurt me." Pedagogically this strategy simplifies everything—refurbishing humans is now off the agenda. No obligation exists to agonize over which particular at-risk groups (gays, atheists, the disabled) warrant forbearance. The message is totally unambiguous and quickly grasped: *anybody* who physically harms *anybody* will be punished.

Lastly, and perhaps of the utmost importance given the historic character of repression, a system of limited government can prevent hatreds from gaining state support, no small matter since only government can legally confiscate property, imprison, or execute. This is absolutely critical since it is one thing to loathe thy neighbor's faith but quite another to have the neighbor arrested for heresy. This bulwark against intolerance is often tricky to navigate in practice since conflicts among private individuals often in-stigate calls for aggrandizing state authority so as to prevent future hateful incidents. Seldom recognized in such calls for "more state protection" is that newly acquired power can authorize future repression as the political winds change. In the long run it thus might be safer to handle the insults or abuse privately than award government the obligation to stamp out some ill-defined "offensiveness."

It is tempting to denigrate traditional conflict avoiding tactics vis-à-vis pro-moting an idyllic awareness of human variety. Voltaire's adage that the best is the enemy of the good certainly applies here, assuming that a nation of totally tolerant people is even feasible. Those already heavily invested in promoting classroom instruction will surely defend sunk costs against rival nostrums. But, the lofty (and expensive) solution so favored by today's educators remains problemati-cal in light of its brief history. By contrast, what is described here—physical isolation, the role of commerce to reduce animosities, instilling lawfulness and so on—are proven remedies to quell civil strife.

Calibrating Tolerance

Though expressions like "I cannot tolerate him" are commonplace, and certainly suffice for ordinary conversations, such statements are imprecise. Ditto for what the recipient of this intolerance might feel. After all, to exhibit intolerance toward somebody might mean everything from a violent attack to snide jokes while the object of loathing may just perceive a minor slight or, conceivably, a death threat. And, as we shall see, the entire scale can shift to reflect historical circumstances and local conditions. Terminological murkiness resembles the era when "scientists" idiosyncratically used words like heavy or light rather than ten pounds or five pounds. Matters would be entirely different if we had a fixed scientific instrument to assess tolerance akin to the standard meter. This device might, for example, define everything on a 100-point scale, with 100 being unqualified veneration, zero unmitigated disgust, and, conceivably, anything between 40 and 60 deemed "tolerance." An unchanging, more finely gradated scale would then refine though not replace the tripartite tolerance framework discussed earlier. If the educator-favored dichotomous framework were imposed, anything below 49.99 would be "intolerance"; all else becomes "tolerance." Now, instead of ambiguously saying, "I can just barely stomach him," one would instead offer, "my reaction to him is 40.1."

Further precision might entail adding a behavioral dimension since two people may plausibly exhibit equal loathing (say 10 on our 100-point scale) but diverge substantially in their eagerness or opportunity to act. Consider, for example, two staunch anti-Communists. One lacks any present or future contact with Marxists and thus is unlikely to be intolerant. The other, by contrast, is a police chief in a city teeming with Communists. While both are equally (and precisely) intolerant, it would nevertheless be a mistake to treat them as one and the same. Going one step further, educating the former to be "more indulgent" of Marxists is wasteful; if mitigating conflict is the aim, better to concentrate on those capable of imposing harm.

Disagreement on a precise absolute tolerance/intolerance yardstick, let alone the lack of a behavioral penchant measure, begets confusion insofar as people apply identical terms to depict wildly unlike things. The familiar one dimensional crude yardstick can mean what one person finds (barely) "intolerable" (say 49 on the aforementioned hypothetical scientific instrument) is absolutely abhorrent (say 2) to another. Both, technically, are "intolerant" yet their conclusions (and, perchance, willingness to act) diverge sharply. This would be the equivalent of modern medicine classifying people with only two or three categories—sick, feeling so-so, and healthy so cancer is akin to a cold.

Exacerbating matters is that tolerance calibrations, unlike engineering where bridges can collapse if people differ regarding "strong," do not lend themselves to an absolute standard. But, unlike other situations in which hazy benchmarks are adequate (fashion, music, art), here the consequences can be far-reaching. It is one thing to say, "I detest modern art," quite another for African-American pupils to announce that they find their textbooks deeply offensive. Though nobody might ask *exactly* what these outraged students have in mind, or the precise criterion guiding their conclusion, in today's atmosphere merely expressing this ire might bring legal action.

To appreciate the urgency of applying precise terminology, consider Voltaire's grim account of eighteenth-century Irish religious warfare. Here Protestant-hating Catholics spent over two months burying Protestants alive but this was only the beginning. Anti-Protestant zealotry also included "hanging young mothers from the gallows with their daughters strapped to their necks so as to watch them die together, splitting open the bellies of pregnant women and pulling out their half-formed babies to throw to dogs and pigs to eat, placing daggers in the hands of garroted prisoners and guiding the dagger into the breast of their wives, fathers, mothers and daughters, with the depraved intent of creating parricides by this device and thus not only exterminating them all, but sending them all to Hell (19)." That's intolerance!! This butchery certainly might warrant an absolute zero on our 100-point scale.

Now consider a 2005 *New York Times* story captioned "There's No Shortage of Intolerance in the Workplace." The story recounts how white men who once dominated industry were now "lashing out" at new found workplace diversity. And what form did this aversion to newcomers take? Were newly employed women burnt at the stake for displacing white males? The author (Hubert B. Herring) relying on a survey of 623 employees reports that 30 percent of these employees overheard a racial slur during the last year, 20 percent reported ridicule of sexual orientation, and 20 percent were privy to age bias. No evidence is presented that affronts injured anyone or impeded careers. Educators often express a similar "updating" of intolerance to include insults that once would have passed unnoticed to those (like Locke) monitoring hatefulness. One such advocate (Holloway 2003) even maintained that a student's mere exposure to hate-related graffiti was "unbearable" intolerance, and the presence of wounding offensiveness required immediate administrative intervention, notably, augmenting staff diversity and bilingual education. What happened after this allegedly injurious encounter, unfortunately, went unreported.

These examples clearly show how labels mask huge differences. One era's vile oppression might be another's warm acceptance despite identical behavior. Irish Protestant mothers marched to the gallows with their children would have gladly welcomed a repugnance limited to vulgar slanders or anti-Protestant graffiti. Such ill-will would likely be deemed *tolerable* petty nuisances, predictable discord plaguing all multi-religious societies, and not a calamity requiring remediation. Similarly, newly hired female and African-American workers might decades back have once gladly accepted occasional snide remarks as a bearable price for obtaining better jobs.

From one perspective this progression from, say, torture to off-color jokes is less indicative of "intolerance" than a sign of progress, the equivalent of, say, bubonic plague being replaced by obesity as the foremost public health challenge. Contemporary illustrations regarding overheard slurs and the like certainly fail to demonstrate that *serious* hatefulness lingers on despite Herculean remediation, so we must redouble our efforts. Making tasteless jokes about women is hardly comparable to burying them alive. A more accurate lesson to be drawn from these two cases is that, on average, virulence has shifted from zero to, perhaps, 47 and the behavior component has likewise moved from energetic murder to just maligning. Over centuries, happily, the entire scale has moved upward, at least in the U.S. Unfortunately, our crude lexicon does not permit this grada-tion—intolerance is just intolerance.

An ill-defined vocabulary can have serious ramifications. This crude categorization—intolerance is intolerance is intolerance—without the necessary calibration now means a world perpetually mired in hatefulness. After all, since (a) everybody can detect offensiveness and (b) slights are integral to society, those stamping out intolerance are both doomed to fail and be relegated to lifetime employment. If one truly craved a hate-free environment, relocating to a cave and ceasing all outside contact is perhaps the sole solution. Perhaps only then would there be no slights, rebukes, derogatory remarks, harass-ments, disconcerting pictures, or anything else displaying less-than-perfect appreciation.

Still, even then, despite total isolation, perceived abhorrence might linger. It will always be true that some people have exceptionally thin skin, a few are even paranoid, so no amount of effort can rid life of intolerance. To appreciate the ease of "experiencing" persecution despite all tangible contrary evidence, consider 1987 survey data regarded *perceived* political freedom in the United States (Gibson 1992). When asked if government would permit a national strike, three-quarters of all respondents said that it would ban such actions though, of course, no laws forbid it, and the government has never proposed stopping such a strike. Furthermore, 64 percent of African Americans and 40 percent of whites believed that they could not secure official permission to hold a public meeting to protest government policy though, of course, plain-to-see public protests are commonplace. These survey data suggest that perceived "intolerance" does exist but, truth be told, this is nonsense, though its psychological impact may nevertheless be real.

The barrier to creating an intolerance-free world grows even more formidable if we apply the standard of what a single person might perceive. That is, if ninety-nine people find, say, a magazine cartoon with a racial theme innocuous but one mysteriously decides that it is "intolerable," does this single adverse response demand remediation, i.e., removing the offensive cartoon or securing an apology from the cartoonist, the magazine publisher, the person selling the magazine and so on? And would such an apology then bring acceptance? Even if we reject the single, most touchy person standard, the matter is settled given that nearly everything can, in some form or shape, be insufferable to somebody under some circumstances.

It is also true that while heightened tolerance is, at least in principle, widely desired, powerful financial and political incentives often push in the opposite direction. Laws penalizing employers for hostile work environments, even holding them responsible for the casual slights of other employees now rewards uncovering intolerance. Overhearing a bawdy joke might be sufficient to bring riches. Walter Olson (1997) recounts innumerable instances in which judges and juries, applying ambiguous laws, generously compensated these "intolerance" victims. In one extreme case a forty-seven-year-old Missouri woman received a $50 million dollar settlement when fellow Wal-Mart employees offended her with risqué talk. She herself admitted to using similar language, and nobody had actually sexually accosted her though at one time a supervisor tried to kiss her. Just hearing offensiveness garnered $50 million (73). Similarly, advocacy groups opportunistically seeking incidents to energize their followers and raise funds quickly see "intolerance." Offense might come from a crude TV skit, a public figure's inadvertent remark, or just about anything, and in a world where the on-the-lookout recipient is the final judge of what truly offends, this settles the case.[2]

There is an irony here regarding simultaneously promoting tolerance together with ethnic, racial, sexual, linguistic, and similar group identities. This is especially relevant for educators who often assume (without any evidence) that heightened group consciousness can facilitate near utopian tolerance levels. For example, the National Coalition Building Institute (NCBI) has since 1984, often with U.S. Department of Education cooperation, organized hundreds of campus programs promoting diversity. In many instances, universities themselves actively assist the NCBI. Among its key goals is to teach participants how to appreciate their ethnic uniqueness while recognizing how they, as a group member, have suffered from internalized oppression and discrimination. In other words, the ideal graduate of such lessons is somebody who is proud and victimized. Instruction is also given on handling bigoted comments and behavior (http://www.ncbi.org/campusprogram/).

Left unsaid in this noble-sounding effort is that aims easily clash: the more heightened the group awareness, the greater the sensitivity to affronts, the greater the likelihood of discerning hostility from others. It would be as if a supposedly helpful medicine really exacerbated the illness, so unaware doctors upped dosages as health deteriorated. For example, an African American with a razor-sharp racial consciousness is, in all likelihood, far more likely to detect racial slights than a black person lacking this keen identity. If we add multiple firmly held self-concepts strongly anchored in race, ethnicity, religion, sexuality, economic status, and so on, the opportunities for perceived "intolerance" multiply exponentially. Now, thanks to a well-meaning though misguided effort, life suddenly overflows with previously unnoticed hatefulness.

Coerced Tolerance?

As noted, social tranquility recipes necessarily entail *some* compulsion or threats of coercion, both private and public. Panhandlers might be obnoxious but nearly everyone forbears punching them since that breaks the law. One might similarly refrain from shooting a rambunctious neighbor out of fear that this might prompt personal retribution. Threatening force may be distasteful to those infatuated with harmony, but it is vital, and tolerance in and of itself cannot guarantee tranquility: something more is *always* necessary.

But, can such compulsion, in the name of enhancing social tranquility, even extend to imparting tolerance, a gun-to-the-head version, so to speak? Consider the anti-Semite who proclaims, "Jews disgust me, and I want to murder them all!" Can we *force* this anti-Semite to be more accepting in his or her private beliefs? And, if this effort proves successful, can we deem imposed forbearance the genuine article or perhaps just an imposture? By the same token, can we impel a teacher who personally loathes homosexuality to extol appreciation of gays so that he or she outwardly appears "tolerant"? Is this "a tolerant teacher" or closer to an actor giving a performance?

Those reflecting on predicaments generally eschew coercion despite its practical allure. Voltaire, like Locke, dismissed such forced acceptance as bogus: "For man is under no obligation to believe or not to believe. His duties are to respect the laws and customs of his country...." (2000, 49). The modern philosopher Preston King (1976, 9) similarly argues that authenticity presupposes personal autonomy, an opportunity to accept or reject (he uses the term "acquiescence" to denote situations lacking choice). One can also safely assume that educators would reject compulsory parroting at least in principle though career advancement certainly seems to require "getting with the program" in public.

This philosophical dilemma is hardly abstract, and harkens back to tumultuous earlier eras when monarchs dictated religious orthodoxies on the pain of execution. If education is state-mandated, and if, say, teachers lecture students to view homosexuality positively, children *are* being compelled to be tolerant. (And by implication, force extends to teachers required to be enthusiastic, lest they be considered laggards). State-coerced tolerance is hardly hypothetical. In 2000, for example, the California state legislature enacted two laws (AB 1785 and AB 1931) mandating the State Board of Education to develop a civic education so as to promote student appreciation of California diversity. AB 1785 which addressed the training of certain teachers spoke of diversity based upon "race, color, religion, nationality, country of origin, ancestry, gender, disability or sexual orientation." Meanwhile, AB 1931 allocated state money for school fieldtrips to locations promoting ethnic sensitivity, overcoming racism and other ways to quell hatred (Foster 2000).

Duress acknowledged, can parents who abhor this message object on the grounds that since their offspring lack the requisite volition, instruction is impermissible brainwashing? Might they refuse permission, for example, if their children were under school auspices to be taken to a gay rights center to learn about how gays are mistreated? The dilemma is quite real since upset parents risk legal sanctions if they keep children home.

Separating autonomy from coercion grows complicated in practice. If, for example, teachers are relentlessly upbeat about homosexuality, what *exactly* separates forced indoctrination from inoffensively explicating facts? Does fervently repeating a point five times make it "coercive"? Might stubbornness—not formal lesson content—decide. That is, for the gullible, everything, no matter how mild, is quickly absorbed, while the staunch believer remains impervious to hectoring. Variations in learning ability are also relevant. It might be pointless to expect the slow learners to navigate complicated distinctions, so beliefs must be pounded in. For ten-year-olds, lessons about accepting Muslims may, conceivably, be brainwashing; for eighteen year olds, this may be less true since they possess the power to disagree, so genuine tolerance is possible.

Complexities aside, it is still arguable that classroom instruction, regardless of mildness, *inherently* entails irresistible pressure. Educators alleging "children can decide themselves" are patently disingenuous save in lackadaisical schools where all learning is nonchalant. If the "correct" views regarding who deserves acceptance (or rejection) are to be imposed from above, the situation resembles acquiring reading and writing skills. Dunces, meanwhile, receive extra help or even punishment until lessons sink in. Only an exceptional twelve-year-old could bravely announce, "I reject being forced by my teachers to endure gays since this violates my moral autonomy!" Such a resister will unlikely be taken seriously; more probable, he or she will be classified as defiant, even a "slow learner." If such bottom-up resistance grows, teachers will probably redouble their effort since, as most educators will announce, students themselves certainly lack the wisdom to assert contrary views.

These dilemmas clearly apply to punitive sensitivity training in which parties guilty of (real or alleged) offensiveness receive psychological counseling to soften (supposedly) hateful hearts. Increasingly popular in the workplace and on college campuses, it is viewed as a kinder, gentler technique for quelling prejudice than, say, fines or incarceration. Attempts to eradicate sexism, homophobia, racism, and nearly anything else suggesting aversion to so-called "at-risk" groups are standard. Critically, lessons are usually non-voluntary, often the least draconian option for, say, a student caught writing racist graffiti or a mandatory element of freshman orientation. Intentionally remolding inner thoughts, even in the face of resistance is explicit, and practitioners seem oblivious to comparisons with totalitarian tactics or similarities with the novel *1984*.[3]

If personal autonomy is, indeed, necessary for "true tolerance," then we could expect individual differences to emerge across similar circumstances. There is certainly no logical reason why autonomous individuals would reach identical decisions regarding what deserves tolerance or its opposite. Much depends on personal values, circumstances and weighting evidence—certainly two people can honestly disagree on, say, whether unsafe sex should be criminalized (rendering it intolerable) or just handled via voluntary education (which implies that non-compliance is tolerable). This idiosyncratic element acknowledged, is it improper to pronounce an effort to "promote tolerance" a failure if some people reject pro-tolerance admonitions? Such a sweeping conclusion rests on the shaky assumption that the educator's categorizations—what does or does not deserve toleration—apply equally to every pupil across infinite situations. Even if this authoritative strategy could be abstractly defended as socially necessary in a strife-filled world, then whether educators possess the necessary training to impose a specific agenda remains doubtful. Learning "to be tolerant" is wholly unlike mastering arithmetic. The individual's right to reject erstwhile "be more tolerant" messages is profoundly important when judging the success and failures of these lessons, a point to which we shall return in chapter 4.

Imposing this one-group-at-a-time tolerance, versus treating the topic more abstractly, highlights the practical issue of which groups in particular, among countless potential candidates, warrant attention. There is certainly no official, expertly devised "must be tolerated" list to guide pedagogy, so that if instructionally consistency is desired, it must be imposed. If such an authoritative list were to be developed, hundreds of contenders would surely demand classroom time, a situation akin to quarrels over including countless ethnic groups demanding that history textbooks memorialize them.

The upshot of this let-everyone-freely-decide approach is, undoubtedly, incompleteness and confusion, a situation parallel to "personalized" history lessons. Now, some children might be told to cherish African Americans, Muslims, the handicapped, beggars, and those unable to speak English. Elsewhere exemplars would be Native Americans, Jews, the physically disfigured, the Irish, Hispanics, and gays. Meanwhile politically conservative teachers with a different agenda dwell on Christian fundamentalists, the military, abortion foes, the police, and Republicans. Again, one can only imagine the political turmoil when lessons become grab bags of personal biases and whatever seems temporarily alluring.

Regardless of forcefulness, or choosing exemplars, the key issues remain: how important is it to reshape inner beliefs so as to promote social tranquility? Is this cost commensurate with likely benefits? And of the utmost importance, in the final analysis, how can teachers know for sure of their achievement? Locke's "Letter" spoke to this point directly regarding the futility of imposing religious faith: "Such is the nature of the understanding that it cannot be compelled to the belief of any thing by outward force. Confiscation of estate, imprisonment, torments, nothing of that nature can have any such efficacy as to make men change inward judgment that they have frame of things." (Locke, *Works,* 6:1, 12, cited in Vernon, 1997, 17). It is only reason and evidence, Locke argues, that might alter belief. To push ever harder is pointless, and a recipe for civil discord. From this perspective, the most that involuntary exposure can accomplish is hypocrisy and deceit.

Locke's case appears persuasive even today. To wit, children (and adults) might outwardly agree, for example, to prize Islam without reservation, but deep in their heart they might hate it, and, fearing retribution, they prudently acquiesce. Yet, the hopelessness of forced conversion is hardly settled as a practical matter, and a still relevant rejoinder to Locke surfaced almost immediately following his cautionary missive. Jonas Proast, a chaplain at All Souls College, Oxford, just as convincingly claimed that while brute force cannot transform inner opinion, compulsion can bring people to consider reason which would, ultimately, successfully reverse private belief. And for Proast, coercion was, as a practical matter, to be "moderate," requiring, for example, church attendance via fines, not torture which he admitted would be ineffective (see Vernon, 1997, chapter 1 for a more detailed depiction of this counter-argument). More generally, the entire weight of social institutions can mildly and relentlessly facilitate conversion. Years of church-contrived religious encounters (e.g., hearing Handel's *Messiah*) and unavoidable, innocuous-seeming inspirational public ceremonies might ultimate sway the village atheist. Schools routinely follow this "mild" pathway in inculcating patriotism (e.g., legally mandated U.S. history courses, flag saluting). Interestingly, Locke himself admitted the efficacy of gentler compulsion but averred that this might only lead to hypocrisy or "accidental" conversion.

Whether Locke or Proast is correct is, of course, entirely a factual dispute, but a very difficult one to resolve since private views are unknowable. Conversion targets might themselves be perplexed regarding their true inner opinion, and these can fluctuate according to circumstances. Secret disbelievers can certainly survive relentless "reeducation" efforts by just skillful parroting, yet it is equally true that totalitarian brainwashing can be devastatingly effective despite resistance. Grand principles cannot supply answers; everything depends on the practical dexterity of the indoctrinators, the imposed doctrines, opportunities for defiance and countless other tangible factors.

This debate's implications are deceptively consequential. If pressure illegitimately violates individual autonomy, as some have argued, and uncovering true beliefs remains problematical, why then invest scarce resources—conceivably billions—in this quest? Is this not, as Locke, argues, also a prescription for civil discord among those who cherish freedom of conscience? Why risk that as one gentle admonition after the next fails, well-meaning educators will adopt yet more stringent measures? Or is Proast correct: a steady stream of moderate admonitions, pleas, entreatments, and mild rebukes will eventually triumph. The less complicated rejoinder to this uncertain pathway is to concentrate instead on outward behavior, even accepting hypocrisy, totally apart from private thoughts.

Limiting Tolerance

Tolerance theorizing is almost entirely one-sidedly positive—the appetite for it appears insatiable. J. S. Mill famously insisted that without tolerance, the free exchange of ideas is impossible and thus truth, and, ultimately progress, is thwarted (Tinder 1995, ch. 1 discusses Mill's and similar truth-based justifications at length). Halberstam (1982-83) observes that defenses invoke just about any value—stability, equality, truth, religious salvation among others—while proponents range from the religiously pious to Marxists plus a healthy helping of utilitarians. Paul Kurtz adds creativity, peace, innovation and an absence of fanaticism to this list (Kurtz 1995/1996). The distinguished philosopher A. J. Ayer even asserts, with scant empirical data, that irrationality begets intolerance (1987, 83). Endorsing intolerance is, apparently, akin to defending bestiality. Oddities like Jonas Proast, who rebuked John Locke's renowned "Letter," are airbrushed from intellectual history though a few scholars insist that he out-argued Locke (e.g., Vernon 1997, ch. 1).[4]

It is not as if (selective) intolerance lacks scholarly champions. Recall Locke's fulminations against Catholics and atheists. J. S. Mill, freely admitted the need to constrain tolerance, for example, public drunkenness and similar immorality were impermissible (Mill 1947, ch. V covers a multitude of properly intolerable behaviors).[5] The psychiatrist Kai T. Erikson (1966) argues that reviling outsiders, even if unreasonable, helps cement internal cohesion and is thus necessary for civil society. More generally, it is plain to see that a misguided knack for bearing evil can have ruinous consequences. African Americans living under Jim Crow segregation were probably counseled, "just learn to live with it despite the inconvenience." No doubt, many European Jews mistakenly believed that Nazism was tolerable, an aberration that would quickly pass. Nevertheless, those keen on building yet one more tolerance defense prefer to skip over qualms regarding gracious welcomes.[6]

That being said, however, *in*tolerance is unequivocally the historic human default option. Forbearing cities like seventeenth-century Amsterdam are famous because they flourished amidst seas of religious persecution, and all the justly renowned pleas of Milton, Locke, Voltaire, and others would go unwritten unless heretics were genuinely threatened. A Darwinian penchant for survival would suggest that aggression toward outsiders may be useful. Without this proclivity to defend "us" against "them," humanity may have been doomed. Why do we so quickly criminalize abhorrent personal behavior? Or wage civil war? It is ironic, then, that intolerance defenses are so rare while persecution upholders, like the barely remembered Proast, go unread. It is almost as if tolerance cognoscenti hope to change the world by pretending that the opposite is some odd aberration. Who wants to learn why the venerated St. Thomas Aquinas advocated slaughtering religious heretics if they refused to mend their ways? (*Summa Theologiae,* "Utrum ritus infidelium sint tolerandi," cited in Oberdiek 2001, 70). Better to keep the shaky idealistic enterprise on track.

Demarcating the tolerable from the intolerable via grand principles is difficult. Philosophers for centuries have labored and failed to achieve a universal consensus. No two people are likely to concur on every detail, and shifting circumstances renders formulations obsolete. Nevertheless, the arduousness of achieving some ideal do-not-tolerate registry or an enduring abstract demarcation standard does not authorize fleeing the subject altogether. Nor does this task's formidable nature permit educators to insist that doing "something," however muddled or wrongheaded, to quell pending chaos moves the enterprise forward.

The place to begin is to acknowledge the distinction between tolerance/intolerance formulae privately heeded versus menus conveyed via public instruction. Parents, friends, co-workers, and other private individuals can certainly, without any restriction, plead, beseech, and admonish or even psychologically counsel those awash in hatefulness. The opposite is equally true—we can all hector friends and family to be more intolerant. Indeed, it is even arguable that intolerance, not acceptance, towards the vices of loved ones is a moral obligation, a sign of true compassion.[7] For example, ignoring a child's drug addiction in the name of "tolerance" abdicates parental responsibility, and hardly deserves praise as live and and let live acceptance. We may disagree with each person's menu, but this quarrel cannot justify state intervention. To take an extreme case, parents may pressure their offspring to tolerate suicide bombers, and while most would judge this instruction ill-advised, both as a matter of principle and practicality, this parental guidance cannot be thwarted. Again, it is futile to formulate, let alone enforce, private tolerance/intolerance standards.

Matters are, however, quite different when government enters this realm. Unlike a friend in pleading for greater acceptance of nearby undocumented workers, the state can exercise enormous power in these matters, and as such must be held to a more stringent standard. One can always ignore friendly advice; this is less true given the state's power to punish, even kill those who disagree.

How, then, is *public* instruction to be handled? This is hardly hypothetical even if schools cease teaching tolerance as a separate subject. Even limited governments are, after all, legitimately concerned about schools conveying the "right" views on patriotism, national loyalty, respect for law, civic decorum, and countless other worthy dispositions touching on tolerance. Matters become far more complicated when "teaching tolerance" formally enters the pedagogical agenda. Can teachers wrestle with all the bewildering dilemmas in a few hours per week (at most) and with an audience often incapable of grasping the subtle arguments that inevitably infuse this topic? Of course, one simple escape route is to drop the topic altogether as too burdensome for already over-extended schools. But, at least for the moment, assume that the curriculum does include explicit tolerance instruction. What topics get included or ignored?

Focusing on the decision-making process surrounding the instruction itself, and not commencing with content, avoids awaiting land mines. From this perspective, determining *what* is taught is secondary to *who* decide and *how* the choice is made. In a democracy the answer to the "what" question must be: politics decides, or, concretely, elected officials adjudicate though accountable bureaucrats may ultimately choose. This pathway inheres in the very idea of *public* education. In theory, this is no different than deciding that, for example, grade schools will teach spelling but not religion, geography but not computer games. This is true even for private schools insofar as states always mandate minimal requirements. To be sure, churches, secularists, ethnic/racial/sexual organizations, and activists of all ideological stripes can offer advice, but the ultimate choice must be political.[8] This rough and ready solution simply acknowledges the democratic character of American education. Moreover, lobbying is a First Amendment right, and certainly applies to tolerance fans. This is no different than, say, publicly pushing for any other educational policy.

Critics might object that this solution pushes everything backwards to an era when kings or popes settled orthodoxies by fiat. The specter of a budding dictatorship misleads, insofar as it conflates the imposition of choices (inescapable in any situation) with it being "undemocratic." Besides, democratically decided choices would occur across thousands of schools, each with their own proclivities, each with their own varied interests, and none of these entities would be legally obliged to add tolerance to their curriculum (and, of course, parents are free to flee or resist noxious lessons). To reiterate, political resolution occurs only if formal tolerance instruction is authorized, and one cannot assume a stampede to embrace this panacea. One might personally appreciate homosexuality and believe that appreciating it should be added to the curriculum, but imposing this view via public education must first survive an arduous civic gauntlet.

Prohibited is privately distributing messages directly to teachers and pupils, bypassing local school boards or state department of education oversight. This is hardly a radical departure from traditional education policy—even spelling pedagogy requires some top-down, publicly accountable administrative consent. It is an ideologically neutral solution, too—all factions must bargain via identical channels (though with unequal resources, of course) to achieve aims. To appreciate the latter point's appeal, imagine the likely outrage among today's tolerance devotees if creationists surreptitiously visited classrooms to proselytize rejecting Darwin solely at the invitation of sympathetic teachers who then hid this activity from parents.

Political resolution, moreover, says nothing about the wisdom of outcomes or the reasonableness of attending deliberation. Legislators (or, more likely, bodies with the delegated responsibility) might make horrendous mistakes or rely on wrongheaded claims supplied by ill-informed lobbyists in chaotic public assemblies. No matter—what is paramount is that decision-makers are *accountable* for their errors and, critically, these are correctable as circumstances changes and superior arguments emerge. No doubt, a violence-inspiring lesson plan would quickly be abandoned, if only because responsible officials feared voter retaliation. By contrast, non-accountable pedagogues lack incentives to

mend their ways if entreatments prove disastrous. This flexibility is what tolerance (or at least its classic version) is about—navigating details within specific
contexts to achieve a reasonable tranquility, not abstract perfection. To insist on
permanency on one or another registry is pointless save for Utopians. Adjustments are always ongoing, and politics is markedly well-suited to muddling
through this quagmire.

A political solution's great virtue is the protection it affords against majority
despotism subtly inserted into the classroom to unsuspecting students, no small
improvement given the historical record of what happens when orthodoxies are
forcefully imposed. This advantage flows from the fact that U.S. politics, with
its multiple access points and concurrent majorities, favors compromise if not
gridlock. Neither an impassioned majority *nor* minority can dominate while,
thanks to decentralization, the defeated can readily seek refuge elsewhere. And,
given limited government power (and a watchdog free press), it is extremely
unlikely that noxious views will be jammed down anybody's throat, even if one
is unfortunate enough to reside in enemy territory. It is all too easy to forget these
bulwarks against tyranny since they now seem so "natural" and irreversible. In
practical terms, for example, those demanding classroom lessons for respecting homosexuals and those who insist the opposite can both triumph, albeit in
different settings and with likely watered-down messages. Though each may be
nervous when glancing at the other's civic triumphs, the upshot is that diverse
opinions co-exist. Political fragmentation and a multiplicity of views hardly
guarantee a tolerant society; it merely ensures that resisters are not prisoners of
an inescapable orthodoxy.

Conclusion: Making Choices

Analysis began by noting the plethora of choices awaiting tolerance crusaders. Though easily ignored, they are unavoidable. As in building anything of
consequence, prodigious planning is necessary lest the project succumb to chaos.
Earnest enthusiasm cannot suffice and, contrary to some allegations, American
society hardly verges on mayhem, so even hasty plans outshine passivity. The
necessity of laying the groundwork acknowledged, what questions demand
resolution before investing yet more precious resources?

First, and of the utmost importance, which tolerance definition, of the two
versions we have broadly outlined, warrants application? This often seemingly
offhand choice has momentous consequences. Electing the "classic" tripartite
version in one sense facilitates the quest, given that abhorrence toward almost
anything is quintessentially human. Now, glossing over flaws in the name of
quelling strife is unnecessary. Teachers just admonish students to endure the
loathsome, a well-practiced response familiar to everyone. But, arduousness
remains. Countless fine-grained distinctions regarding what is insufferable
versus what is barely acceptable are required. Continuous adjustments are also
indispensable—today's abomination may be venerated tomorrow and one's
criteria can certainly shift as well. Bestowing tolerance requires work.

The dichotomous formula so favored by educators is likewise a mixed burden. It is certainly straightforward—one either likes or dislikes. Its claim to expel hatefulness is also seductive in a society seemingly mired in endless strife. Unfortunately, this twofold framework avoids life's ambiguities, and while teachers can command shades of gray to vanish, they are inescapable in daily encounters. Sooner or later, graduates of these lessons will find themselves confused, even paralyzed, when encountering what is neither perfectly good nor unambiguously horrible.

Choices also concern the proportion of tolerance instruction, of any stripe, in the overall recipe for social tranquility. The potential amelioration menu is extensive, ranging from legal sanctions to physical separation, even stoicism. High-sounding principles need not supply a successful mix; achievement depends on specific circumstances and available resources. Quelling religious hatreds by preaching cultural sensitivity may also be futile. A better option might be to supply incentives to alleviate the violence, for example, designing marketplaces to facilitate cooperation. The key question should be, "How can people peacefully live together," not "How can we best teach tolerance." This training may be critical, but it is unrealistic to expect miracles from this single approach.

A third quandary is calibrating tolerance/intolerance. References to, say, hatefulness, are frustratingly inexact. Hostility could mean, conceivably, everything from intent to kill to a penchant for minor insults. Since all societies breed friction, it is pointless to insist that life be intolerance free. Acknowledging differences of degree is critical, and the tolerance vocabulary must reflect gradations. As one might establish minimally acceptable air pollution levels, baseline standards might be set regarding acceptable repugnance. Educators might then work towards reducing ethnic/racial frictions to "good enough" levels, not banishing antagonisms altogether. In light of history, what applies in one setting might not be useful elsewhere. Horribleness changes. As pointed out earlier, seventeenth-century about-to-be murdered Irish Protestants might have gladly welcomed just being insulted.

Fourth, what are suitable coercion levels in achieving tolerance? Must people be compelled to appreciate the loathsome or can we just settle for outward appearances, even hypocrisy? This is an especially vexing question when educating youngsters since it may be impossible to distinguish "teaching facts" from "brainwashing." This is not just a matter of abstract principle; schools routinely forcefully impart lessons about, say, patriotism or morality. Upping the coercive element brings its own risks even if ultimately successful. Not only is it difficult to determine whether outward agreement signifies private concurrence, but efforts to remold inner thoughts can foment divisiveness, as bloody religious wars amply demonstrate. Venturing into "thought reform" is always risky, and especially if we cherish limited government.

Finally, while preaching tolerance effortlessly captures the rhetorical high ground, abominations abound, so unavoidable choices regarding the demarcation of the acceptable from the truly loathsome are required. This is a nightmarish problem, one not solvable by fiat or recourse to lofty principles but one that is inevitable. In the context of education, especially when publicly funded, these dilemmas must be resolved democratically, not by unaccountable advocates imposing views by circumventing official supervision. This resolution will be, predictably, a messy, contentious route, but the alternative is unacceptable in a democracy. Educators, then, must adhere to publicly decided upon rules regarding what deserves classroom attention, though wise choices cannot be guaranteed.

Notes

1. A noteworthy addition to those favoring the "appreciate difference" definition is the Gallup Poll. Beginning in the spring of 2003, Gallup began using a "Religious Tolerance Index" to assess views towards varied religious groups. This five item scale included such items as "I always treat people of other religious faiths with respect" and "Most religious faiths make a positive contribution to society." Gallup has already employed this measure and it will doubtlessly be embraced by others given Gallup's imprimatur. The upshot, conceivably, will be to stigmatize those having *any* reservations about *any* religion (Winseman 2004).

2. The acceptance of discrimination claims bereft of any hard evidence, let alone a precise legal standard is illustrated in a December 8, 2005 Associated Press story with the headline," Poll: Nearly one out of six employees claim bias" (http://msnbc.msn.com/id/10385843/print/1/displaymode/1098/. These reports of "victimization" were treated at face value and inspired a call for more workplace diversity training. Never mentioned was the possibility that at least some perceptions may have been groundless, a result of harmless misunderstanding or just contrived for purposes of litigation.

3. Kors (2000) offers an illuminating account of this enterprise. What is especially notable is that "thought reform" efforts exist apart from any crime or even documented offensive behavior. It is just assumed that evil lurks in the heart of oppressors (especially white males), and these potential evildoers may be totally unaware of hidden proclivities. Sensitivity training is thus a preemptive strike to insure social harmony. Ironically, this "bring social tranquility" agenda often entails highly inflammatory statements directed against whites in general and white males in particular as if they are the root cause of human misery.

4. Though formal defenses of intolerance are exceedingly rare in today's push towards extending tolerance, Waldron (2003) carefully examines several possibilities. One particularly noteworthy defense concerns whether those who demand total compliance with their views, e.g., Muslims seeking state adoption of *Sharia*, warrant tolerance. Conceivably, a liberal society might reject such an imposed orthodoxy.

5. Today's one-sided treatment of Mill as the unabashed tolerance champion is remarkable given his own limited commitment to "anything goes." His focus was largely on personal eccentricities and certainly stopped far short of banishing moral strictures from public or private life. According to Cowling (1990) Mill was quite authoritarian insofar as envisioning a society run by "better minds."

6. Though scholars, and virtually everyone else, flee devising a "do not tolerate" registry, such a list does occasionally surface. Jonathan Peal, a rabbi from Queens,

N.Y., took the plunge in a New Jersey newspaper editorial. He called for intolerance of child-abusers, wife-beaters, drug pushers and abusers, gossipers, thieves and malingerers, chronic liars, hypocrites and cheaters, ingrates, as well as racists and those engaging in gratuitous violence (Pearl 2004). Unfortunately, this inventory favored murky categories and is hardly exhaustive.

7.   The potential harm done in the name of "tolerance" is probably immense. As we shall eventually see, various personal vices are sometimes "tolerated" when ethical principles would counsel stern rebuke. This topic is briefly but superbly explored in Stetson and Conti (2005, 144-47).

8.   Perhaps the most difficult detail in this argument concerns unelected judges. In principle, these judges are politically accountable via administrative devices (e.g., modifying their jurisdiction) and, ultimately, impeachment. Nominally, then, a judicial ruling mandating specific tolerance instruction would qualify as legitimate in our reasoning. Yet, such edicts may be impossible to overcome via normal politics save time-consuming litigation or even a constitutional amendment. Much depends on how far a judicial decision strays from statutes.

3

Preaching the Tolerance Gospel

"If you have the law, argue the law. If you have the facts, argue the facts. If you have neither the law nor the facts, confuse the issue."—Old "country lawyer" adage

We have depicted how educators characterize tolerance, namely dichotomizing this concept into the appreciated (tolerance) versus the loathed (intolerance). A twofold demarcation is, however, only the departure point in launching a far more encompassing pedagogical enterprise whose implementation will, allegedly, ensure domestic social tranquility, if not world peace. Here we dig deeper and extract the major, undergirding, barely articulated themes. At the outset, we admit to an unsympathetic, if not hostile, overview. We are, however, unapologetic. The stakes here, if only the opportunity costs when neglecting traditional academics, is huge and advocates enjoy far more freedom to make outrageous claims than FDA scientists reviewing putative miracle cures. Somebody has to put the endeavor under the microscope, and since devotees themselves shun their responsibility, we assign ourselves the task.

Several caveats are necessary before beginning. First, our accounts derive from what promoters themselves offer plus mass media stories. Ongoing classroom instruction is beyond our scope; conceivably, what transpires in lessons may diverge from what educators claim as teachers themselves look askance at these pedagogical admonitions. It is also unclear just how much classroom time is actually allocated, though advocates boast about how their magazines, seminars, and similar activities draw teacher admiration.[1] Moreover, culling is not executed according to a scientific formula though it is extensive. Analysis merely aims to provide an overall, if somewhat impressionistic, overview. Finally, the educator-led "teach tolerance" project is hardly a coherent philosophy advanced by a single organization. It is a decentralized, moralistic movement, and, as such, lacks a single, canonical text. We merely assemble commonplace themes, and we cannot claim that every proponent endorses each of these ideas, though we suspect that differences are relatively minor.

Attitudes are Fundamental

Transforming attitudes lies at the heart of this quest and it is further assumed that what is outwardly expressed authentically reflects inner beliefs. It seems almost inconceivable to pedagogues that people lie or otherwise hide private thoughts. This rudimentary framework—verbal acquiescence in accepting differences insures social serenity—certainly appears so axiomatic that marshalling supporting empirical data is gratuitous. This wondrous outcome is settled by fiat without agonizing about possible complexities. Conspicuously absent is a discussion of the attitude-behavior link, a critical part of this equation that chapter 5 explores in depth. As social science theory, this framework is remarkably reductionist.

There is also an accompanying upbeat, if naïve, vision of human nature: since people are born without prejudices and hatreds, a blank slate (or *tabula rasa*, in Locke's terminology), successful transformation simply entails intercepting competing "bad thoughts" that, sadly, intrude from a strife-filled world. It is an optimistic Rousseau-like perspective; to wit, people are born inclined to embrace uniqueness but everywhere people battle each other.[2] More remarkable, even when tolerance fans admit that people are born disliking differences, reversing these inclination is readily achievable. As Bruce D. Perry (2002), who is both an MD and a Ph.D., put it, "Once a child learns that differences make other people interesting, stimulating, and capable, she becomes more comfortable with the world" and this, we are assured, begets tolerance. This is light years distant from the Madisonian, pessimistic version underlying the Constitution, specifically, people naturally seek to tyrannize others, and this is irreversible and tenacious, so it is government structure, not futile appeals to goodness or refurbishing human nature that sustains liberty. This sweeping view of human malleability is Marxian in character and one can only wonder how its champions would fare in the Middle East or the Balkans.

Arriving at a blank slate interpretation often involves some remarkable fancy intellectual footwork. *Hate Hurts* (Stern-LaRosa and Bettmann 2000), a seemingly research-based book sponsored by the well-heeled, prestigious Anti-Defamation League, begins with a theory of society in which everything is, ultimately, socially constructed and therefore manageable: "Noticing differences is biological. Forming attitudes about them is social. The good news is that we can shape how children value the differences they perceive" (14). Though conceding that even infants instinctively recognize human variations, biologically anchored perceptions are still treated positively: "…babies at this age instinctively enjoy and appreciate differences" (18). When agonizing over why toddlers perceive some groups harshly, for example, believing that black males are more often punished, the authors quickly explain that children must have absorbed racial prejudices from adults, the movies, or similarly hate-laden environmental influences. Alternatives explanations are absent, that is, children actually encounter these shortcomings or that distaste, not appreciation, may be biologically instinctive. Everything, positive or negative, is pushed into the Rousseau-like Procrustean bed.

An almost religious quality in the rescuing of youngsters from impending hatefulness abounds, its fervency akin to eras when missionaries baptized heathen infants to save their souls. This enthusiasm was conspicuously illustrated in 2005 when the Anti-Defamation League (ADL) together with the Miami-Dade Family Learning Partnership instigated a project in which all thirty-two thousand babies born in Dade County, Florida that year would receive books depicting the immense variety of human eyes and noses (some 32,000 types!) to encourage respect for differences. As Frances Tropp, associate director of the ADL's southern region put it, "If we could reach children before they developed biases and prejudices, while they were still young, then we are ahead of the game" (Bierman 2005). Whether or not it is possible to shield youngsters from corrupting bigotry via distributing bewildering picture books overflowing with noses and eyes is, needless to say, an unanswered scientific puzzle.

Psychology is equally central in calibrating inflicted harm. Recall earlier pleas by Locke, Voltaire, and other forbearance champions, that extending acceptance is vital to stop the slaughter of religious heretics, or at least to keep them out of jail for innocently practicing their faith. That the objects of intolerance might feel ostracized or shamed was irrelevant—the issue was life or death. Today, by contrast, at least for true believers, there is a conflation of torture (even execution) and psychological distress, no matter how minor. In an odd sense, the right to be free of troubling "insensitivity" has been raised up to an unalienable right, perchance more important than life, liberty, and/or protection of property. Disparaging words make people feel rotten, decrease self-esteem, and this wounding is inherently reprehensible. Discomfort now becomes the modern gold standard for evildoing.

It is also assumed that inner scars will someday, in some form, have socially detrimental outward consequences—physical abusiveness or murdering classmates. One leading compendium of anti-hate nostrums was explicit regarding this self-esteem/mayhem link: "People who feel good about themselves exhibit less prejudice and discriminatory behavior than people who don't" (Stern-LaRosa and Bettmann 2000, 267). A Harvard psychiatrist averred that even encountering mild prejudice may bring enough emotional damage to disrupt normal functioning (Poussaint in Bullard, 1996, xiv). Zero scientific evidence is supplied regarding how low self-esteem begets future harm. Since data on self-esteem abounds, and heightened self-appreciation may be delusional, the omission is yet more shoddy social science.

Also postulated is that people are naturally thin-skinned about verbal slights, no matter if the disrespect was unintentional and that thickening a person's skin is an illegitimate solution to combating hostility. Actually, the opposite is prescribed—tolerance requires thinning the skin by heightening racial/ethnic sensitivities. With so many hurting opportunities, normal human interaction requires endless vigilance. *Hate Hurts* (Stern-LaRosa and Bettmann 2000) offers a seemingly endless parade of perilous off-hand remarks made by children, many of which sound innocuous to the untrained ear, for example, referring to an exam as *lame* (217) since this term demeans an individual's physical handicap.

In a world where insulting terminology constantly shifts and much depends on who uses the label, navigating these waters can be nightmarish. "Queer" and "dyke" can be hateful unless expressed by homosexuals and then they may become badges of honor.[3] According to one California newspaper report (Harris 2004) October is now nationally recognized as "Queer History Month" but what if a youngster calls a classmate, "you queer!" Who decides when usage constitutes an insult? Whether the banter occurred within earshot of a gay person appears irrelevant—words hurt even if not heard.

It is almost as if educators are constructing a *cordon sanitaire* in which children can live their lives without ever hearing bad words. Diane Ravitch (2003) recounts how textbook censors screen out anything potentially discomforting, from controversial terms like abortion to less-than-flattering descriptions of events or people, since, it is assumed, that mere exposure psychologically debilitates fragile youngsters. Ravitch's *Appendix I* provides nearly thirty single-spaced pages of such "damaging" words and phrases, terms like barbarian, crazy person, dummy, fat, and lady. Recall Victorian sensibilities when women at the dinner table were deemed so delicate that merely mentioning a chicken's anatomy (breast, leg, thigh) was impolite, so the offending body parts had to be replaced by the more sexually neutral white and dark lest the fairer sex faint.

Significantly, there is no cost-benefit analysis for banishing distress. Educators hope to concoct an idyllic world devoid of well-intentioned rebuke (or "tough love") let alone well-intended mocking humor. A lesson proffered by the popular *Teaching Tolerance* magazine recounts the damage done by teasing obese children about being fat. The essay acknowledged that childhood obesity was rampant and unhealthy, but medical dangers aside, teasing was objectionable since it lowered a person's self-esteem and horizons (Aronson 2004). In another case, a hefty student complained that after being admonished that it wouldn't hurt for him to lose a little weight, he now understood the meaning of discrimination (Hossain 2004). Ironically, self-images unscathed by criticism are branded "healthy" though taunting aimed to inhibit medically dangerous behavior is now certified as "harmful." That discomfort from scolding might be short-lived, a worthwhile price for being motivated to shed pounds, perchance superior to drugs or unsustainable diets, remained unsaid. Sustaining pristine self-esteem clearly outranks better health in calculating well-being.

It is also notable that the burden for change always falls on the person expressing the hurtful view, almost never on the person with the alleged defect. This is true even where the trait that draws aversion is reversible, for example, an unkempt appearance or slurred speech, and change might even be beneficial. Nonetheless, sensitivity educators tacitly assume that pretending that this unpleasantness does not exist helps build a better society. The see no evil, hear no evil doctrine is carried to absurdity and, conceivably, serves to lighten the responsibility of those who could help others.

Sensitivity educators further promote feelings of "acceptance" to contravene sound instincts. Instruction thus increases the likelihood of personal harm or group strife, the very outcome lessons supposedly mitigate. For example, immediately following 9/11 many Arab children attending a Brooklyn, N.Y., public grade school only a short distance from the fallen World Trade Center towers felt fearful, a condition compounded by slurs from non-Arab classmates and neighbors. Nevertheless, thanks to speedy sympathetic teacher interventions, Arab pupils soon felt at ease, assured that Arab ethnicity drew respect in today's tumultuous world (Rose 2001/2002). Advice regarding caution in dangerous situation, not reassurances of zero danger, might have been more helpful.

In *Hate Hurts* (Stern-LaRosa and Bettmann 2000, 48) the lesson about homosexuality seeks to root out "unconscious beliefs in myths and stereotypes" among children that prompt irrational fears of gays, even homophobia. Nothing is said to these youngsters about gays justifying apprehension. One can only imagine how apprehensive parents or teachers are safely advising children about pedophiles.[4] Sara Bullard (1996, 25) excoriates a friend for "intolerance" when locking her car doors in a lower-class black neighborhood though, of course, the much higher black crime rate is uncontestable (and some places now require locked car doors!). Unfortunately, though anxiety and suspicion may instigate discomfort, these instinctive human reactions are often indispensable in potentially dangerous situations. Like pain, unease is an innate survival mechanism. Promoting inner tranquility to achieve "tolerance" can also be a cost-inefficient alternative to, say, learning to manage touchy encounters or tips on disguising hostility-evoking traits.

A simplistic "political theory" underlies this moralistic movement: (1) a harmonious society absolutely requires instilling appreciative personal dispositions, the earlier the better and (2) once a penchant for accepting the once disliked is ubiquitous, peacefulness will triumph, both at home and abroad. Yet again, a simple reductionist, feebly supported set of homilies supplies guidance. A story in the *American Teacher,* a United Federation of Teachers publication, was explicit: "Respecting the individual and celebrating religious, cultural and ethnic diversity here and around the globe—these are the true enemies of terrorism, values that would make the events of September 11, 2001 all but impossible if they were more widely shared" (Rose 2001/2002).

Educators accepting this rudimentary but grandiose conflict theory do so in accordance with expert advice. The National Association of School Psychologists in an effort to quell post-9/11 civil discord expressly adopted this framework, noting that America's darkest moments (e.g., mistreating people of Japanese ancestry during World War II) flowed from intolerance and hatred, and that lashing out against innocent people only exacerbates future violence. Most pointedly, by showing mutual respect we can strengthen communities at home and thus "show the world that American values will endure now and forever" (http://www.nasponline.org/NEAT/tolerance,html). In short, tolerance on the part of the aggrieved party is the superior way to fight terror and, conceivably, tolerance was the proper stratagem to prevent possible sabotage during World War II.

Sara Bullard, a founder of the Teaching Tolerance project, an immensely influential organization to judge by its proliferating activities and publications, goes a step further (Bullard 1996, 12-14). She argues that virtually every misfortune, from poverty to drug abuse, from suicide to world peace, is traceable to the intolerance that arises in families bereft of love and exemplary behavior. As she put it, "Clearly, our diverse democracy will grow into a companionable place only if we plant the seeds of peace in our own homes" (13-14). In an instant, *sans* any proof, every traditional bulwark of American-style democracy, for example, the rule of law, limited government, economic abundance, elections and a free press, are subordinated to family therapy. A few pages later (42) she blithely contends that the only difference between tolerant and intolerant people is early family life. In this cosmology civil strife can be held at bay if only we assist dysfunctional families by promoting love. As is commonplace in this literature, the potentially dangerous tension between government intervention in family life and personal liberty is scarcely noticed.

It is difficult to exaggerate how obsession with inner thoughts to the neglect of all else can lead the entire enterprise off on wild goose chases. It is almost as if the outward expression of appreciation is the decisive, supreme cosmic force in human affairs. As Marxists fixated on the ownership of production, as Freudians obsessed over repressed sexuality, educators see worldly strife as flowing from explicitly voiced interpersonal hate. Personal repugnance has now become the root of all evil, a one-factor theory of history. Organizers of one Louisiana high school bigotry reduction project even depicted the Crusades, the fighting in the Balkans, plus the rest of the world's violence as resulting from insufficient tolerance (Fryer 2003). A similar analysis (Fleming and Gilmore 2000) went so far as to claim that the Holocaust was traceable to slurs about Jews, an analysis oblivious to countless exceptions and maddening causal complexities. That anti-Semitism might, for example, derive from marketplace competition or top-down organized scapegoating, and that verbalized religious hostility itself was largely epiphenomenal, escapes notice.

The facile substitution of "intolerance" for specific ideologies that resulted in immense carnage is also worth noting. It is not communism, fascism, or rampant nationalism per se that instigates mass slaughter; it is the underlying aversion to what differs that is the genuine culprit.[5] Alvin F. Poussaint, a clinical professor of psychiatry at Harvard, explicitly claims that intolerance has killed or enslaved millions, and this same dangerous virus still festers in the U.S. as evidenced by assaults on homosexuals, women, and other disparaged groups. Significantly, Poussaint believes this ailment (and he does apply a medical framework) can be fought by enacting civil rights laws and pursuing affirmative action (*Teaching Tolerance,* 1996, foreword).

Nor do these educators broach the possibility of "bad feelings" and inter-ethnic distaste (including racist slurs) being nearly universal, a normal though annoying feature of human interaction, and such loathing seldom erupts into genocide, let alone violent civil conflict. Surely the United States has long had a sub-culture in which anti-Jewish remarks (and derogatory "ethnic humor" more generally) were commonplace. As we suggested in chapter 2, the objects of this aggression enjoy multiple defensive measures besides pleading with their enemies for greater forbearance—for decades, blacks living in the Jim Crow South simply migrated northward rather than preach forbearance to nar-row-minded whites (an undertaking that undoubtedly would have aggravated hostility). Moreover, how would tolerance-minded educators teaching about the Holocaust respond to the proposition that contemporary European anti-Semitism flows principally from militant Islam, not insults, so publicly silencing bigots scarcely matters? Surely any robust conflict theory must include additional (and rival) explanatory factors if it is to rise above sloganeering. Yet one more time, essential complexity is absent.

Appreciating Diversity

Tolerance (or intolerance) cannot be abstract; one must display it to *something* in particular—one cannot appreciate everything or nothing. Instruction must involve concrete referents, and, assumingly, these phenomena are, for one reason or another, currently under-appreciated. Recall that Locke pleaded for allowing Quakers and Baptists to worship freely; he did not hail the ben-efits of having "multiple theological viewpoints." In principle, the potential "need-to-tolerate" menu is limitless, and, to compound this abundance, today's proliferating advocacy groups virtually guarantee scores of candidates seeking entry. Even proponents of ideas currently beyond respectability, for example, terrorism, can insist that they too deserve an invitation to the Pantheon (and, in fact, terrorism does have its defenders as legitimate self-defense). What, then, in particular do these educators *specifically* welcome, and of greater significance for democratic schools, are these choices cogently justified? Might there be a parallel with prestige university admissions—thousands submit credentials for rigorous scrutiny, but schools accept only a handful. Or, is the selection process more haphazard, one in which "successful applicants" gain entry for reasons that seem capricious or just whim or ideological factors?

When educators extol what today deserves appreciation, they inevitably begin by referring to "differences between people" ("diversity" is a synonym for this phrase). The Santa Barbara County, California school superintendent is typical: "Learning tolerance for human differences is never an easy task, but those who work with young people must try to help them do so." Further on he adds, "The themes of tolerance of and respect for all people and cultures are very important for our students to learn and understand..." (Cirone 2001) Thus, to reject the inherent goodness of (unspecified) human differences is, *ipso facto*, to practice hate and discrimination.

But, what variations among thousands explicitly warrant heightened approval? Scanning countless lessons plans, pleas, and heartfelt admonitions uncovers a medley of candidates deserving "greater appreciation" though, as a brief sampling will reveal, only a small handful of applicants repeatedly survive the final cut. The PBS lesson plan mentioned in chapter 1 specifically speaks of regional, linguistic, and socioeconomic differences. The terms "Arab," "Middle East," and "Muslim" also briefly occurred in the context of offering tips on eradicating "ethnic stereotypes." One typical California junior high school program spoke of color, race, sexual orientation, and socio-economic background (Losi 2005). Meanwhile, a Minnesota grade school, in a program involving some 20,000 students statewide, zeroes in on skin color, racism, and cultural differences (Her 2003). A post-9/11 statement issued by the National Association of School Psychologists seeking to calm troubled waters noted predictably the need to show acceptance towards Arabs. It then went on to extol the welcoming of different races, ethnicities, sexual orientations, and "those with special needs" (http://www.nasponline.org/NEAT/tolerance,html). Holloway's (2003) detailed overview of tolerance-promoting nostrums repeatedly singled out race, ethnicity, culture, class and gender variations as requiring pedagogical attention. Similarly, the book-length *Hate Hurts* (Stern-LaRosa and Bettmann 2000) in the chapter "Some Things That Make People Different From One Another" highlighted gender, sexual orientation, race, religion, culture, ethnicity, and, lastly, differences in ability (the polite phraseology for the disabled).

This litany of those deserving candidates initially seems obvious to those immersed in today's academy but there is nothing inevitable about these compilations. Keep in mind that the purpose here is to offer concrete, practical advice to dodge future strife, not just celebrate abstract human dissimilarity as one learns to appreciate nature. Unfortunately, once we move beyond glittering generalities, and especially as children grow up and encounter real-world evils, these classification frameworks will surely shift with the political winds and thus prove a confusing guide. To be blunt, children receive a crude, oddly selective taxonomy, and while it is arguable that such simplicity is appropriate for youngsters, avoiding the subject altogether might in the long run be less mischievous. Educators might also reasonably insist that fabricating *any* catalogue of "what needs tolerance" will be problematic and too filled with maddening exceptions to apply systematically.

An interesting example of student bewilderment of just what deserves "inclusion" occurred in a Florida high school's effort to organize a "Day of Silence/ Tolerance" promotion (Catalanello 2005). When this event (which included wearing black) sought to honor gays, it brought opposition from a local Christian minister who saw it as a pro-homosexuality ploy. Defenders asserted that it was not just about gays, but about everybody, and to make this point they offered a "Pledge of Tolerance" which students could voluntarily sign during lunchtime. This affirmation read, "We pledge to make our school and community a better place by showing tolerance to all regardless of race, culture, religion, sexual identity *or any other characteristic*" (italics added). In other words, tolerance is just a blank check lest *somebody* be excluded.

This open-ended approach can become a nightmare. The categories themselves, for example, race, ethnicity, etc., are crude to the point of inaccuracy across myriad circumstances. Classification can be controversial, even insulting. Are voodoo and Scientology, let alone witchcraft and paganism, bona fide religions? Even the seemingly hard and fast category of "sex" grows murky given modern surgical miracles permitting sex changes, so we now have people who are "male" or "female" in degrees or as matters of personal preference. Advocacy groups sometimes divide on what certifies authenticity in such matters (the term "authentic" usually betrays disagreement, as in the phrase "authentically black" which suggests that some blacks are not really black). The U.S. Census Bureau has long wrestled with defining "race" and has almost abandoned this search since people themselves define racial identities in myriad, quite personal ways. There is no legal definition of race, and short of large-scale DNA testing, considerable latitude exists for self-classification.

Meanwhile, more than a few academics insist that "race" is meaningless, an injurious social construction, and should be dropped from public discussion. Two similar-looking people can diverge in their racial/ethnic identity—one sees herself as "black," another as "Latina." Outward indicators can deceive—a Spanish-sounding name need not indicate Spanish ancestry if it was acquired by marriage (the reverse is also true insofar as family names are occasionally legally Anglicized). There can be opportunism as when people adopt iffy identities by alleging ancestral traits to receive government benefits targeted for the disadvantaged. Cultural variations are often nuanced, and a mischaracterization invites rebuke; even correct labeling might be deemed patronizing insofar as it denies uniqueness. Upper-class Cuban Americans who are often indistinguishable for those classifying themselves as "white" might be outraged if treated as poor Mexicans though both may be officially labeled "Hispanic."

Specific context can powerfully shape group identities. A handful of students of Mexican ancestry in an all-white school can view themselves as Mexican; the same students in a setting where Mexican immigrants dominate can, instead, emphasize their regional origins within Mexico, length of U.S. residence, social status, or any number of traits barely having anything to do with Mexican ethnicity. Powerful self-identities may be nearly incomprehensible to uninformed outsiders. For example, naïve teachers might falsely assume that Jewish students share a common culture and religion, yet variations in parent national origins, home language, religious orthodoxy, and rabbinical loyalty can breed warring factions. Some ultra-Orthodox Jewish students might refuse to recognize fellow more secularized co-religionists as "Jewish." In such instances discerning key definitional traits may require careful study, and crude terms like "religion" are irrelevant.

It is also true that since these myriad to-be-cherished traits are generally non-exclusive, they can be assembled in endless combinations and political advocates often demand multi-trait labels to signify authentic distinctiveness. This is a world in which Hispanic disabled lesbians might allege themselves to possess a culture poles apart from what English-speaking African-American male homosexuals enjoy. Must pupils welcome each and every combination, or are some deservedly "less important"? What if bisexuals insist that "homosexual" inaccurately captures their unique lifestyle and are offended when lumped together with gays? To repeat yet one more time, this fracturing taxonomic approach encourages mind-boggling confusion for uncertain pedagogical ends. It might be more advisable for teachers to counsel treating people as people regardless of race or sexuality.

Nor is it self-evident just how to portray each trait, other than that this account must be uniformly favorable. For example, when exploring African-American culture, what *exactly* should be explicated and from what historical perspective? Should slavery be depicted as an unmitigated human disaster or should free blacks who surmounted hardship be acknowledged? What about recognizing black slaves who voluntarily served in the Confederate Army? Such details are hardly trivial to various racial/ethnic groups. Given that groups seeking better classroom treatment have multiple leaders, all with varied agendas, how is a sensitive educator to select "authentic" voices? When teaching black history, the range of perspectives is formidable, everything from Afro-centrism to accounts stressing traditional religious and family values. A few black leaders might be enraged at the very mention of Booker T. Washington given his "conservative" views.

Compounding this awaiting perplexity is that many of the educator-favored categories are largely legal, often affirmative action-based, and differ from what people themselves use. "Hispanic" may comprise a legitimate "ethnicity" in textbooks celebrating diversity, but among millions from Mexico, Central and South America, "Hispanic" is almost irrelevant: Guatemalans see themselves as distinct from El Salvadorians, and millions of so-called "Hispanics" speak Indian dialects or Portuguese, not Spanish. Many can barely speak Spanish. Ditto for "Asians," a heterogeneous people, diverging profoundly in religion, culture, and appearance. Lumping together, say, Vietnamese, Chinese, Koreans, and Japanese people so as to show respect via organizing an "Asian potluck dinner" will likely bring indignation, not harmony.

Those monitoring academic fashions will undoubtedly note that the identity menu derives largely—if not exclusively—from post-modern theorizing commonly found in English departments, and far less from what actually transpires on the street. Significantly, identity champions never admonish students to think of themselves as "Americans" though this indisputably is *the* core identity of nearly all students. Nor is there any discussion of geographical self-classification (e.g., being a New Yorker) though this, too, is commonplace, as is shown by the fact that Americans encountering each other overseas inevitably start conversations with "Where are you from?" not "What's your sexual preference?" Equally absent from this menu is family identity, one's connection with relatives and ancestors. As was true with national identity, family loyalties have long anchored civil society and are far more useful and psychologically satisfying than one's erotic inclinations.

The major flaw in this commonplace category *carte du jour* is that it is unclear whether, in fact, candidates for inclusion are sufficiently at risk to justify selection. The implicit assertion is that those singled out *might* be vulnerable to hatreds, or have once encountered aversion, but present-day repression is just blithely asserted as if it were plain to see. This is not to say that people distinguishable by race, ethnicity, sexuality, and the like are totally immune from tribulations. But if the applied standard were any amount of harm, everybody deserves the welcome mat including white Christian soldiers whose feelings are occasionally hurt by harsh condemnation. The appropriate—though never asked—question is whether those gaining this "official" protection are the *most* endangered, and if threatened, the impetus to help them is justifiable according to explicit criteria, for example, frequent bodily assaults or property confiscation.

This "who needs tolerance?" is both a moral and empirical question, and the empirical portion requires tedious scrutiny. Not every sect or group claiming harm is credible, and even the most honest soul may exaggerate or minimize nasty encounters. Nor can it be presumed that the classroom is a suitable place to solve these problems, pressing as they may be. How are schools to address the friction between secular and fundamentalist Muslims or between Jewish families refusing to accept interfaith marriages? The world overflows with antagonisms, but much of it scarcely means anything to most schoolchildren who cannot possibly grasp what the complicated conflicts entail.

However one might ultimately resolve invitation-list dilemmas, the key point is that educators fail to address these quandaries, let alone supply convincing justifications. As a practical matter this flight from judgment may be wise since, admittedly, transforming the school into a "tolerance courtroom" to settle the list of aggrieved-claiming finalists would be a nightmare. Educators are unqualified to adjudicate claims and counter-claims by the hundreds regarding who today is *unjustifiably* loathed. Are gays unfairly persecuted in every regard, and how does this mistreatment compare to, say, anti-Semitism? What if this oppression is largely invisible to all but the most hyper-sensitive, a matter of contentious perception or mired in linguistic interpretation (as whether "Polish jokes" constitutes ethnic harassment where no listener is Polish)? In the final analysis, educators seemingly pluck favorite "victims" from thin air or from the speculations of far-removed academics. This is a far cry from earlier eras when visiting the public gallows or jails settled the question of who was being persecuted.

Combating Stereotypes

Paralleling this quest for instilling respect for differences are efforts to expose and expunge what educators call stereotypes. In this context, stereotype use is tantamount to intolerance, and it is commonplace to apply the term "victim" to those stereotyped, even if victims are oblivious to the alleged slight. One quite typical web-based tolerance site made "Busting Stereotypes" the primary order of business in its Five Lessons for Teaching About Tolerance" (www. educationworld.com/a_lesson/lesson294.shtml). In effect, educators proclaim that the world abounds with differences, and we are obligated to cherish variety, but they simultaneously reconize that to acknowledge *some* differences is harmful behavior, and these latter categorizations are "stereotypes." The obvious assignment, then, is to discern which particular labeling is commendable versus hurtful and, since assembling an exhaustive list is impossible, at least elucidate some guiding principles.

Unfortunately for would-be guidance seekers, explications conveniently sidestep the distinction as if it were self-evident. One might wonder whether the famous quip about pornography also applies to stereotypes: I may not be able to define it, but I know it when I see it. The website Tolerance.org offers parents a ten-step program to boost tolerance. Lesson Two, second only to "talking about tolerance," advises parents to point out stereotypes in movies, TV shows, computer games, and the like. "Lunatics" illustrates one such nefarious stereotype. What, exactly, makes "lunatic" a stereotype is, however, left to the imagination so that a well-meaning father or mother trying to draw the line between lunatic versus insane or wacky is left befuddled. Would purely psychiatric terminology, for example, "schizoid personality disorder," escape rebuke? A similar vagueness characterizes PBS's advice to teachers when combating hatefulness: "Use strategies to analyze stereotypes in media (e.g., recognize stereotypes that serve the interest of some groups in society at the expense of others; identify techniques used in visual media that perpetuate stereotypes)" http://www.pbs. org/americaresponds/tolerance.html.

But when tolerance experts do on rare occasions confront it, the result is usually unsatisfying since solutions are largely wordplay, not useful criteria. One lesson plan (Fleming and Gilmore, 2000) defined stereotype as depictions permitting zero deviations while generalizations allow exceptions. This is quite different from, say, what the *Oxford English Dictionary* offers regarding stereotypes, namely a preconceived oversimplified characterization.[6] To illustrate this distinction, Fleming and Gilmore list "Chinese ride bicycles" as a below-the-surface (and assumingly pernicious) "stereotype" since, assuredly, there must be a least one Chinese person out of a billion who has never ridden a bicycle. Supposedly, this training helped promote international understanding among students, though it is hard to imagine how knowing that a few non-bicycle-riding Chinese exists improves ethnic perceptions.

Significantly, the oft-given defense "but such stereotypes are generally true" is irrelevant in this banishment crusade. Consider several offending sex-related stereotypes offered in *Hate Hurts* (Stern, LaRosa and Bett 2000, 44-5):

Girls are compassionate and gentle.
Boys are strong.
Boys are more naturally athletic.
Girls don't hit.
Boys don't cry.

Surely only those totally divorced from plain-to-see reality will deny that these statements are *generally* true and, more important, supply handy shortcuts in navigating life's choices. A coach who organized a sports team that refused to recognize sexual distinctions surely invites needless tribulations (e.g., girls regularly losing when strength mattered). Ironically, girls abhorring rough-and-tumble sports might be compelled to participate so as to "banish stereotypes" and their lackluster performance might only deepen the "stereotype," an outcome hardly desired by those seeking to rid society of invidious comparisons. Only coaches pursuing a non-athletic agenda could remain employed in this "sensitive" environment. To be sure, an occasional girl might be a champion wrestler by beating docile, crybaby boys, but everyone would recognize that this was exceptional and confessing male superiority—documented in wins and losses—hardly a sign of hatefulness.

This cosmology assumes that stereotypes result from ignorance, not reality and, significantly, this connection is beyond empirical analysis. Thus, is a student who observes that students of Chinese backgrounds academically outperform African Americans—since he or she regularly encounters this pattern, reads about it in reputable books and magazines, and hears others confirming it from this perspective—is guilty of factual inaccuracy. This reasoning, with its virtually inescapable culpable verdict, is deceptively consequential, for it awards the tolerance-minded educator *permanent* authority to refurbish "bad" thinking. A hapless stereotyper, protestations and documentation aside, will be told again and again à la *1984* that 2+2=5. Going one step further, if educators cannot close racial gaps in academic attainment, along with all the other disconcerting and patently obvious inequalities, then perhaps these tolerance experts can banish them by forcing people to deny their existence.[7]

Rooting out stereotypes can take bizarre twists when those seeking betterment zero in on minor cognitive adjustments. It is as if we could improve the world simply by reclassifying what instigates strife. The Tolerance Minnesota project, for example, combats racism among early grade school children by teaching students that familiar racial classification labels, that is, black, white, brown, are factually "wrong" and terminology such as pink, tan, and similar fine-grained color distinctions should be substituted. That is, "black" is a (bad) stereotype since, quite plainly, those labeled "black" are not technically black-colored but various hues of brown. The project's director alleges that applying a multi-color skin palette will help avoid hateful race-based name calling and thus insure tranquility. This and similar anti-intolerance programs reached some 20,000 students in Minnesota during 2002 (Her 2003). Left unsaid is that applying intermediate (or "mixed") racial categories has long been resisted (especially as U.S. Census categories) by nearly all mainstream civil rights organizations as an insidious ploy to fragment African-American political influence. It is also a recipe for befuddlement given the multiplicity of skin tone characterizations or imprecise vocabulary (for example, distinguishing an "olive complexion" from "swarthy").

The "war" on stereotypes can occasionally turn Kafkaesque. For example, the PRIDE Alliance, a University of Redland (California) gay group held a Drag Ball so as to raise funds to promote tolerance and fund scholarships for gay students. Five hundred people were expected to attend, many of them heterosexual. As is typical in such drag shows in which men impersonate women, entertainment veers towards outrageous kitsch. Several performers regularly worked at local clubs and one ("Bridgette") weighed in at 320 pounds and was to wear a cheerleader's costume in his act (Harp 2005). A naïve straight student attending his or her first drag queen event might see such "dangerous stereotypes" of gays as heavy drinking, cross dressing, sexually tinged rowdiness and campy "effeminate" behavior. One can only be reminded of Groucho Marx's famous quip: Who do you believe, me or your own eyes?

Commonplace illustrations infusing this literature also make it apparent that negative assessments are "dangerous stereotypes" regardless of documentation or careful qualifiers. The assertion's harmful consequence, not its factual validity, thus determines categorization into "laudable difference" versus "stereotype." To contend, for example, that African Americans are generally more crime prone than Asians is, at least in this taxonomy, to demonstrate "intolerance" regardless of data accuracy or the "generally" qualifier. A well-meaning educator might also chastise the speaker by insisting that this statement is factually false since not all blacks are criminals and many Asians are wrongdoers. Even if this teacher conceded the statement's overall accuracy, the intolerance accusation will probably stick since the statement's likely (unconscious) goal was destructive, that is, diminish the self-esteem of African Americans. Stating indisputable facts, then, can be tantamount to expressing hate.

In some lessons even acknowledging admirable group traits can exhibit "harmful stereotyping." To say, for instance, that students of Chinese ancestry excel at math is "destructive," for it implicitly stigmatizes the non-Chinese for being innumerate. Avoiding stereotyping pitfalls is thus futile since even lavish praise might hide invidious comparisons no matter how pure the motives. Savvy students will prudently retreat to banalities or silence. The less astute, unfortunately, will probably invite frequent reprimands for offering even the most innocuous seeming "insensitive" observations. It is no wonder, then, that everybody, teachers and students alike, prudently gravitate toward glittering generalities about "differences."

Safely navigating this stereotyping thicket is clearly impossible, and this is equally true for children, parents, and teachers. There are *no* reasonable, distinct guidelines, let alone grand principles, to assist in avoiding "hurting innocents." Murky standards thus award immense power to those in positions able to certify some remark or picture as "a stereotype." This is but a new (and surely improved) censorship tactic reminiscent of the day when official censors enjoyed carte blanche. Now a frank though admittedly awkward classroom discussion of "hot button" issues such as race or gender is "legitimately" banished, since it "promotes stereotypes." Worse, pupils themselves will learn to fear anything, no matter how educationally valuable, if there is any hint of "controversy," lest they commit hatefulness by even raising the subject. Since nobody can predict what will be "controversial," discussion will occur entirely outside the classroom or in secret. One can only be reminded of how Soviet citizens adapted to the reigning Marxist orthodoxy—a world of euphemisms, deceit, and cynicism.

Relativism

Tolerance-minded educators seemingly welcome human diversity in all its fullness. Such a sweeping admonition to accept *all* human differences without distinction is, obviously, nonsensical. Gradations are inescapable; nobody is perfect. Making distinctions regarding better or worse is vital, if tolerance-devoted educators are to refute critics who castigate them for preaching unqualified moral relativism. This is hardly an abstract dilemma given deeply rooted cultural values, though those dominating the discussion might momentarily brush it aside. How will a teacher respond to a clever student mischievously asserting that the Ku Klux Klan is just as "valid" as civil rights organizations since both advance group rights? More important, how can tolerance aficionados defend themselves against those who insist, as per classic tolerance, that instruction must dwell on odium in navigating this terrain, or at a minimum, acknowledge that even the acceptable might be imperfect?

Advocating gracious acceptance standards does not automatically assent to "everything is all equally good" relativism. As a wine connoisseur might enjoy all wines, he or she may still believe that some wines are superior to others or simply that he or she personally prefers some vintages over others. One can, after all, brag that America is a great country without implying that all other nations are despicable. Gradations of culture, sexuality, and just about everything else are possible without demeaning, save perhaps to strident egalitarians insisting that any hierarchical distinctions are pernicious. Details regarding standards are critical. It is obvious, for example, that Western civilization is superior *if* one seeks scientific accomplishment versus cultures in less developed nations where other quests are more central. All rankings are contentious, but it is absurd to argue that simply admitting any value-ordering automatically condemns the less favored.

Though it would take scant courage to say, "while nearly all groups or beliefs offer something of worth, certain things *are* better, at least to me, given my personal preferences," this nuanced reasoning is unusual among those preaching the tolerance gospel. Advanced instead, though often implicitly, is that everything is *equal*, so, for example, homosexuality, bisexuality, and heterosexuality are merely "different," and diverge not one iota in legality, morality, or contribution to civil society. In fact, recognizing qualitative variations can be tantamount to harmful insensitivity or even hatefulness. In something called the "Declaration of Tolerance" pledge which Tolerance.org offers as its version of the Pledge of Allegiance, students must recite, "Tolerance is a personal decision that comes from the belief that every person is a treasure." Moreover, and of the utmost importance, equal worthiness *must be recognized by others, even those who reject equivalences* (http://www.tolerance.org/101_tools/declaration.html.). A heterosexual student cannot passively escape reproach with, "I'll put up with gays though I think they're immoral." To be certifiably tolerant now requires, "I believe that gay and straight are just as good." Though seldom noticed, this shift is momentous, incredibly costly, and as we shall see in chapter 6, a surefire recipe for avoidable strife.

To be fair, the phrase "equally good" seldom appears in appreciate-diversity appeals since owning up to unabashed relativism invites rebuke. Nevertheless, since there is never any effort to differentiate between what warrants respect, let alone formulate criteria for this task, disclaimers are, frankly, a subterfuge. More common are less inflammatory though blanket admonitions for "respect" or "validation" that, in the absence of any qualifications, imply the equality of everything, or of unmitigated moral relativism on the sly. This is the educational world where everybody receives graduation honors and valedictorians exceed a dozen. One philosophy professor cleverly side-stepped the relativism label by just dividing the world into good and bad: "Our idea is that to be a virtuous citizen is to be one that tolerates everything except intolerance (cited in McDowell and Hostetler 1998, 43).

Bullard (1996, 29-31) promotes judgmental leveling by deprecating its opposite, namely peoples' harmful proclivity to rank. This ordering of educational attainment, income, appearances and talent (among other traits), it is alleged, may provide succor in today's contentious, competitive environment but, alas, ultimately breeds prejudice. Equally invidious is "...a myth of certainty that defines the world in rigid measures of right and wrong, good and bad, success and failure" (53). Better to ignore distinctions, even good ones, lest this bring hurtfulness. Even the bumper sticker "My child is an honors student" (23) is interpreted as invidious ranking. In the final analysis, occasional qualifier aside, it is unlikely that children told to "value all people" will independently impute that some people require a higher valuation and, if such a "we are superior" judgment were uttered, it will probably be viewed as unwelcome aversion.

The dexterity in promoting moral relativism can be prodigious and, to be frank, often underhanded. Consider, for example, how Teaching Tolerance.org, a major provider of pedagogical material, wrestles with homosexuality in "Lesson 9, The Power of Words." Obviously, it would be a tactical blunder to recognize openly that homosexuality and heterosexuality exist on the same moral plane. Instead, as the aim of the exercise announces, "Students will begin to explore some of the effects of compulsory heterosexuality on various aspects of society." Further along the lessons asserted that, "The privileged status of heterosexuals frees them from having to deal with labeling, which is part of the privilege." A tutorial is then proposed in which the world is turned upside down: children explore how society would function if homosexuality, not heterosexuality, were the norm (e.g., having gay parents). Afterwards students in a role reversal exercise are asked how they would personally feel if homosexuality were *compulsory* (italics added). Everything ends when teachers ask their students how they can alter language or behavior as a result of these fresh insights (www.teachingtolerance.org/words). Step by step, including manipulated emotions (forced gay sex!), children are led down a path in which homosexuality becomes a morally neutral option, implicitly on a par with wading through a restaurant menu.

As was true in characterizing stereotyping, a proclivity to rank is transformed into a mental health disorder, hopefully remediable by arduous though absolutely vital therapeutic intervention. Moreover, not only does this ranking inclination harm those being ranked but it also can deepen into self-hatred, and as the drug addict finds solace in destructive heroin, self-haters gain comfort by attacking those who differ in color, religion, or any convenient difference. In other words, a white who insists that blacks are genetically unequal to whites is but scapegoating blacks to ameliorate feelings of loneliness and self-depreciation (Bullard 1996, 51-53, among others).

This leveling is undoubtedly partially explainable by intellectual laziness: considerable effort is required to discern, let alone defend, bona fide distinctions, and few educators are knowledgeable enough to differentiate culture, sexuality, or whatever else is rankable. Gradations also breed acrimony insofar as few like to be told that their culture or religious beliefs, while "good," is nevertheless comparatively inferior. And, to be frank, youngsters may be incapable (or disinclined) of navigating fine-grained distinctions, so teachers simplify to the point of gross exaggeration. As one fourth-grade teacher blithely summarized it when describing "The Rainbow Christmas," a play designed to promote tolerance and diversity, "We need to be open-mined and tolerant of everybody, no matter what their beliefs are and where they're from" (Hutter 2005).

Nonetheless, over and above the convenience of escaping judgment, the affirmations among educators that everything is *really* equal seems genuine. It is almost as if everything, one's culture, sexual activities, language, eating habits, parenting style, socio-economic status, are matters of personal taste. Students in this environment may never hear (at least positively) once commonplace terms like "normal," "natural," "conventional," or "customary." Thus, as some people favor vanilla over chocolate, others prefer to be homosexual over heterosexual, and to praise one as better than the other signifies exclusion, insensitivity, and countless other synonyms for hatefulness.

Cultural relativism, not surprisingly, is typically interwoven with the multiculturalism that is all the rage in American schools.[8] This symbiosis is critical insofar as it permits almost any lesson, even biology or arithmetic, to serve as a forum to preach this "appreciate *all* differences" message (though, to be fair, exceptions are granted to such things as "hurting others" though these are never precisely defined). This perspective involves far more than just the obvious "all cultures are equally good," though this element is obviously paramount. As Alvin J. Schmidt (1997, 3) notes, today's multiculturalism implicitly transforms what might be construed as universal, bedrock principles undergirding American society and transforms them into "mere beliefs," no different than, say, arguments over whether Beethoven sounds better than Mozart. Hence, there is *nothing* intrinsically superior about rule of law, the existence of objective knowledge, fixed moral standards, the subordination of group rights to individual rights, legal equality, democracy, and nearly all else that defines our culture. It is not that these values are bad though, there are some who insist that anything associated with Western civilization is evil; rather, these values are not deemed inherently superior or even better insofar as they lead to more favorable practical outcomes such as economic prosperity or longevity. For the more advanced there are lessons on how to detect hidden cultural bias, for example, how the entire idea of "merit" is just a tactic of for white European cultural domination. Classroom exhortations to obey the law can now be reduced to "everything is just a matter of opinion, with no one sentiment superior to another."

Such intellectually complicated messages, for example, competing notions of legal obligation, are not themselves expressed to grade-school children. Instead, multicultural advocates repackage this equality of everything into "fun" exercises in which the implied idea is that the world is a smorgasbord wherein each has his or her own undisciplined predilections. In one extensive California project, for example, students learned that people all over the world celebrate the same things for the same reasons but just do it differently. To drive this point home, with all the appropriate food, music and decorations, children celebrated Kwanzaa, Chinese New Year, Japanese Children's Day, Passover, and Cinco de Mayo. Not surprisingly, according to the organizer, "The kids love it." Meanwhile, "religious" tolerance for sixth-, seventh-, and eighth-graders is explored with a lesson on "Myths, Deities and Icons" (Cirone 2001).

This unwavering insistence on equality of everything that somehow enters the tolerance Pantheon, which itself is hazy, is, obviously, a difficult position to defend when educators are forcefully confronted with this relativism charge. When on rare occasion they do encounter this rebuke, rejoinders suggest a paucity of thoughtfulness. Consider one such "response" offered by two scholars whose work appeared under the auspices of Columbia University's Teacher's College (Heller and Hawkins 1994). When recounting those lambasting their Teaching Tolerance project for lacking a moral center, and thus, in principle, making it equally applicable to tolerating pedophiles, child molesters, and rapists, the authors supply a straightforward answer—their lesson plans *never* sought appreciation for pedophiles, child molesters, and rapists. These experts are, apparently, literalists who miss their accuser's point—it is *the absence of exclusionary principles* informing this framework, not damnation of particular off-hand odious examples that is so troublesome.

Distorting Reality

It might be tempting to treat this campaign as an isolated school subject akin to once-a-week classes about health in which teachers warn students about dangerous unprotected sex. Though this characterization may occasionally be correct, this is certainly not what tolerance pedagogues intend. Promoting a gracious welcome to just about anything ideally is supposed to infuse the entire curriculum, even subjects like math and science. After all, hatefulness can erupt anywhere—bullies can belittle those failing algebra while biology teachers might make off-hand remarks demeaning women—so success demands a policy of total immersion. This full-time character further requires that schools enlist parents, advising them on how to correct stereotypes expressed at dinner table discussions.

The insertion of "tolerance" into every nook and corner of schooling is deceptively consequential given the barely noticed intellectual "baggage" arriving with advocacy. To be blunt, inculcating this version of forbearance *requires distorting reality*, grievously so in many instances. The unfortunate upshot is that in erstwhile efforts to remediate social problems, schools unwittingly undermine their core academic mission of imparting knowledge. It is not that teachers want to mis-educate students. Rather, "learning to be tolerant" demands myriad factual suppositions and oft-repeated exemplars, and many of these are patently false or, at best, uncertain despite heartfelt contrary assertions. It is far more likely that children will grow cynical versus becoming tolerant.

Nowhere is this reality subversion more glaring that in this literature's relentless reaffirmation that "diversity is our strength" mantra. Proclaiming it is absolutely *de rigueur* in this mission and it is ubiquitous. A National Association of School Psychologists press handout is typical: "America is strong because of our diversity. Known as the great 'melting pot' of the world, American democracy is founded on respect for individual differences. These differences in culture, religion and ethnicity have contributed to the strength and richness of our country" (http://www.nasponline.org/NEAT/tolerance,html). More is involved than gratuitous speech-making. This diversity-equals-strength link is essential for justifying all the attentiveness awarded "diversity." Though never explicitly articulated, the syllogistic logic is unambiguous. We are strong because we are diverse and since educators helps sustain this diversity by urging tolerance towards the different, educators thereby contribute to national vigor. Conversely, those denying these differences or advising assimilation are weakening America.

Not only is this statement factually uncertain if not patently wrong but its constant reiteration *sans* supporting evidence, let alone a willingness to debate veracity, sets a dreadful example for what education supposedly entails. There is a relentless anti-intellectualism disguised by fashionable edu-jargon, for example, ethnic jokes are mechanism of social control (Stern-LaRosa and Bettmann, 208). It is scarcely an exaggeration to say that stylistically (though certainly not substantively) this oft-repeated phrase resembles a theological stricture, a dogmatic proposition exclusively anchored in a faith authoritatively handed down to settle disputes axiomatically. As a slogan it mimics the German *Arbeit Macht Frei* or *1984's* "War is Peace" whereby constant repetition pounds the malleable into ideological compliance. Thus, if a parent objects to spending too much classroom time on appreciating ethnic differences vis-à-vis learning mathematics, the pat "authoritative" rejoinder is that diversity lessons quell hatreds, and thus build a stronger America. Is that aim less important than mastering long division?

No logic or historical reason connects population heterogeneity with national strength or any other virtue. A far more plausible case is that endless appreciate-variety admonitions would be totally *unnecessary* if the United States, like Japan or Norway, were a homogeneous nation. The need to instill approval is but a consequence of having abundant diversity, and a costly obligation one to boot. No reason exists to suppose that multi-ethnic, multi-racial, or multi-religious societies are inevitable or peaceful. In fact, one study of eighth-grade public and private schools in New York and Fort Worth, Texas found that pupils in ethnically diverse schools felt more threatened by those with unpopular views and this resulted in decreased support for civil liberties. Many nations have traditionally "solved" their diversity by banning immigrants who rejected the dominant culture or by forcing assimilation among newcomers. Brutal civil wars are often about ethnic separatism. The entire sustain-separate-identities enterprise can, moreover, be judged a tax on societies that have mixed populations though, admittedly, this "tax" may be justifiable in terms of long-range benefits. Surely the money spent for bilingual education and sundry other accommodations for those beleaguered by mainstream America would be unnecessary, if we all spoke the same language or embraced the identical ethos.

Those pouring ever more funds into tolerance education seem oblivious to the idea that this tactic brings tangible costs, especially opportunity costs, while vague benefits seemingly exist in some idyllic future. Consider, for example, the case of Ligonier, Indiana in which the influx of Hispanics aggravated student adjustment problems for the local school district (Hull 2005). This promote diversity approach was not cost-free—a local foundation provided some $490,000 for the cultural education, of which $182,539 went directly to teachers for cultural awareness projects. Schools also have added expensive bilingual instruction. Yet, what are the demonstrable benefits beyond some hazy "educating the community"? None are offered. A more convincing case would be that it might be wiser to limit immigration and allocate the $490,000 to teach core subjects with demonstrable benefits.

The cheery image of every group bringing something uniquely valuable to our collective table might be suitable for a grade-school textbook, but this upbeat message fails to survive close, open-minded, empirical scrutiny. When academics do venture into this territory (see, for example, Vogt 1997, chapter 5 for a one-sided literature overview on so-called "contact theory") a prodigious effort is made to undercover the slightest upbeat finding while discomforting data is typically dismissed as flawed (e.g., racial/ethnic interaction was not "meaningful"). Frequent examples of inter-group contact making matters worse never enter analysis; failures only instigate calls for more research. Meanwhile, suggestions to facilitate contact benefits verge on the utopian, for example, abolishing academic tracking so whites cannot easily see less academically talented blacks congregating in separate classrooms. There is a philosopher's stone quality to this forced contact endeavor—that magical device that would turn lead into gold.

The urge to avoid offensiveness cannot obscure unsavory historical facts. Irish immigrants of the mid-nineteenth-century brought nonstop drunken brawls and crime to many cities. Today's Mexican arrivals similarly burden innumerable Southwestern towns with crushing health care and crime costs while violent turf battles with black gangs grow commonplace (*WorldNetDaily.com,* 2006). We can thank the Italians for delicious pasta, but not their contribution to organized crime. Why else, both in the past and today, would anti-immigration groups flourish? Did these movements reflect a mass psychosis totally divorced from reality? Hardly—immigration has *always* brought tribulations, and many of these persist. Governments have spent *trillions* to lift African Americans out of poverty with uncertain outcomes, and in a full accounting of having to accommodate immigrants might, conceivably, show an unpleasant reality. To insist that every ethnic or religious groups made an unambiguous—let alone equal—contribution to our national well-being is, to be frank, absurd, and will only bring snickers to the faces of perceptive students.

In some instances, contributions of some ethnic groups might be, on average, *negative* insofar as the accompanying liabilities overshadow benefits. Though this conclusion might be tactfully omitted in scanning the ledger, it undoubtedly has ample truth. Robert Putnam, the distinguished Harvard researcher recently suggested that those living in ethnically diverse communities are less likely to trust others, and social trust is a key building block energizing civic life. He admits that this conclusion is an unwelcome one, but one that still must be acknowledged. As he put it, "We act as turtles. The effects of diversity are worse than what has been imagined." This is even true where differences may appear slight to outsiders—civic life is more likely to thrive in homogeneity (Lloyd 2006).

The value of diversity in education may also be grossly overstated. Diversity proponents have long labored to demonstrate this benefit, but such efforts seldom, if ever, survive close scrutiny. A recent United States Commission on Civil Rights report's overall conclusion drawn from this research literature for primary and secondary schools was that the academic and social benefits of diversity were minimal or inconclusive. This was particularly true for minority students (USCCR Press Release, November 28, 2006). To be sure, these conclusions were not unanimously accepted by the Commission, but opponents generally remain at a loss in showing clear-cut advantages that justify the enormous costs to implement diversity.

History strongly suggests, on balance, the mischievous impact of diversity. Some multi-ethnic empires such as Austro-Hungary under the Hapsburgs were relatively peaceful and tolerant for much (though not all) of their existence but this required constant difficult adjustments. In other instances, e.g., modern-day Great Britain, peaceful co-existence does generally occur though achieving it required centuries of bloody conflict among the Welsh, Scots, and others (though the influx of non-white immigrants has rekindled strife). But, on the other side of history's ledger are far more societies violently choking on "diversity." Obvious illustrations include: Yugoslavia for at least half a millennia; India both before and after the end of colonialism; modern-day Sri Lanka, Kashmir, and Lebanon; the Basque secessionist movement in Spain; Northern Ireland for centuries plus dozens (if not hundreds) of strife-torn societies in Africa, the Middle East, and Asia. Recall chapter 1's depiction of the religious turmoil that plagued Europe; newspapers and TV news daily recount the bloody battles between Iraqi Shiite and Sunni Muslims and, occasionally, massacres involving between Muslims and Christians in Indonesia, Sudan, Russia, and elsewhere. Peaceful multi-ethnic societies draw our attention largely because they are so exceptional. Again, to aver that diversity is the recipe for tranquility is blatant nonsense for anyone who pays attention to the real world.

The contentious character of mixed settings conceivably explains why many groups reject all but the most superficial encounters with outsiders. The Amish, for example, prefer isolated, relatively homogeneous rural settings, free of modern distractions where their children can be raised according to strict religious ideals. Hasidic Jews similarly go to great lengths to separate themselves from diversity, even though they might be living amidst people of greatly varying backgrounds. In both instances, well-intentioned efforts to build bridges to outsiders are resisted as subversive tactics undermining community cohesion. Nor are these religious groups anxious to welcome outsiders in order to educate them about their cultures. Mixed marriages are often viewed as a family disgrace among countless religious sects and ethnic groups. Among certain ultra-Orthodox Jews, teaching non-Jews about sacred texts is a crime to be tried in a rabbinical court.

Recent empirical research from England where multiculturalism is vigorously state-enforced also casts serious doubts on this contact-will-bring-peace hypothesis. Writing for the Commission for Racial Equality, the chair, Trevor Phillips (who is black), concluded that people are happier when with people who are similar racially and ethnically. Those living in ethnically diverse areas are, moreover, less trusting, and this can readily lead to inter-racial disturbances. Phillips goes on to suggest that the solution to this strife may lie in building broader senses of identity that transcend religious, racial, or ethnic identities (Easton 2006).

It is also equally foolish to argue that America was built, and continues to thrive, on a multiplicity of newly arriving cultures, religions, or whatever. America originated as a jumble of religions and economic classes but initial circumstances does not imply that diversity was actively sought as one might, for example, seek a varied, balanced diet as the pathway to health. Many of early settlers explicitly migrated to the New World to *flee* their diverse, enmity-filled surroundings; the Puritans left Holland since it was *too* tolerant and thus posed a threat to community cohesiveness. Outsiders were always greeted with suspicion, not welcomed.

The Founding Fathers fatalistically accepted a plethora of quarreling factions and deep religious divisions, but this was a harsh reality and an *unfortunate* impediment to a non-tyrannical civil society. This disadvantage was to be surmounted via government structure (as per Madison, *Federalist # 10*)—checks and balances, separation of powers, and federalism—not family therapy. There is nothing in our early history about promoting tolerance by the way of redirecting human nature. The Founders would be appalled by the notion that refurbishing family life was the correct pathway to political progress, and would certainly resist any state intervention to promote loving parents.

Relentlessly heeding this mantra probably renders many academic subjects unteachable, if intellectual consistency is the aim. How can a history instructor treat periodic race riots, Indian wars, violent religious clashes, and a horrific Civil War fought along multiple fault lines while simultaneously recognizing that "diversity is our strength"? Or the tribulations of congested, filthy cities during the latter half of the nineteenth century as scores of immigrants arrived? Did their arrival instantly uplift those already here by tutoring natives how to cook matzo ball soup or pizza? One might actually get that cheerful impression when reading textbook accounts of immigrant contribution. Meanwhile, are English teachers to abandon grammar and spelling so as to avoid stigmatizing those challenged by standard English? Must geography lessons hide gigantic gaps in economic accomplishment across nations in order to avoid injuring the self-esteem of students whose ancestors resided in these troubled areas?

Pushed to a *reductio ad absurdum*, the "diversity is our strength" dictum can almost single-handedly destroy education since it forces *everything* involving group variation to be positive. Its most strident relativistic fans might go as far as to insist that *no* group or culture possesses any defects. This pedagogical enterprise subordinates facts to emotions, so "Is it true?" is replaced by "Does it make people feel good?" Even the venerable escape route of "some people say this, others disagree, but the evidence points this way" falls short when the aim is to promote social tranquility. The parallel with teaching communism under Soviet rule is obvious: twisting of reality to satisfy an ideological agenda becomes *de rigueur*. Teachers thus face an unappetizing menu of lying, selectivity, or just mouthing empty-headed slogans in lieu of serious instruction (e.g., African tribalism is unambiguously wonderful since it helps enrich our folklore).

Tolerance devotees also seem obligated to teach a prescription for our turmoil that will only exacerbate matters. This is analogous to pre-modern medicine when cures like arsenic or mercury were often worse than the disease so that visiting the doctor was lethal. To wit, at this campaign's intellectual core lies the supposition that harmony can be best achieved by knowledge and, best of all, interaction among those who differ from each other. Sara Bullard (1996) articulated this commonplace theme: "...we must actively reach out to others whom we would normally avoid. We must intentionally cross racial, religious and economic bounds, and take the risk of entering each other's lives for the purpose of discovering some connection between us" (76). In other words, harmony is just a matter of exposure.

This message is a wonderful and nearly painless marching order for pedagogues seeking world betterment. Now, rather than bedeviling hapless students with academic tedium, teachers can herd their charges to museums showcasing exotic cultures, invite representatives of marginalized groups to propagate the faith and most easily, inundate pupils with pictures, strange foods, foreign folk tales, plays, occasional non-English words, and all else that highlights human variety. The more ambitious can try the Southern Poverty Law Center's "Mix It Up At Lunch" project where students attempt to reverse the familiar self-imposed school lunchrooms racial segregation. This once involved some six thousand schools in all fifty states in 2003 (PR Newswire 2003). The most ambitious tactic is, of course, mandatory school integration so that whites, blacks, and perhaps Hispanics can interact to cherish each other so as to quell racial strife. Breaking down "artificial" barriers may even entail eliminating academic tracking and forcefully diversifying after-school clubs (like cheerleading) that have traditionally attracted students of similar backgrounds.

Unlike most truisms where personal experiences lend credibility, this one flies in the face of what educators, students, and everybody else knows to be indisputably true and, for good measure, what is carefully documented by first-rate research. Schools in which students of mixed backgrounds, especially racial and ethnic differences, are pushed together by court orders are seldom tranquil. Re-segregation to escape the "benefits" of getting to know those who differ is typical. Even in San Francisco, a city famous for celebrating diversity, when a 1982 court-ordered settlement mandating racial/ethnic integration expired in 2001, many parents fled the alleged benefits of cross-group contact. In the space of only four years, the number of ethnically identifiable schools jumped by two-thirds despite administrative efforts to sustain diversity (Fulbright and Knight 2006).

The "white flight" research literature is absolutely conclusive here. James Coleman and associates scrutinized enrollment trends in sixty-seven of the largest central school districts between 1968 and 1973 and reported major white out-migration to the suburbs (cited in Armor 1995, 176). A different study found that in 1,200 school districts any type of interracial contact motivated whites to flee (cited in Armor 1995, 177). The very prospect of encountering differences across race was often sufficient. In a case study of four cities, between 42 percent and 57 percent of white students compelled to attend predominantly black schools were "no-shows" on the first day of classes (cited in Armor 1995, 179). Court ordered integration is routinely ignored. By 1990, the white enrollment in Atlanta's public schools had dropped to below 10 percent while in Dallas it was 18 percent and this "blackening" of urban public education is hardly extreme (Armor 1995, 72). This pattern is both common and unrelenting. Charles T. Clotfelter's (2001) detailed statistical investigations found that white flight still continues despite years of celebrating diversity and is unrelated to district size or metropolitan area population.

Ironically, re-segregation usually involves fleeing groups whose erstwhile contribution is celebrated in these tolerance lessons, that is, African Americans and Hispanics. One can only imagine if it were possible to "integrate" gay students as one might achieve racial balance.[9] Heartfelt admonitions aside, white parents generally refuse to have their offspring mingle with blacks and Hispanics. The costs clearly outweigh alleged rewards and this is true for millions over decades. The predictable "expert" rejoinder is, of course, that aversion is ignorance-based, and that only if parents and children would open their hearts to what experts pronounce appreciation would soar. The impediment, then, is "dangerous stereotypes," not a reality in which black and Hispanic children disrupt learning or commit crimes.

A far better case is that group separation is generally more "natural," and while we may bemoan people keeping their distance, such separation *helps* promote peace (many historic ethnic enclaves such as Jewish ghettoes were partially self-defense measures). Admonishing people to appreciate difference would be irrelevant if society were organized around separated homogeneous enclaves. Or, if such hectoring were pursued in heterogeneous settings, it would be wiser to praise those whom one never encounters—a perfect, risk-free tolerance pedagogy. Convincing American fifth-graders that Kurds are a terrific people will always be "successful," since they are unlikely to meet any Kurds. Success in cooling animosities is less likely in, say, many German cities where encountering Kurds is often unpleasant.

Going one step further, homogeneity is generally what people themselves desire provided this option is voluntary and self-segregation is cost-free. To the extent that neighborhoods reflect the desire for like-minded people to congregate with one another, schools will be relatively homogeneous, so forcing children to travel from these enclaves to achieve social engineering objectives might be excessively costly (particularly if these aims are disliked by recipients). Let us not forget that the father of Linda Brown, the plaintiff in the historic *Brown v. Board of Education* (1954), sued to keep his daughter in a neighborhood school versus having her bused miles away.[10]

No doubt clever students will ask their teachers why governments must force diversity on businesses and colleges if diversity is so inherently valuable. After all, the number of statutes, court cases, consent degrees, and ongoing litigation here is enormous, so diversity, perhaps like the speed limit, required legal coercion. A truly bright student might go even further and ask for statistical proof that policies such as affirmative action or court-ordered busing have, on the whole, benefited America, especially given the huge costs. One can only imagine a teacher confronting such a contentious student, particularly since the pro-diversity data here are inconclusive, at best.[11]

What is crucial about this teacher-conveyed misinformation is not that it is wrong. To some degree much of education, especially in the sciences and history, is often factually incorrect given evolving discovery. Far more relevant is that misinformation is (or should be) easily recognized as such by educators. It requires effort to deny an obvious reality. That recipients of misinformation are compelled by state law to heed these messages only compounds this sin. If the opportunity costs of mis-education are factored in, the endeavor's costs are gargantuan. This is willful advancement of propaganda over genuine education and, as such, a far deeper corruption than just garbling a fact or two.

Conclusions

It should be clear that the campaign's underlying theoretical structures are exceedingly flimsy. The conceptual problems we elucidated in chapter 2 are blithely ignored, let alone resolved. These passionate arguments are pure, unqualified assertion. Cited scholarly research is entirely one-sided, flippant, and undoubtedly convincing only to the already convinced. Endlessly repeated assertions, for example, "diversity makes us strong," are so patently false, so out of touch with everyday reality, that one can only wonder where these putative education experts live. An infatuation with offhand reductionist explanations (e.g., unhealthy home life begets civil strife) are almost comical. What, pray tell, might the sentence, "We will only attain freedom if we learn to appreciate what is different and muster the courage to discover what is fundamentally the same" *possibly* mean? (Heller and Hawkins, 1994). What happens when students hear such gobbledygook? This is not a scientific enterprise that resembles, say, the war on cancer. As we have frequently noted, it often has an evangelical flavor.

For those who view education as the rational acquisition of knowledge, the emotionalism that infuses this enterprise is remarkable. Teachers are now obligated to serve as amateur therapists, not stern taskmasters drilling students in traditional subjects. One celebration of tolerance spoke glowingly of how teachers could shield sensitive pupils from psychic harm, even raising this task to the *ultimate* pedagogical aim in a democratic society (Paley 1991, iii, italics added). "Good teachers" help build equitable, inclusive, caring communities in a world rife with divisions, even helping their charges become citizens of the world (Carnes 1991, vi). One can only imagine how teacher/social activists wrestle with the pain that comes with mastering boring subjects where failures—if not painful humiliations—are integral to learning.[12]

A likely below-the-radar impact of instruction is to undermine the very idea of "normal." This is especially ironic since teacher colleges were once "Normal Schools" established to impart society's norms. Alas, today's teachers schooled in multicultural, tolerance-oriented instruction tell their pupils that there is nothing normal, only different, and each difference is both legitimate and worthy of respect. For a few educators, the very acknowledgement of "normal" may be synonymous with hatefulness. Maybe schools of education might be fittingly renamed "Abnormal Schools." This relativistic message is, of course, nonsensical and will eventually be perceived as such, but in the meantime once-in-a-lifetime opportunities to absorb basic values are wasted, if not subverted. Time that was once spent in "good citizenship" (i.e., proper deportment, respect for authority, decent manners and all else comprising civil society) is now redirected towards superficial travelogue-like activities so as to "learn" the value of diversity. Juan is to be treated well not because he is a human being and all people deserve respect; Juan deserves respect because he is different.

The panacea's very simple-mindedness may explain popularity. A Gresham's Law plausibly applies to what experts concoct: *ceteris paribus*, the easiest to grasp, easiest to apply proposal will outshine all rivals regardless of supporting evidence or, worse, continuing disappointments. Achieving universal betterment merely entails hectoring students that "differences are good" and outward aversion is tantamount to strife begetting hatefulness. A particularly disturbing example of escape from a difficult reality occurred in one California school district following the murder of a black student by three Hispanic students (Bender 2005). This is a law enforcement problem for which ample, tried and true, resources are already in place. At worst, more security guards might be hired or surveillance equipment installed. Instead school administrators elected a perfectly safe and likely ineffectual solution: they paid the Southern Poverty Law Center $25,000 to teach tolerance. That even a 99.9 percent success rate with this program cannot stop an occasional murder seems off the agenda. It's just easier to preach the tolerance gospel.

"Curing the world of hate" also supplies a handy, politically convenient substitute for genuine learning. This is especially valuable given today's criticism that America's schools are doing a slipshod academic job vis-à-vis our economic rivals. An ingenious educator might thus say, "Yes, the Japanese run circles around us in math, but we are toiling extra hours to build a better society, and what is more important?" Needless to say, it would be exceedingly impolite to note that Japan also has the advantage of being a homogeneous society and goes to great length to keep it that way, and uniformity may contribute to academic proficiency. And, since campaigns to impose racial and ethnic diversity in schools are relentless, and the predictable outcome is miniscule, the quelling-hatefulness job is guaranteed lifetime employment.

The comparative ease of pursuing this quest bodes poorly for future reform. It is just too enticing to redirect energies to create more administrative overhead whose only purpose is to sermonize. In terms of protecting teachers inadvertently overstepping innumerable complicated work rules, let alone angering quick-to-anger grievance groups, preaching this Pollyannaish gospel is also bullet-proof politically. Consider the potential dangers awaiting teachers who forcefully separate black and Hispanic students to reduce playground chaos. A single complaint will doom the measure, no matter how effective. Few students may learn anything in an out-of-control school, but no career suffers from just lecturing delinquents about diversity.

Why is resistance so mute?[13] We can only speculate, but one plausible explanation is that its aim is so lofty, so idealistic, that challenging it resembles the proverbial assault on motherhood and apple pie. Who could possibly oppose cherishing varied people, mental health, loving families, heightened self-esteem, making up to once-oppressed people, sympathy for the marginalized, and all the rest that this glittering crusade promises. No parents want their children "taught hate," though they may be unaware of just how the enterprise has twisted "hate" beyond all recognition. Tolerance advocates have captured today's high moral ground and are unlikely to be dislodged no matter how feeble their accomplishments.

Notes

1.   Participants occasionally describe the enterprise's scope, though these claims require caution given their fund-raising purposes. Nevertheless, for example, the magazine *Teaching Tolerance*, according to its publisher, the Southern Poverty Law Center (SPLC), is mailed free twice a year to some 600,000 people involved in education while "thousands" of its multi-media kits are also distributed. This organization also awards $1,000 grants to second-grade classrooms to assist in

teaching tolerance and some 1,000 schools on average apply for grants. Meanwhile, the SLPC claims that some 80,000 schools here and abroad use its Teaching Tolerance classroom material (Bender 2005). The well-funded Museum of Tolerance likewise energetically distributes teaching materials and conducts seminars for educators. The website www.ccsf.edu/Resources/Tolerance/res.html lists some seventy-one other websites possibly helpful in this campaign, and these, in turn, provide a gateway to countless like-minded others. Whether teachers seriously heed the myriad messages is unclear, but there is no question that they are bombarded by pleas.

2. Embracing a blank slate conception of human nature is not, however, universal among advocates. Sara Bullard (1996), an oft-cited author contends, "We are intolerant not because we are ignorant or racist or ill, but because we are human" (3). If that assertion is, indeed, correct, than the whole purpose of her book, *Teaching Tolerance,* is wasted, a project akin to creating an aggression-free society. This assertion is probably intended to mean that inculcating tolerance faces formidable obstacles. But elsewhere (12) she suggests that intolerance is not hard-wired into the human psyche. In any case, her musings again illustrate this enterprise's lackadaisical approach to theory building.

3. Favorable use of "queer" is commonplace in universities, both as a group name and in research ("Queer Studies"). A California lesbian motorcycle group recently sought court assistance to register "Dykes with Bikes" as an officially recognized name since the state considered "dyke" offensive and thus legally impermissible (the lesbians won). Slight shifts in usage can play havoc when dealing with the overly sensitive. People of Spanish ancestry have used various terms of self-identification—Hispanic, Hispanic ethnicity, Hispanic origin, Latino and Latina (sometimes combined into Latino/a). Moreover, yesterday's slur can be today's proud badge of identity, for example, the term "Chicano" was once an insult. Now we have university-based Chicano Studies programs.

4. Defenders of this sanitized perspective can always argue that pedophilia is not exactly homosexuality, so "appreciating gays" does not put anybody at risk. Such hair-splitting is clearly dangerous when advising youngsters totally unable to distinguish, say, adults with a penchant for socializing with young boys from clever child molesters.

5. Those monitoring today's ideological battles will grasp the covert agenda—by fingering "intolerance" as the preeminent guilty party for the slaughter of millions, the biggest killer in the modern era, Communism, implicitly slides off the hook (as do National Socialism, tribalism, and nationalism). Not only does this word shift comfort those on today's left, many of whom are ardent tolerance education fans, but it also helps escape a serious paradox: modern tolerance training and Communism *both* endorse human malleability as the *mandatory* pathway to a Utopia-like, better society.

6. Distinguishing between differences and stereotypes is quite solvable statistically via means and standard deviations. One could label as "stereotyping" statements about distributions with a small (precisely specified) standard deviation or some other statistical formulae. Needless to say, however, this objective approach is seldom readily applicable and, more critically, educators generally seem uninterested in such rigor preferring instead seat-of-the-pants characterizations.

7. The fancy conceptual footwork expended to deny reality can be inspired. One popular ploy is to dismiss an undeniable truth by "explaining" it away. If women perform less ably than men in mathematics, for example, just claim that these gaps, though self-evident, are not "real" since women lack equal opportunity. Similarly, differences in crime rate by race merely reflect unequal enforcement

and a biased criminal code, not some Platonic reality. Elsewhere, the world is not what it seems since all standards are "arbitrary" so a success is really a failure and vice versa. Or, in post-modern terminology, it is "merely" socially constructed and thus amenable to infinite, equally valid interpretations.

8. Multiculturalism deeply penetrates modern education so much of the tolerance "agenda" is accomplished without ever uttering the word "tolerance." The multiculturalism mentality has now even entered the national policy agenda more widely. These potentially destructive consequences are carefully explored in Gottfried (2002, especially chapter 4).

9. The issue of integrating gay students is not hypothetical. New York City created an all-gay high school—the Harvey Milk School—so as to provide homosexual students with a safe, sensitive setting. Given New York's liberal political climate, one can only assume that this was done after failed attempts to convince heterosexual students of the benefits of having gay classmates. Such failures, however, are unlikely to dampen enthusiasm for the belief that mixing is advantageous.

10. The workplace offers abundant proof regarding homogeneity. It is no accident that many industries and work crews are comprised of people speaking the same language sharing a common culture. Such uniformity reduces possible verbal misunderstanding and undoubtedly facilitates efficiency, regardless of what workforce diversity champions allege. One need only visit many urban McDonalds or other restaurants to witness how all-Hispanic crews productively interact. Homogeneity's usefulness is best revealed indirectly—workplace diversity must be government-imposed, and those who refuse are punished.

11. Manufacturing bogus claims regarding the alleged benefits of diversity is predictable given that livelihoods depend on this supposition. Thousands of careers are built around its promotion as are dozens of publications. One can only be reminded of the fate of Marxist academics in the Soviet Union after the collapse. Truth may set you free, but it can also bring unemployment. Farron (2005) offers a masterful analysis of the common deceptions surrounding this topic in the face of undeniable reality.

12. The negative impact of "touchy-feely" instruction can be deceptive. For children from homes encouraging academic achievement, stressing empathy at the expense of academics probably does little harm. For those children from disadvantaged environments, however, the early "escape" from academic rigor and discipline is probably disastrous. Appreciating varied skin tones while not acquiring literacy skills will undoubtedly perpetuate poverty. The disregard for objectivity may also "feminize" schools and push young boys away from learning. None of this seems to bother diversity training devotees.

13. Challenges from professional educations are seemingly non-existent. Serious objections exist largely in Christian-oriented books (see, for example, Gaede, 1993; Stetson and Conti, 2005; and McDowell and Hostetler, 1998). This opposition fails to filter into the scholarly mainstream since an unfashionable, unabashed Christian evangelical tone infuses these critiques. In today's scholarly world, impassioned Christianity is tantamount to intolerance.

4

Empirical Foundations

*"In no other field [than education] are personal experiences and ideology so fre-
quently relied on to make policy choices, and in no other field is the research base
so inadequate and little used"—National Research Council, "Improving Student
Learning," 1999.*

The educator-led quest for "more tolerance" manifests itself as a collection of
slogans and heartfelt admonitions, but it ultimately rests on complicated, social
science-based theories. Advocates rarely acknowledge theoretical foundations,
and might even be incapable of articulating them if pressed, but foundations
nevertheless exist. Of the utmost importance, connective tissue is empirically
verifiable, and as in bridge construction, success requires firmly securing each
element. A bit of success here or there proves little. Unfortunately, those educators preaching "tolerance begets tranquility" only focus on small outcroppings,
typically upbeat anecdotal testimonials, ignoring or assuming away less visible
steps on an arduous road, a situation perhaps comparable to engineers irrespon-
sibly inviting people to cross a half-built bridge while explaining that finishing
the project was just too troublesome.

That American schools are mired in academic mediocrity makes justification
all the more vital. Opportunity costs are huge and victory against hatefulness
is hardly preordained. Imagine holding pedagogical experts to the rigorous
standards that pharmaceutical companies must satisfy before marketing claimed
cures. A proposed tolerance remedy would receive laboratory scrutiny and then
be field tested with the results closely monitored before doctors could prescribe
it. Benefits would have to be unambiguously positive while negative side-ef-
fects bearable prior to certification. Sad to say, a huge gap separates promoting
tolerance versus FDA drug approval. The pharmaceutical certification parallel
seemingly never even occurs to educators. This "medicine" for our alleged defects is just glibly heralded, and to demand supporting evidence might appear
as tacit "hatefulness."

The project's underlying foundations are as follows. First, teachers can impart
tolerant attitudes ("cherish differences") via explicit classroom lessons, and
children correctly grasp the messages versus garbling them into something else.
Moreover, tolerant inclinations persist despite contrary peer pressure, life expe-

riences, and multiple, age-related cognitive changes and all else that typically undermines early learning. Second, these enduring perspectives regularly shape behavior versus just being empty platitudes. Finally, this childhood exposure is sufficient to establish social harmony *generally*, that is, those educated for tolerance build a tolerant society.

These requirements are, admittedly, arduous but this project entails no less. Verification may also be impractical, and so the entire enterprise may ultimately rest on unscientific optimism. After all, who can predict the reaction of those claiming to value Islam should Muslims again kill thousands of Americans? We shall further see that confirming evidence is often woefully incomplete and at best derives from studies having little to do with this particular version of tolerance per se. No doubt, tolerance-minded educators will reject this exacting approach as pre-ordained toward failure and thus antithetical to harmony. Nevertheless, stacking the deck objections aside, accepting anything less only substitutes sloganeering for science. A hard-headed perspective is especially relevant given that so many educator-supplied nostrums have proven useless, and have even exacerbated matters. Prior skeptical scrutiny of the type supplied here might have avoided these failures.

Can Tolerance be Taught?

Tolerance messages obviously can be conveyed—students by the thousands hear entreatments and participate in countless build-appreciation exercises. Unfortunately, as any classroom quiz will confirm, mere exposure is hardly identical to *absorbing* lessons. The real question, then, is what happens following these admonitions? For subjects like reading and mathematics, mandatory standardized tests calibrate impact so we know that math lessons occasionally come to naught. Given that teachers are attempting to push students away from the tenacious inclination to disparage those unlike themselves, the odds are especially discouraging. Assessing tolerance instruction is further daunting since SAT-like tests for acquiring an appreciation of differences are nonexistent. Evidence can come only from a tiny handful of scholarly studies or informed speculation.

The experimental format would permit impact measurement. Analysis would begin by ascertaining students' initial tolerance-related attitudes. Pupils would then be randomly divided with an experimental group (E) receiving the appreciate diversity instruction (the stimulus or "S" in technical language) while a control group (C) would hear nothing. This message's content would be specified exactly so that impromptu asides of what deserves respect would be forbidden. After a specified time (say, six months), the attitudes of all students would again be determined. Resources permitting, monitoring would continue for years, a situation comparable to periodic basic skill tests.

Zero differences in outcome hardly doom the quest. A null result merely means that a particular lesson plan of myriad possibilities has proven ineffectual. Educators would then return to the drawing board. This is comparable to drug research—cures often emerge only after endless dead ends. To shun this scientific strategy as too troublesome or unnecessary since "we know it works" is, in effect, to imply that the enterprise is fundamentally *un*important.[1] What if medical researchers *sans* any hard evidence, blithely sold their pet cancer cures? They would properly be labeled quacks, even arrested for fraud.

This particular scientific approach is, admittedly, hardly trouble free. Students in the experimental treatment might share experiences with control group members or some in the experimental condition may have been absent during these lessons. A salient outside event, for example, a well-publicized local hate crime, could distort outcomes. The initial random division may have failed to create comparable conditions, so variations in teacher aptitude, classroom atmosphere and the like could inadvertently muddle results. What might work in the ninth grade may fail if applied in the sixth grade given cognitive differences. Nevertheless, as in large-scale tests of drugs, extensive analysis across varied settings and time periods would undoubtedly go a long way in demonstrating this approach's contribution to quelling incipient hatreds. This is certainly (or should be) the pathway taken before implementing new ways to teach everything from spelling to safe sex.

What evidence, then, exists that instruction accomplishes its ostensible betterment aims? If we limit ourselves to the educator-favored definition of tolerance—near blank-check appreciation of diversity—the answer is *no scientific proof whatsoever*. When empirical research does occasionally grace these exhortations, it serves as mere window dressing to give the aura of "science." Put bluntly, thousands of hours and lots of money flow into uncertain, untested schemes. A learning curve is thus impossible—educators must permanently grope around in the dark. Admittedly, some unpublished research project might supply confirming evidence, and teachers might have noticed genuine improvement post-tolerance lessons, but in a field overflowing with research across dozens of journals about curriculum impacts, this neglect is indisputable. One would assume that champions would publicize even shaky, impressionistic confirmations.

To appreciate the non-scientific character of this advocacy despite a style hinting otherwise, consider Linter's (2005) effort to use photographs to instill appreciation for diversity (tolerance) among 175 students in grades one through four over a four-month period. The researcher presented pictures of children from around the world engaging in activities assumed to be familiar to every youngster. Both before and after viewing these images, students offered accounts of how they judged people unlike themselves. Teacher-supplied narratives stressing the gap between those portrayed and the American students accompanied a second set of images. One showed wheelchair-bound boys playing basketball, another depicted a Muslim girl dressed in a headscarf, and a third showed South American children residing in what appeared to be a garbage dump. The aim throughout was to elicit how these Americans felt when encountering people dramatically dissimilar from themselves. The experience was often an eye-opener—a few had not even heard the term "Muslim."

Children typically reacted with unease, though several could relate personal experiences to what they saw (e.g., recalling having seen a disabled person). For the most part, however, the reaction was one of recognizing the dreadfulness of life elsewhere. If the aim was to demonstrate that "people are different," the mission was vividly accomplished. It came as a genuine surprise that people could live without supermarkets, decent sanitation, electricity, or doctors. Many wanted these deplorable conditions improved, and a few volunteered to help personally. The investigator noted that children often struggled to comprehend what they saw and felt threatened, if not repulsed.

Did this exercise promote greater classroom or community tolerance? Did schoolyard fights between blacks and whites vanish? It is impossible to know. There are no statistical data and precise attitude change is never hypothesized, let alone determined. Analysis is reassuringly long on vague optimism but very short on confirmation. The author repeatedly asserts that this encounter altered perceptions and, at least momentarily, connected disparate lives—a proposition that is technically beyond falsification since any data would "prove" this assertion. Everything is just imputed, not measured, let alone proven. As Linter put it, "They were able to sympathize with the images in the photographs and, in childlike ways, begin to understand the lives of others in a nonthreatening, nonjudgmental way." No doubt, at least in the author's eyes, this project was a success insofar as it challenged students to visualize a world contrary to their own which, it was assumed, would engender appreciation of what might otherwise be feared at home. And, if "...students realize that similarities are often found through differences" they may be less likely to physically abuse or harm those who are different.[2]

The absence of scientific confirmation does not, alas, prevent sweeping contrary claims by presumed experts. Consider, for example, John H. Holloway (2003), a project director at the renowned Educational Testing Service, and as such someone who should be acquainted with the rules of empirical inquiry. In his brief analysis of building ethnic and racial tolerance he concludes, "Research has shown that school-based programs can promote racial tolerance among students" (86). Preceding this upbeat assessment he offers a litany of *possible* remedies for interracial conflict—multiculturalism, conflict resolution training, recruiting a diverse staff, better teacher training, especially in cultural diversity among other nostrums. Unfortunately, there is a lack of hard evidence in the essay itself and the citations appear either largely irrelevant to the question at hand or provide no support whatsoever. Zero uncertainty occurs about the interventions working, nor are there any warnings about how troublesome it might be to prove these assertions. The awaited triumph over hate thanks to strong doses of multiculturalism appears to be an unchallengeable article of faith.

Going one step further, it is also unclear from this cheerful literature that these messages are uniformly absorbed as teachers intend. Not a single account of this enterprise includes "tolerance test" results, let alone an awareness of the need for before/after comparisons.[3] The need for such a progress-measuring instrument appears totally unwarranted—everything revolves around just making the effort. This is akin to math instruction without quizzes, a strategy that perhaps explains its allure to both teachers and students. Evasion does have its benefits. One could only imagine if most students flunked such a test if one indeed existed. Equally relevant, with no test there are no potentially embarrassing gaps across racial or ethnic groups that reflect poorly on parents and teachers.

The absence of studies seeking confirmation that these lessons calm turmoil may also reflect a widespread inability among professional educators to understand even the rudiments of scientific investigation. That is, the simple experimental formula is unknown despite its popularity beyond education. Consider, for example, one such "study" at a South Carolina college of education (Stevens and Charles 2005). Keep in mind that this effort is one of the very, very few that even attempt to measure impact. Specifically, to assess the effectiveness of the school's effort to educate teachers who could teach tolerance after graduating, fifty-one students (nineteen of whom were self-selected since they sought extra credit) drawn from two "Foundations of Education" classes watched a film, *The Shadow of Hate* that celebrated diversity and tolerance. Students then wrote essay answers to four broad questions afterwards, for example, "What is the relationship between power and discrimination?" and "...did you learn something about US history?"

These answers were then scrutinized to evaluate whether the film's message about endless discrimination and hatreds directed toward the less fortunate sank in. Judged by the snippets the authors provide and the cheery conclusion, the exercise was a resounding success. Prospective teachers learned about how the dominant abuse their power, how so many varied people faced discrimination, and how all children needed equal treatment. Measured by even minimal scientific standards, this is shoddy research. Among other flaws, key concepts, for example, tolerance, appreciating diversity, were left undefined operationally (or if defined, specifics were not provided), and the film's content is never sufficiently described, so that the reader cannot know what, exactly, the students saw and how this exposure was linked to any outcome. Nor was there any formal coding scheme to score answers. The researchers themselves apparently judged responses, a clear conflict of interest in seeking objective confirmation. Nor was there any control group. Prior knowledge was never ascertained, so we have no idea of the exercise's net impact (descriptions of the college's curriculum strongly suggests that the film merely reinforced an already pervasive multicultural agenda). Finally, it appears that student responses were not confidential, and given that this was classroom-related, students probably voiced what they sensed instructors expected.

Though speculative, as with so much instructional effort regardless of subject, a great deal hints that transmission may be imperfect. Even in relatively ambitious programs, the time allocated is relatively small (though hardly cost-free given competing needs), and this hardly suggests lessons taking root among children. Occasionally telling third-graders that, "all students are equally talented academically" is unlike daily drills on the multiplication table. Moreover, and relevant for a possible long-term impact, these terse lessons are not written on blank slates; the opposite is more likely to be true. The battle is arduously up hill. The learned classroom message may settle into the students' memories as, "my teacher says that all cultures are the same" and absent relentless repetition, grow hazy with time. "Do-good" catchphrases probably come to resemble glittering religious strictures (e.g., "honor one's parents") now and then announced on ceremonial occasions. Or like so much other instruction, even oft-repeated history and science, inattention and intellectual laziness leads to everything going in one ear and out the other.

Particularly troubling is the possibility that youngsters may be mentally incapable of correctly grasping these often counter-intuitive messages in which the loathsome is now to be cherished for no reason other than it is different. That grade school pupils must wait until they mature further before it is even possible to learn intellectually demanding subjects is indisputable, and no reason exists to suppose that this principle does not govern this tolerance instruction. Older children outshine younger ones in their tolerance views (see Avery 1992 for a brief overview), and this relationship suggests a cognitive development link. Extensive research on children's moral development shows that some subtle, let alone contradictory ideas, are just beyond third graders so that no amount of instruction can prove successful. The core idea underlying all tolerance conceptions—the paradox of appreciating the odious—in all likelihood puzzles pre-adolescents viewing the world in black/white, good/bad terms, and even among the more mature, it may bewilder the less intellectually gifted. Early grade school admonitions are thus comparable to trying to teach algebra to those overwhelmed by arithmetic.

Moreover, and this can only be speculative, reinforcing *in*tolerance at an early age may be far easier given children's natural propensity to spurn the dissimilar. This certainly fits well with studies of childhood moral development showing a natural tilt towards "us" versus "them" worldviews. Schools are hardly inclined in this "good-bad" direction (though some religious schools may disparage non-believers) but encounters elsewhere can serve as *de facto* instruction to loathe those who are different. Even the most upbeat tolerance-infatuated educators, especially when pleading for additional resources, acknowledge this swimming-against-the-stream problem though their enthusiasm remains unabated. By the time youngsters are even mentally capable of learning to "appreciate differences," they have been watching hundreds, possibly thousands of hours of television whose message often contravenes what teachers announce. A fourth-grade lecture on appreciating swarthy foreigners may be too little, too late for somebody who has spent hundreds of hours battling grotesque aliens while protecting America via video games.

Perhaps the most "positive" outcome that be reasonably expected is that pupils now sense what is permissible publicly, a skill comparable to learning to repress slang terms denoting human anatomy. Savvy students recognize that a rebuke awaits them if they call classmates "fat" or "queer" or voice invidious racial or ethnic comparisons ("stereotypes") in earshot of teachers. Considerable indirect evidence confirms the charge that publicly affirming diversity is little more than the "correct," socially acceptable response—a confusion of "ought" with "is." For example, studies of interracial friendship show that whites grossly exaggerate their personal closeness to blacks. One inquiry (Steinhorn and Diggs-Brown 1999) calculated that if whites were to be believed, every black in America would have five or six close white friends. Other data (reported in Farron 2005, 189) found that while 40 percent of whites reported having a close black friend, only 6 percent could name a black friend if specifically asked to provide names. Needless to say, such claims regarding personal commitment to diversity are not credible.

Educators would naturally contend that suppression of outward hostility is a genuine accomplishment, a harbinger of future appreciation, and therefore laudable. Educators may conceivably be right, though it is equally true that their assertion is unanswerable based on their data. Nevertheless, it remains clear that the teacher-supervised class or lunchroom is not the world and, equally important, pushing these allegedly harmful words underground need not predict subsequent hurtful behavior. Opportunities for hypocrisy abound. Criminals routinely lie and can certainly master the outward appearance of being law abiding when police are present. We shall have more to say about this attitude-behavior link below.

Even more remarkable is that rough impact measures are feasible, though these might fall short of strict scientific standards. Schools collect data on violence and severe disciplinary sanctions, and these can be juxtaposed against tolerance instruction. To wit, if fewer interracial schoolyard confrontations erupt after presenting a program, the intervention plausibly helped though this evidence is only correlational, not causal. School records on classroom attendance, drop-outs, and academic achievement among intolerance targets provide further opportunities for indirect assessment. In fact, champions of teaching youngsters to be more tolerant of gay students often point to missed classes and truancy as evidence of the need for intervention. At a minimum, tolerance advocates could collect student and teacher impressions following these lessons. If the promised improvement transpired, surely *somebody* would notice and write about it in contrast to the far more familiar response of simply heralding alleged remedies. Perhaps educators have so little confidence in their endeavors that they prefer to reaffirm, not test, impact.[4]

Though these diversity-infatuated educators have failed to assess their nostrum's value, researchers employing an alternative conception of "tolerance" have inquired about successful transmission, and efforts here may shed light on the enterprise more generally. These investigators reject an appreciation of human diversity as "tolerance" in favor of a willingness to permit unpopular groups to express themselves in a democratic society. This is the "classic" understanding of tolerance depicted in chapter 2 since it only requires "putting up with" what is disliked, not embracing it. For example, those who dislike homosexuals still can qualify as "tolerant" if they would permit gay organizations to hold a rally or publish a newspaper. Of the utmost importance, this definitional shift from appreciating to enduring entails a far *lower* tolerance threshold since, obviously, there is no obligation to like the once disliked. If this easier-to-embrace tolerance cannot be imparted, or improvements are only minor, the odds of success for the more demanding "appreciate diversity" version must surely be nearly zero.

A particularly ambitious and scientifically rigorous effort was executed in 1991 and involved 274 seventh- to ninth-grade students in an urban and two rural settings (Avery *et al.*, 1992). Tolerance was operationally defined using a "content-controlled" measure: students were supplied a list of groups from both sides of the political spectrum (e.g., American communists, peace activists) and instructed to select those they disliked. This differs sharply from the stress on racial/ethnic aversions with which education experts are infatuated. Students then answered six civil liberties-related questions regarding his or her least liked group, for example, permitting group members to run for elective office, teach in public schools, and give a public speech. Additional attitude data on self-esteem, authoritarian tendencies, and views of the curriculum plus demographic data were also collected. So as to ensure that the selected least-liked group was "real," students were asked how personally threatened they were by their most disliked group.

The tolerance lesson plan received by some students (the "E" group) was extensive, far more than a handful of vague appreciate diversity exhortations. There were eight lessons of two-to-three-day duration, and entailed multiple pedagogical techniques—case studies, role playing, simulations, mock interviews, as well as forays into history. Attention further focused on past victims of intolerance (the Holocaust, for example), the roots of intolerance, the meaning of human rights, including limiting these rights, relevant court cases, and such thorny quandaries as freedom of conscience. Teachers explained both the long-term and immediate consequences of intolerance. It is hard to imagine a more sophisticated and intensive explication of this complicated subject in a school setting.

Did this ambitious enterprise succeed? Some movement occurred toward tolerance among those exposed to this curriculum versus those unexposed. Still, while statistically significant, the shift was modest—most students went from mildly intolerant to mildly tolerant. Hardly any intolerant students became new-found civil liberties champions. Researchers sensibly suggested that preexisting dispositions acquired in the home and elsewhere significantly limits school-based instruction. Of particular relevance for the educator-favored version of tolerance, with a single exception (Nazis), perceptions of disliked groups failed to improve post-curriculum exposure. This implies that inculcating a new-found appreciation for a once-loathed group—the aim of educators—will not necessarily result in that group winning additional civil liberties. The most that could be hoped for, then, is that the disliked will be endured, not necessarily appreciated. There was some good news, however: instruction could reduce perceived group threats, and this did engender willingness to grant civil liberties. A further interesting though pessimistic outcome was that among more authoritarian students, exposure to these lessons provoked reaction in the *opposite* direction! Apparently, learning about past hatefulness and the like can awaken fears about present circumstances.

Though our excursion into school-based tolerance instruction has been brief, this literature generally counsels pessimism. Writing after a decade of tinkering with classroom-based tolerance instruction, Avery (2006) cautions that schools are not the panacea. Finkel's (2000) overview suggests that successes are relatively rare and shifts likely reflect large-scale economic change and generational replacement. To be sure, this gloom is not the final word, and several researchers have successfully boosted tolerant attitudes slightly, at least temporarily, by offering arguments on its behalf (e.g., Gibson 1998; Marcus et al. 1995; Gibson and Gouws 2003, ch. 6) while others have demonstrated that manipulating the context of situations can have salutary effects (e.g., Kuklinski et al. 1991). Industrious researchers may yet devise techniques to push youngsters towards extending civil liberties to those voicing noxious views. Such tiny rays of hope are predictable since, after all, the possible combinations are virtually limitless, and something will always work in the short term given sufficient experimentation. In light of all possible lesson formats (lectures, role-playing, field trips), available target groups, teaching styles and what types of students receive these entreatments, educators can spend a lifetime tinkering with ways to save humanity from hatefulness.

Still, it is one thing to manipulate half-formed attitudes in controlled situations for a captive audience, quite another to redirect deeply felt views when individuals leave school. Certainly no reason exists why those eschewing tolerance would seek to alter their allegedly "unhealthy" views. Few parents whose children remain unexposed to these tolerance lessons will supply this instruction at home or hire tutors as they might remediate deficiencies in academic subjects. Adults wanting to incarcerate communists for just speaking their minds are unlikely to return to school to "correct" their views as one might take classes to acquire employment-related skills. Intolerance might, conceivably, undermine democratic society, but for most intolerant people this proclivity is hardly akin to a painful illness motivating a trip to the doctor.

If we go beyond specific experiments to impart tolerance one classroom at a time, and examine more general indoctrination efforts, the evidence here is equally dismal. Consider the record of American colleges in their relentless efforts, many of which are compulsory, to expose students to the benefits of diversity and multiculturalism. Does this do any good? Fortunately, extensive data on the impact of this effort exist—reports from nearly 8 million students at 1,300 institutions—and the result show *no* benefits (see Farron 2005, 190-91). Affirmative action-related lawsuits involving the alleged benefits of campus diversity also seem silent when it comes time to present hard evidence. Nor is there any reason to suppose that the long-term impact of this quest will be any different from what transpires today. The bottom line seems to be that classroom hectoring to "respect those who are different" and all the rest just wastes time.

Perhaps the best overall argument in the education-begets-tolerance arsenal is that a moderate relationship exists between this disposition (variously defined) and education. But, that well-documented fact acknowledged, it does not follow that pushing people to spend more hours in school guarantees the Promised Land. In fact, one book—*Tolerance and Education* (Vogt 1997), which spends over 200 pages and endless scholarly citations into untold potentially relevant research literatures trying to find this precise link, tirelessly asserts that, indeed, it does somehow exist, yet positive results never materialize. As is typical among educators, the reasoning seems to be that since education can mold people's views, it certainly can (in some ill-defined way) reshape views on tolerance though, alas, proof positive remains elusive.

A far more credible view is that the talents facilitating educational accomplishment—superior cognitive ability, openness to new ideas, and the like—also encourage tolerance, so schooling per se is not the primary causal factor. One review of this link (Sullivan, Avery, Thalhammer, Wood, and Bird, 1994) refers to the minimal impact of civic instruction on promoting tolerance so the high tolerance-education link is spurious. Nie, Junn, and Stehlik-Barry (1996, 70-72) show empirically that tolerance (defined as extending civil liberties to the unpopular) heavily depends on cognitive capacity, and schooling *cannot* alter innate intellectual ability. Tolerant people get more education, not the reverse. It is also arguable that schooling also imparts public norms, so those advancing educationally simultaneously learn what is socially acceptable, and expressing "tolerance" is unquestionably a cherished value. In other words, schooling helps people to give the "right" answer apart from whether they really believe it.

Nor is the exact formula by which education builds tolerance (assuming that it does) well understood, and sorting everything out may be unachievable for contemporary social science. Recall our observation about all the possible ways to teach tolerance, and this complexity is only the beginning in a comprehensive approach. Research reveals that tolerant dispositions seem closely intertwined with other psychological factors—dogmatism, civic interest, self-esteem, moral development, among others—so rooting out intolerance entails extensive change far beyond what might be practical in classroom settings, assuming that we can untangle these traits. Factors bearing on instructional accomplishment are likewise considerable, for example, teacher credibility (see Goldenson 1978, cited in Sullivan et al. 1994) or the classroom intellectual openness (see Torney, Oppenheim, and Farnen 1975, cited in Sullivan et al. 1994). Compounding this insufficiency of existing knowledge is the absence of a compelling political concern—legislators are hardly demanding more funds for a Manhattan Project-like quest despite the alarms sounded by agitated pedagogues.

If we evaluate tolerance promotion enterprises in the context of other school-based efforts to redirect students, pessimism further deepens. Countless well-meaning, intensive educational efforts are directed at children—everything from anti-drug crusades to promoting safe sex—and even acclaimed successes usually fall far short of unanimity, and unanimity is what is required here if society is to be hate free. Multimillion dollar efforts to reduce teen pregnancies, for example, are heralded in spite of modest reductions. Thousands of students graduate illiterate despite eight or more years of schooling! That inculcating tolerance via schooling hardly enjoys the support levels for these other more pressing crusades should also encourage modest expectations.

Our last concern here is whether these lessons will endure, assuming that they are correctly absorbed. Given that this enterprise is relatively young, a clear, scientifically derived answer must wait though, sad to say, it is unlikely that researchers will track these changes given their disdain for even far simpler empirical research. Nevertheless, everything we have examined thus far suggests that these lessons will fade from memory. Unlike, say, learning math, no tangible, marketplace rewards exist for embracing this tolerance worldview and, as we suggested earlier, internalizing upbeat beliefs about those who differ can be personally risky (e.g., refusing to avoid those with a reputation for crime). A message so contrary to peoples' nature hardly seems a good candidate for entering the psychological DNA. Intolerance may be a "disease" but the school nurse cannot quickly inoculate children against hatefulness as youngsters might receive a vaccine against polio.

If we look beyond this specific tolerance quest, and examine the persistence of attitudes more generally, the prognosis is gloomy. Zaller (1992, ch. 4) explored the subject of survey-measured attitude stability at length, and concludes "...instability in people's attitudes over time is one of the most deeply worrisome, if not routinely emphasized, finds of modern survey research" (64). This is, moreover, hardly surprising in a world overflowing with new and contradictory information. Responses to questions about valuing diversity, one strongly suspects, are little more than off-the-top-of-the-head responses reflecting the immediate environment, and could easily change the next moment as the situation changes.

In sum, schooling may shape tolerance but this hardly demonstrates that schools can battle hatefulness. At most, tolerance in its less demanding version can be *slightly* and only occasionally boosted, and even then, only with *intensive* intervention. Occasional alarmism aside, this mission certainly is not the school's prime objective, and much that transpires in the school is beyond what educators can control. Powerful trends may work in the contrary direction and, ironically, some of these are also educator promoted. Alleged cures may be contributing to the disease. Various studies (e.g., Avery et al. 1992) have, for example, demonstrated a close connection between perceived threat and intolerance, and as schools increasingly grow more ethnically diverse, often as a result of educator-welcomed, court-imposed integration, inter-group tensions may mount, and tolerance recede.

Do Tolerance Attitudes Predict Tolerant Behavior?

Repeated attention to attitudes aside, the ultimate prize is (or should be) tolerant *behavior* since it is pointless to fashion "good intentions," if dispositions have zero to do with society-wide intolerance. The attitude-behavior link should thus be central for any amelioration project. As a practical matter, adding behavior elements is straightforward since what always instigates calls for heightened tolerance is intolerant public behavior—an ethnic slur, spray-painting racist graffiti, and the like. Indeed, it requires extra effort to assess inner dispositions versus observing and then confronting what is plain to see.

Unfortunately, as chapter 2 noted, the right disposition is reflexively equated with tolerant behavior with scarcely any recognition of possible tensions between thought and action. This unjustified conflation can involve some clever wordplay, for example, when Pennsylvania State University defined "intolerance" as "an attitude, feeling or belief in furtherance of which an individual acts to intimidate, threaten or show contempt for other individuals or groups based on characteristics such as race, ancestry...or veteran status" (cited in French 2006). In other words, any negative behavior towards those in these specified protected entities is assumed to flow from "intolerance," not some other cause, for example, a squabble over money. There is no need, then, to inquire about attitudes causing behavior—behavior perfectly reveals the underlying attitude, at least according to this formulation. A few even go a step further and insist that thinking, in and of itself, is all that matters, a sort of psychological condition akin to dangerous dementia. Nevertheless, to ignore behavior is a colossal error, as if reality existed only in peoples' minds. It is certainly true that given a choice between living amongst people who were only attitudinally tolerant versus those who behaved tolerantly, the latter is preferable. Surely members of unpopular groups are more worried about physical assault than others thinking "bad thoughts." Intolerant thinking is important *only* if it leads to intolerant action.

A substantial research literature across myriad situations shows that a one-to-one correspondence between the two seldom exists (see, for example, Deutscher, 1975; Crespi, 1971, Oskamp 1977, among others). Liska (1975, vii) observes that this inconsistency has long been reflected in popular clichés like "talk is cheap" or "practice what you preach." One relevant review (Deutscher 1975) noted studies showing major inconsistencies among trade unionist utterances and action, cheating among college students, how urban teachers actually taught versus claimed classroom practices, and people's actual health practices as opposed to verbal assurances. Other studies showed, as one might expect, a double standard regarding alcohol consumption, employers boasting about hiring handicapped workers, and even what mothers claimed about raising offspring. Books recounting human hypocrisy would fill a library and reversing this proclivity is probably beyond what educators can even hope to accomplish.

Even if tolerant attitudes and behavior were perfectly correlated, this fact does not in and of itself foretell persecution of those potentially at risk from the intolerant. The social and geographical distribution of hatreds may mitigate this sturdy attitude-behavior connection. For example, imagine rampant homophobia among youngsters with this disposition on the edge of becoming hateful behavior. Are gays therefore in danger? To recall our discussion of alternatives to tolerance in chapter 2, the answer is, "Not necessarily." For one, gays might be unavailable as targets, or if present, homophobes may fail to recognize them as such (being "closeted" has long shielded homosexuals from abuse). We cannot expect those at risk to be masochists and remain in hostile environments, let alone announce the very traits that draw the ire of others. Disliked ethnic (and religious) groups have traditionally clustered and avoided outsiders for safety reasons, and this strategy renders pervasive unsympathetic attitudes irrelevant. Gays may also avail themselves of the time-honored way of preventing unfriendly views from becoming hurtful—threaten violent retaliation or otherwise raise the cost of anti-gay behavior, so again, rampant homophobia poses little problem, save among those who insist that others *must* think highly of them.

Avoiding a behavior-based test of lesson effectiveness can deceptively exaggerate the benefits of educational intervention. This sleight-of-hand can easily pass scientific scrutiny and thus provide a comforting conclusion that schools can quell hatefulness. This would be accomplished if, perhaps, teachers intent on demonstrating success might well gravitate to garnering appreciation for those posing minimal direct personal threat to their students.[5] For example, in a school seething with racial hostility between blacks and whites, teachers prudently preach about respecting Native Americans leaving racial antagonisms untouched. Such a program—targeting stereotypes about Native Americans—can thus be an unqualified "success" by the standard of only altering hateful attitudes without regard to specific situations. Going a step further, adding appreciation for the disabled, the elderly, those unable to speak English, panhandlers and recent immigrants might yield spectacular seeming accomplishment, though schoolyard strife between African Americans and Hispanics continues unabated. The lesson's aim, of course, *should be* to quell the problem at hand, not construct some vague mental utopia, but that is far more likely to come up short, if not generate unwelcome controversy.

It is not that the attitudes and actions are totally disjoined—words and deeds occasionally do match. The key question is *when* we can expect aversion to differences erupting into hateful behavior, not the existence of these attitudes per se. Research suggests several situations in which there is a close connection, but these findings are hardly good news for tolerance instruction devotees. Drawing on extensive research Crespi (1971) asserts that thinking and behavior often closely correspond in tightly structured, repetitive situations such as consumer purchases or voting. That is, a young Democrat will increasingly vote Democratic the longer he or she remains a Democrat. This is brand loyalty in advertising parlance. Similarly, attitudes and behavior are more likely to be congruent when an attitude is ascertained in close proximity to behavior—party affiliation is asked a day or two before the election.

But, tolerance-related encounters are seldom as structured as supermarket shopping or selecting between clearly party-labeled candidates. To continue with our homophobia example, those disliking gays have multiple options short of venting repugnance. Of the utmost importance, these encounters are generally infrequent given people's natural inclination to avoid the disagreeable. Even in close quarters he or she might avoid contact entirely, and if such contact is unavoidable, minimize it or coolly handle it short of overt antagonism. Such self-segregation is ubiquitous in schools where students prudently sidestep potentially conflict-laden situations. The homophobe might even refuse to believe that this person is really gay, or rely on time-honored tactics in inescapable unpleasant exchanges—fake cordiality or just lie! The upshot, then, is that while homophobia clearly exists, predicting its specific consequences is problematical, and reprehensible behavior is not inevitable. Perhaps after dozens of such encounters, attitudes and behavior would more closely align, but in what precise direction is pure speculation, and this assumes a willingness to seek out troublesome situations.

The time proximity requirement is an even more formidable impediment to alignment. Attitude-behavior links can also deteriorate over time, even if once solid, particularly as new attitudes are developed and fresh circumstances arise. Instruction may not be relevant for decades, and schools cannot totally guide their students to resist future temptations. The power of immediate, unforeseen circumstances can be formidable—an otherwise tolerant individual can become a dangerous bigot when intoxicated or egged on by a mob. Lots can happen as conditions develop—tolerance towards Islam was far easier pre-9/11; who knows what threats to civil peace might emerge when today's youngsters mature? Can educators anticipate specific future threats? Hardly. If early indoctrination guaranteed steadfastness, few religious adherents would ever abandon their faith, and the hours spent instilling religion far exceed what is devoted to inculcating tolerance. In other words, it is the exclusive, almost naive emphasis on childhood attitude change as the remedy for future (unpredictable) strife that draws our ire.

Even if attitudes did accurately foretell behavior, *which* attitudes in concrete circumstances are decisive? Only rarely is a single attitude all determining, and social situations always involve multiple dispositions with new attitudes being added (and perhaps subtracted) over a lifetime. Connections among a multiplicity of views can fluctuate depending on numerous unanticipated conditions, all of which are well beyond the reach of tolerance devotees. This is a question decided by laborious research across untold settings, not by fiat or wishful thinking. One might, for example, generally be fond of gays but this positive disposition might be momentarily trumped by, say, revulsion at outlandish homoerotic attire or peer pressure when actually encountering homosexual classmates. Of course, influence can flow in the opposite direction—the intractable sadistic homophobe might tolerate gays if, for example, he or she highly values public decorum when encountering those one disapproves of (one just "holds one's tongue"). That behavior is the product of multiple attitudinal predispositions is fraught with pedagogical implication, given manipulating dozens of attitudes, many of which whose relevance is beyond anticipation. Clearly, such wholesale attitude refurbishment is totally impractical in today's schools.

Awaiting quandaries also exist when teaching diverse attitudes, and vagueness is commonplace in such lessons. Unfortunately for tolerance devotees, opportunities for tolerance/intolerance always arise in more specific, quite complicated settings. Not every child can deduce the "correct" specifics from grand principles, and this gap is frustratingly familiar. Americans overwhelmingly embrace "free speech" but not necessarily for particularly abhorrent views such as communism. Many thieves believe that honesty is the best policy though, perhaps, for other people. Youngsters admonished to appreciate "those who reject our cultures and traditions" can react violently when encountering rambunctious Palestinians dressed as suicide bombers at a campus rally burning American flags, all the while believing themselves to be generally tolerant.

Moreover, glib generalities ("respect all human diversity") so adored by educators inevitably collide or engender confusion in actual practice. Recall that tolerance lessons typically escape controversy by shunning specifics or leaving key terms undefined. Even those wanting to translate their early lessons into concrete behavior may be bewildered in murky future circumstances. Imagine the predicament of white students told to tolerate (undefined) "minorities" but who are themselves a neighborhood racial minority. Are Russian immigrants or women "minorities"? How does one translate "appreciating diversity" when encountering everyday frictions? Should a "tolerant person" praise obnoxious "different" behavior such as aggressive panhandling, or is indifference sufficient? These murky application dilemmas are far removed from arguing about authorizing religious services for seventeenth-century English Unitarians.

When all is said and done, then, we *have no idea* if those expressing the "right" or "wrong" views on appreciating diversity will honor their verbal assurances. This paucity of knowledge even applies in far more scientifically based research (for example, Marcus et al. 1995, 219-220). If anything, the evidence points in the opposite direction—there are just too many other factors impeding a close link between imposed tolerant attitudes and tolerant behavior. Perhaps only among those who believe that attitudes are all that counts can this uncertainty be comforting.[6]

Can Tolerance Education Bring About a Tolerant Society?

Momentarily assume that all previous conditions are substantially satisfied—educators galore join the bandwagon, instruction flourishes, and pupils absorbing these lessons are outwardly tolerant. Is this momentous accomplishment a harbinger of *overall* tranquility, an end to hatefulness plus all the other promised benefits? The answer must still be uncertain, and in all likelihood, this campaign will experience notable disappointments, though it is impossible to predict whether this idyllic future will outshine the allegedly hateful present. One cannot simply cumulate successful individual conversions to the tolerance camp so as to predict some future society. Uniform tranquility involving millions of separate people is not a public policy that can be imposed via majority vote.

That even a tiny handful of tolerance resistors can readily persist is fundamental, and even successful programs will have some failures. Setbacks are inevitable given the nature of schooling. Teachers can endlessly berate youngsters to be tolerant, yet there is absolutely no legal compulsion for them to think "good" thoughts. Stereotyping and the like are *not*, at least for now, crimes, nor is prejudice grounds for denying a diploma. One can only imagine public outcries if, for instance, schools refused to graduate alleged bigots, and this bigotry was defined by liberal (or conservative) school administrators. This possibility of recipient resistance to these "do good" messages is all too easily swept aside by those obsessed by the lure of peacefulness. A relevant parallel would be combating crime by simply imparting respect for law. Such a campaign would probably help but it would be utopian to believe that even endless hectoring could abolish criminality and thus render police and prisons obsolete. A 1 percent failure rate, itself an enormous triumph, still leaves three million criminals. Moreover, since even a few criminals can commit innumerable acts, even a gargantuan reduction in evildoers may fail to eliminate crime.

Recall that tolerance advocates repeatedly speak of "hateful environments" in which a tiny number of miscreants might spray paint homophobic graffiti or ridicule obese classmates. To rid a school of these few "bad apples" would likely be an impossible task short of imposing a virtual police state, hardly what tolerance devotees desire. Upping the proportion of tolerant students from, say, 30 percent to 40 percent or even 80 percent is not comparable to moving from 90 percent to 100 percent and, to repeat, unanimity is vital. Costs will soar when directed at hardcore troublemakers, most of whom have long abandoned heeding what teachers preach (many probably skip class, too).

Nor can educators disillusioned with imperfect (though substantial) outcomes resort to more draconian tactics no matter how ardent their convictions that they are rescuing America from awaiting turmoil. Today's disciplinary menu prohibits corporal punishment, humiliation, and quick expulsion. Ridding schools of bigots only sends them elsewhere and schools have powerful financial incentives to keep troublemakers around until graduation. Even if upping the hours haranguing hapless students were legally permissible, tolerance champions would surely face opposition from other educators (and parents) with competing instructional agendas. For better or worse, though a small amount additional instruction could be added, it cannot be forcefully deepened with sanctions, and this inherent limitation should caution those advocating still more and more.[7]

Recent advances in technology further illustrate what can happen if a campaign falls short of 100 percent, and even substantial progress will never reach 100 percent. In particular, as students increasingly communicate with each other electronically—e-mail, chat rooms, text messaging—fresh opportunities arise for spreading hatefulness. Surveys in 2004 and 2005 conducted among teenagers reported that nearly 35 percent had received bullying electronic messages, and with derogatory comments and insults (McGreevy 2006). That these messages can often be nearly anonymous undoubtedly encourages intolerance. Nor will teachers and parents be able to observe such harassment as they might witness it in hallways or schoolyards. The upshot, then, is that a single hatemonger might conceivably wage an extensive campaign, and provided there are no explicit threats of violence, it is probably unstoppable short of criminal sanctions.

Comparable transformation endeavors from abroad and history likewise suggest skepticism regarding accomplishing a 100 percent effective transformation. The world overflows with failed schemes to "improve" society by reconstituting human nature. Not even the Soviet Union could remold all of its citizens into dutiful communists despite forced population relocation, mass starvation, and firing squads. And imparting a collectivist spirit is arguably just as formidable as overcoming deeply ingrained ethnic or racial aversions. Similarly, modern-day France with its centralized, all-encompassing secularized schooling has fallen short in its efforts to stamp out ethnic/religious antagonisms. To repeat, a miniscule "failure rate" in tolerance instruction still leaves scores of troublemakers, and there is no instance where any nation has been able to transform its population *totally* short of killing dissenters (and even that failed!).

The most obvious practical defect in this idealistic vision is that millions of American will *never* pass through tolerance-infused school instruction. The U.S. is not a closed society in which every adult shares a common, school-produced socialization. For one thing, immigration guarantees that millions of adults will elude this "diversity makes us strong" cosmology.[8] Immigration authorities certainly cannot make "intolerance" a reason for denying entry (and immigrants' claims to "welcome differences" are obviously unverifiable). That countless new arrivals lived in nations overflowing with bitter ethnic rivalries, often aimed at groups already residing here (e.g., Christians, blacks), cannot be dismissed. It is fantasy to expect every visitor from Saudi Arabia, Syria, Egypt, or Iran to believe that the presence of millions of Jews in America is wonderful once they enter U.S. territory. Nor will Hindus from India forget historic disputes with Pakistani Muslims once they clear U.S. Customs. Nor is conceivable that new laws will compel these arrivals to attend tolerance classes and absorb the lessons (there are not even mandatory English classes, and language skill is far more valuable than "learning to be tolerant by disdaining stereotypes"). As for the argument that assimilation will cleanse these hateful dispositions by transforming all new arrivals into "tolerant Americans," this becomes less plausible by the day as today's immigrants find ways to sustain their old values (e.g., following home country TV broadcasts).

The role of immigration in fermenting racial/ethnic strife has been dramatically illustrated in the southern California area as recent Mexican arrivals battle African Americans. In cities like Compton among several other Los Angeles neighborhoods, the murder rate has soared as rival gangs (some 209 Latino and 152 black) struggle for control. Since 2000, more than 5,000 murders in Los Angeles County have resulted from gang disputes.[9] Local high schools regularly witness scrapes between blacks and Latinos, some involving a hundred or more students. These are often coordinated in advance so as to establish "turf" while in other instances it erupts spontaneously over racial epithets or misunderstandings (McGrath 2005). As one might expect given the reluctance of public officials to confront such hot button issues as surging illegal immigration, tougher law enforcement and heightened surveillance, experts have called for more training in cultural sensitivity (Boghossian and Sodders 2005). It is doubtful that a few hours per week on appreciating differences will cool these ongoing animosities, however.

A notable irony here deserves mention. A generous immigration policy will undoubtedly cause social strife as groups with unlike cultures collide and compete over government-supplied benefits such as jobs and contracts. This has always been true, and conflict is an inescapable when attracting varied outsiders. Such discord will probably justify school-based tolerance instruction yet, the very people who instigate the problem, i.e., immigrants, will generally not attend school. At best, their children will be admonished to abandon ethnic/racial hatefulness but this will come to naught if the flow of new arrivals remains unchecked. Even successfully preaching tolerance to these immigrant children might require a minor miracle given language and other culture gaps. Tolerance instruction as the cure for melting pot tribulations will thus always lag one step behind; at most it may prevent hatreds from escalating. We can also assume that "appreciate differences" advocates, probably for ideological reasons, seem unlikely to demand that immigration cease so as to render their job more manageable. A "more the merrier" immigration policy thus perpetuates the problems that tolerance instruction is supposed to cure.

Even leaving aside those who will never encounter school-imposed anti-hate lessons, the obstacles to spreading the tolerance mantra via schooling still remain formidable. Not everyone embraces that supposed idealistic message, and physically fleeing it *is* an option, and one that grows more possible with time. Hatefulness is not yet a certified contagious disease that legally requires mandatory childhood vaccination. Consider a simple example. Imagine that, say, 10 percent of all parents, honoring a religious dictum, are intensely homophobic and wish to pass this belief on to their children. Further picture that teachers told these offspring that homophobia is not only impermissible hate, but that the "gay life-style" requires celebration. Though these incipient homophobes are precisely those targeted, they are also most likely to disregard instruction. For these religious parents "education in tolerance" aimed at instilling approval for homosexuality is tantamount to propagating sin, and it is naive to suppose that parents will defer to teachers on fundamental values. In a sense, parents want to inoculate their children *against* tolerance instruction to make them immune to this schooling.

Upset parents are certainly not helpless. The American educational system by its nature can impede top-down indoctrination, and relevant mechanisms can range for participating in school board elections to non-cooperation. In California's Novato School District when the local school district presented gay-themed skits to grade school children so as to discourage name-calling and bullying, parents sued to stop such instruction (Sack 2002). An even stronger response recently occurred among Canadian Muslims living in Toronto. When their children saw a film about how classmates taunt students with homosexual parents, Muslim parents threatened to withdraw their children from school rather than have them learn to appreciate what they believed was forbidden by their religious doctrines (Leslie 2004).

Aversion to this seemingly peaceable, "non-controversial" message can be quite rambunctious. In 2004, students and parents in the Ashland-Boyd County school district refused to participate in a mandatory "anti-harassment" workshop that resulted from an agreement with the ACLU regarding homosexual students. Hundreds of students skipped the workshop while 324 others were truants on that day. The ACLU has now threatened to seek a court order *compelling* student attendance to learn tolerance. Other cities have witnessed comparable controversies when those sympathetic to homosexuals promote their cause publicly in ways that might reach children (Archibald 2004). The paradox is, of course, that the greater the effort to instill appreciation, the greater the outward resistance, so the greater the "intolerance." Or, teaching tolerance begets intolerance.

Those totally enamored of "appreciate diversity" can easily underestimate the ease by which disgruntled parents can shield their children. Government requires school attendance and the teaching of certain subjects, but deeply upset parents are hardly prisoners of local schools. Unlike English or reading, tolerance instruction of the "appreciate difference" variety is *not* state mandated, and so it can be dropped just as quickly as it can be added. The decentralized nature of U.S. education means that parents disturbed over instructional content can vote with their feet and move to areas with more congenial schools. Indeed, relocation for "better schools," whether for improved sports or advanced placement courses, is commonplace. The explosive growth of charter schools, voucher programs, and especially home schooling further add means to avoid what is perceived as unacceptable brainwashing (Weissberg 2005, 105-115 depicts these options in detail).

The ease of fleeing unwelcome admonitions means that tolerance advocates will often preach to the choir or, equally likely, those who easily disregard it. The volume of pro-tolerance messages will be outwardly impressive but this will only be the appearance of accomplishment. This sorting out will burgeon as instruction shifts from glib generalities ("human diversity") to specifics such as learning to respect Islam. Tolerance education will ironically be most "successful" as measured by such things as workshops and magazine circulation when what is to be appreciated is inconsequential or totally vacuous, hardly what these tolerance crusaders intend when building a hate-free world. Stanley Fish's observation cited earlier is certainly worth repeating: "My General Law of Tolerance is that tolerance is exercised in an inverse relationship to there being anything at stake. The more there is something generally at stake, the less likely tolerance" (1994, 217).

That "appreciate differences" lessons often guarantee civic battles further foretells obstacles in this pathway to permanently quelling strife. The parallel with, say, inoculating children against polio or diphtheria is totally false. Many parents just don't want their children vaccinated. Moreover, political victories are seldom eternal—recall that racial segregation was once legally required, and these tolerance lessons can similarly be abandoned in the face of political discord. Unlike teaching basic, state-mandated skills, there is no compelling educational reason why tolerance instruction must remain part of the curriculum. It may well be yet one more passing fad, soon to be replaced by a new craze or pushed out of the curriculum if academic achievement continues to decline.

Conclusions

Viewed at a distance this educator-led quest for more tolerance abounds with contradictions. On the one hand, we find countless exhortations that teaching diversity makes us strong, that multiculturalism boosts self-esteem, and all the rest. To mobilize those otherwise mired in traditional pedagogical pursuits, appeals are made that evoke images of impending calamities galore for which this tolerance blueprint is the sole effective solution. Judged by its burgeoning popularity, such rhetoric resonates well, and this is true even as budgets become tighter and academic shortcomings grow more apparent. Measured by what infuses educational publications, opposition to this ambitious blueprint is nonexistent.

On the other side of the ledger is an utter disdain for demonstrating the cure's utility. Nor is there much effort to explain why traditional solutions to these tribulations, for example, tougher discipline or separation of warring parties, are suddenly obsolete. The entire enterprise has a religious fervor. Tolerance champions sermonize to the faithful and those who might demand hard scientific proof are dismissed as unhelpful. Nor do these educators seem interested in potentially relevant research outside their discipline. That empirical verification would be straightforward (at least for portions of this enterprise) makes this indifference all the more remarkable. The requisite analytical tools should be familiar to any professional with an advanced social science degree. Such investigations would be relatively cheap too. Surely among the many thousands of schools a few would open their doors to investigators promising to discover cures for disorders plaguing society. It would take relatively little to test experimentally the value of instruction on individual students or examine aggregate statistics in schools introducing tolerance programs. Research conducted by social scientists using an alternative conception of tolerance offers a goldmine of useful possibilities.

While several key elements in this enterprise, namely the link between attitudes and behavior and the long-term tenacity of inculcated values, are less amenable to direct testing, they are sufficiently serious to warrant attention. Uncertainties, let alone the obstacles to future empirical resolution, should dampen enthusiasm for this magic bullet and counsel searching elsewhere. At a minimum there should be government-mandated, fine-print warning labels affixed to these tolerance nostrums telling consumers that no scientific evidence shows any benefit, so let the buyer beware. Ordinary commercial code provisions regarding false advertising are certainly applicable to schools about to purchase pre-packaged "cures." Principals about to spend $25,000 to quell racial animosities by inviting a few speakers to harangue students for a week or two might reasonably request documentation before signing the agreement, even insisting on a money-back guarantee.

One can only wonder if these educators are so steeped in trendy pedagogy that they fail to recognize the fragile link between what generally transpires in society and individual predispositions. In truth, extra effort is necessary to deny plain-to-see reality—social tranquility cannot be achieved one child at a time until 300 million Americans are totally resocialized. Millions of immigrants, many from regions overflowing with religious or ethnic hatreds, arrive yearly and will escape the "diversity makes us strong" mantra. If forcibly exposed, most newcomers will undoubtedly reject these messages as pure fantasy. A half million industrious anti-Semites may be a tiny drop in the national bucket but they can poison civic life.

Surely some administrators are aware that parents have options regarding their children's schooling, and imposing unwelcome ideas about hot button topics such as homosexuality will likely bring flight, not rehabilitated bigots.

Surely they must recognize that no program can ever be 100 percent effective, and a few "bad apples" are sufficient to throw a school into turmoil. If billions spent to eradicate criminality fall short, why should a handful of tolerance re-education programs eliminate racial slurs or demeaning stereotypes? Do these tolerance advocates truly crave a police state in which electronic surveillance will provide irrefutable proof that one student called another, "fatso"? This is visibly a quixotic crusade to anybody save those who reside in the most isolated ivory towers.

No doubt project defenders will condemn this analysis as excessively harsh. Our conclusion will defend our assessment in detail but for the moment all that need be said is that educators have a terrible record for school-based social engineering. Hugely ambitious and expensive schemes to ameliorate racial discord via forced bussing, race-sensitive curriculum and manipulating teacher certification tests, and countless other nostrums have proven ineffective. The ever-popular campaign to cure allegedly shoddy education received for young girls seems to be an academic calamity for boys (see, for example, Sommers 2000). Extending civil liberties to students in the name of making schools less authoritarian so as to encourage creativity and spontaneity has undoubtedly undermined the discipline necessary for learning. To be skeptical of yet one more high-sounding educator-championed scheme, then, hardly seems out of place.

What, then, might account for this odd situation, an energetic pushing for an uncertain remedy when the obstacles to success are so apparent? The answer, we submit, is that this is politics, not a medicine-like cure. Though the lesson may ostensibly be about "appreciating differences" it is really about venerating *some* differences while denigrating others. That attitudes may have little to do with future behavior is irrelevant if attitude change is the aim. In a nutshell, it is the continuation of politics under the guise of building a better world. Chapter 6 will consider these oft-hidden aims in greater detail.

Notes

1.   A noninterest in calibrating impact does not necessarily mean an indifference to outcomes. These lessons may have less visible, more humble objectives, for example, insulating school administrators from future litigation. That is, in a suit by parents of harassed children, school administrators might defend themselves by insisting that they acted to prevent harm before it occurred. These exercises further offer controversy-free opportunities for school officials to burnish resumes by advocating attention-getting pedagogical fads. Promoting the appreciate ethnic/racial/religious differences theme also permits schools to convince various easy-to-anger groups that schools recognize group cultural achievements. As such, tolerance instruction is but a time-honored school response to community pressure groups. Successfully implementing these objectives probably occurs, though few administrators might confess to these less-than-noble aims.

2.   Utilizing skits, meals, and art seems commonplace, hardly surprising since such "fun" activities steer clear of awkward contradictions that inhere in addressing tolerance seriously. Another "touchy-feely" example of this risk-free strategy is

offered by a teacher in Iowa (Skophammer 2004) who had her fourth and fifth grade pupils draw pictures based on scenes from their lives on quilt-backed paper. Using words was optional. The students then viewed classmate portrayals. The teacher happily concluded, "They felt acceptance and tolerance for one another's stories and feelings." The teacher also believed that this exercise would help bring peace world-wide. Predictably, there is no confirmation of any impact other than the children supposedly had fun.

3. Recent empirical studies suggest that even children as young as three can distinguish truth from fantasy by utilizing contextual clues. They can sense that tales of Easter bunnies and tooth fairies are fictions, not accurate descriptions. Given that much of these tolerance lessons contradict a plain-to-see daily reality (recall Chapter 3's account of this whimsical world), many children might reject lessons that, for example, claim that all groups are equally talented academically. This research can be found in *Child Development,* vol. 77, issue 6, 2006 and is summarized in *Science Daily* "Young Children Don't Believe Everything They Hear," November 17th 2006 at http://www.sciencedaily.com/release/2006/11/061116114522.htm.

4. A further silence-inducing factor might be a discomfort with science. That the entire enterprise is infused with emotionalism (e.g., avoiding hurt feelings at all costs), a penchant for subjective impressions, and a cultural relativism that hints at an aversion for scientific methods. Conceivably, these educators perceive the scientific as "merely" a Western-style, male pathway to truth. The scientifically inclined may thus avoid this field altogether leaving what passes for empirical research to others.

5. The familiar research tactic of asking respondents about perceived threats does *not* solve this irrelevancy problem since respondents cannot say, "I find none of the choices threatening." The researcher assumes that there must be some menace, and only seeks to find which of several is the most pressing. Thus, even if threats are totally absent, *something* will emerge as "threatening."

6. Researchers rarely address this link, and among the tiny handful who do, most only "suggest" a close link and outright misrepresentation is not unknown, too. Gibson and Gouws (2003, 8) flatly state: "It is by now well established that attitudes are often strongly associated with behavior." The authors cite a meta analysis of many scientific papers showing a correlation of .33 between words and deeds to buttress their point. Not only is a correlation of .33 not evidence of a "close" association, but these other (and unmentioned) studies probably have nothing to do with tolerance and may well reflect those few instances in which a close tie does exist.

7. Some educators have sought to surmount these restrictions by inserting the "appreciate diversity" message throughout the school curriculum. Not only is this a hugely expensive endeavor, but as we noted in chapter 2 and will demonstrate again in chapter 6, this tacit politicization of academic subjects usually inspires the very turmoil it hopes to quell.

8. Immigration numbers are, needless to say, highly controversial. Homeland Security, Office of Immigration Statistics (http//: uscis.gov) put the number of immigrants in 2004 at some 3.8 million though this figure is undoubtedly too low given illegal immigration. It is also impossible to estimate the intellectual "baggage" these arrivals bring, but given that many flee from countries where US notions of tolerance are totally unknown, we can only assume that these residents would not instinctively embrace this "diversity is our strength" mantra.

9. Violent conflicts between blacks and Latinos also plague California prisons and, until a recent court order forbade it, prison authorities addressed this problem with

strict segregation. That correction officers cannot establish peacefulness despite near total control over prisoners' lives strongly suggests that these hostilities may be very deeply ingrained. Similar prison strife has also occurred between whites and blacks.

5

Bringing Tolerance by Criminalizing Hate

"It will be of little avail to the people that the laws are made by men of their own choice if the laws be so voluminous that they cannot be read, or so incoherent that they cannot be understood." —James Madison

Aversion toward those who differ is biologically ingrained. Humans would scarcely have survived without a capacity for violent anger against strangers. Yet, left unchecked these urges are destructive, a recipe for endless turmoil. Tolerance education is among the gentlest stratagems in this multi-front, almost never-ending battle. At the coercive continuum's opposite end is banishing odium via the criminal code—creating an entire new class of offenses called "hate crimes." Admonishing youngsters to cherish their gay classmates and upping the prison sentence for those assaulting homosexuals because they abhorred gays, over and above the routine incarceration, may appear unrelated but both measures seek identical goals. To paraphrase Karl von Clausewitz's (1780-1831) famous dictum that war continues diplomacy by other means, criminalizing detestation is just the most extreme form of the educator-favored nostrum.

As previous chapters delved into intolerance instruction to assess possibilities of achieving this attractive though Herculean task, here we examine the criminalizing option. Ours is a skeptical stance towards an overwhelmingly popular view, a one-sided chorus, so to speak, save a few quibbles over constitutional niceties.[1] After all, who wants to be "pro-hate" and such legislation, it would seem, might do some good. We begin by specifying exactly what certifies an act a "hate crime" versus, say, just an assault or even murder. Analysis then examines varied theoretical quandaries afflicting this enterprise, such things as uncertainties regarding who, exactly, is protected, and how this enterprise can produce antithetical outcomes. We then briefly trace out the emergence of the quest with particular attention to why hatefulness has suddenly become a "problem needing a solution." Can it be that recent years have seen dangerous resurgences of civil strife, or might the explanation lie elsewhere?

After presenting statistical data on offenses, we touch on issues surrounding hate crime data. Despite all the alarmist rhetoric, misdeeds pale in comparison with more humdrum transgressions. What might explain this disjunction between apprehension and the mild statistical record? Or, do the statistics underreport hatefulness? We also explore an awkward issue that occurs repeatedly but conveniently all but escapes notice among proponents of anti-hate legislation—false accusations. We conclude by considering the limits on legalistic approaches, particularly the dangers of totalitarianism wherein refurbishing human nature is the elected pathway to tranquility.

The Meaning of "Hate Crime"

Though personal repugnance has long been recognized as instigating crime, it has not until recently been integral to the crime itself. Demonstrating perpetrator aversion to the victim might only be part of the prosecution, namely establishing a motive when proving guilt. Hate crime legislation alters this tradition by inserting motive to a key feature of the crime, an element possibly drawing tougher sanctions. This is the equivalent of stiffer penalties for robbery if a gun was used. According to Jennes and Grattet (2004, chapter 1) what makes offenses distinctive, regardless of the specific illegal behavior, is that the violence attempts to "...transmit a terrorizing symbolic message to the victim's community" (3). Levin and McDevitt (nd) add a third element, namely that the victim is innocent in provoking the attack and is therefore interchangeable with any other person of his or her characteristics: if one wishes to bash gays, any gay person or gay-appearing person will suffice.[2]

There is no "stand alone" hate crime; the designation is added to a preexisting transgression for purposes of additional punishment (a "penalty enhancer" in legal language). In this regard, American law differs from some European versions where the mere expression of detestation, apart from overt criminality, can itself draw a prison sentence. What about mixed motives—the robber sought money but was also prejudiced against African Americans and thus robbed a black? Frederick M. Lawrence (1999, 10) like other legal experts argues that a "substantial motivation" must exist for the choice of victim, and that without this component, no crime would have been committed. We shall see that this stricture regarding "substantial" can be troublesome in actual practice.

A hate crime therefore involves two victims—the person raped or otherwise harmed and (indirectly) those sharing the victim's traits. Murdering a gay person becomes more than just a killing if the despicable act aims to send a message to other gays that their being gay, in and of itself, deserves death. Victim choice, then, is critical. If a mugger chooses a well-dressed elderly lady because she is unlikely to resist this is just a generic mugging but if the victim is an old Asian woman *largely* because she is Asian, a hate crime occurs. Property damage is also included—burning a black church compounds the arson if the intent is to intimidate African Americans.

A strong didactic element informs the enterprise—the law itself, followed by harsh retribution, serves as a teaching device. This "send a message" component is thus comparable to past public executions in which huge crowds could witness what happens to evildoers. A few go a step further and assert that these enactments reaffirm our collective commitment to racial and ethnic harmony in a heterogeneous society. Eventually, it is anticipated, the fear of sanctions coupled with public punishment will make hatefulness extinct. Promoting tolerance via a legal sanctions element was even explicit when Congress initially debated federal hate crime legislation (Jenness and Grattet 2004, 42).

As was true for pedagogues clamoring for heightened classroom tolerance instruction, proponents here are partial to alarmist rhetoric hinting impending mayhem. One observer insisted that anti-gay hate crimes are in the same league as the AIDS epidemic in which hundreds of thousands of homosexuals died, and he feared that the spread of AIDS will only exacerbate this violence (Berrill 1991). A group called the Civil Rights Coalition used the terms "festering" and "horrifying" to depict hate crimes in contemporary America (Civilrights. org nd). One Congressman endorsed the first federal hate crime law, the Hate Crimes Sentencing Act (HCSA) since it would "...help protect Americans from the most insidious types of crimes, those that are motivated by hatred of a person merely because of their race, their religion or ethnic background." A second congressional champion spoke of today hatreds as "...a form of poison spreading through our land. It affects people physically and psychologically" (both quoted in Jenness and Grattet 2004, 53).

Paralleling doomsday language are sociological studies documenting the deeply pernicious personal impact of misdeeds (summarized in Lawrence 1999, 40-41). Central to this view is that the victim, as a result of an unchangeable trait (e.g., skin color) can never escape potential harm, and this factor deepens the suffered injury over and above what occurs following a non-bias driven crime. Commonplace psychological impacts include depression, anxiety, feelings of isolation and hopelessness, and multiple other psycho-physiological symptoms, many of which can linger for years. One scholarly analysis goes so far as to claim that hate crimes are equivalent to terrorism (Weisburd and Levin 1994). Racial minorities particularly, it is alleged, are psychologically hard hit. Here being assaulted due to one's race can reawaken painful histories of prejudice and group-based violence, even triggering long dormant feelings of subservience, cultural inferiority, and oppression. Resultant feelings of stigmatization can also lead to self-doubt and a fear of contacting dominant group members, even high blood pressure and drug addiction among other ailments.

The lengths to which hate crime champions will go to justify this legislation can be Kafkaesque. A proposed 1999 federal statute, sponsored by dozens of prominent Democrats spoke of how hate impeded the flow of interstate commerce, even hindering the search for employment while the ensuring violence perpetuates the badge of slavery. The proposed bill announced that "existing Federal law is inadequate to address the problem" and such violence is "deeply" divisive. Despite the availability of FBI statistics showing just the opposite, hate crimes were deemed serious and widespread (H.R. 1082, 1999). Hyperbole aside, however, the particular legislation failed to become law.

Though the legal principle undergirding hate crime is self-evident, its translation into concrete policy can be troublesome. As in classroom tolerance lessons, ambiguities are everywhere, and these inevitably invite quarrels. For one, what, exactly, is "a community," let alone one that needs special legal safety apart from all the other protective statutes? Surely groups like Asians or the disabled are not club-like entities with membership rosters. A least some "community identities" (e.g., religion) are matters of individual choice, not unalterable physical characteristics, and religious groups occasionally debate exactly who belongs. Nor are religious identifying symbols always visible. Recall teacher confusion when going beyond "those who differ" in specifying who warrants tolerance. Dozens of traits could potentially provide the basis for a "community at risk," and while teachers might muddle through, lawmakers cannot hide behind vagaries lest courts nullify the statute as too vague.

Moreover, if some people deserve hate crime protection while others are denied this safeguard, how are these lines to be drawn? That this task is seldom of interest to those other than advocacy groups, the end result is more likely to reflect savvy politicking, or even administrative whimsy versus scientific standards. Overweight people may be singled out for harassment (perhaps since this trait, unlike many others, is obvious), but since the obese lack energetic advocates, no laws will be passed to protect them. Might feeling at risk, even paranoia, warrant inclusion to protected lists, regardless of objective evidence regarding risk, or must advocates statistically demonstrate a focused epidemic of criminality? Must the police thoroughly investigate victim identity claims when considering a possible hate crime, for example, certifying that a bisexual really is, indeed, a bisexual or an alleged Jewish person was born to a Jewish mother or lawfully converted?

Matters become even more complicated since specific group traits typically receiving protected status often lack precise legal definitions, and ordinary people similarly can diverge in perceptions.[3] Laws must be plainly understood, and if ordinary people—let alone potential criminals many of whom have less than average intelligence—are bewildered, the legal code can hardly send the correct message. To appreciate the complexities associated with race, consider that a person who is one-quarter black will still be perceived as "African American" while a person with a single Asian grandparent but three white grandparents will probably be seen as "white." Legislation inevitably protects "religion" but there are endless disputes over what, exactly, constitutes a bona fide religion. What if unlucky targets believe in Scientology, Ethical Culture, witchcraft, or countless other cultish faiths that explicitly deny the religious label? Can a completely secular Jew insist that he was assaulted due to his "ethnicity"? Several states include both religion and creed in statutory language, but how, exactly, does creed differ from religion (Lawrence 1999, 178-89)?

Even where legal "community" definitions exist, they are seldom helpful in the course of daily existence. Government agencies offer dozens of jargon-laden pages regarding what constitutes a disability (e.g., being legally blind) and some of the "minority" categories (e.g., Pacific Islander, Aleut) would undoubtedly baffle most people. If the U.S. Census Bureau remains perpetually perplexed by "race" or "ethnicity" after decades of trying, how can the would-be predator navigate these tribulations when selecting among victims? It may thus be nearly impossible for a "tolerant" career criminal to avoid hate crimes regardless of high-minded intentions. This is hardly the same as leaving the gun home when robbing a convenience store so as to minimize jail time if caught.

These complexities can easily plague what would appear to be a straight-forward trial. A clever defense lawyer could, for example, argue that roughing up a drag queen (female impersonator) was not based on "sexual preference" since not all drag queens are homosexual. This sharp attorney might contend that a loathing for "unconventional appearances" instigated the assault, and this category is typically outside of state or federal coverage. Linguistic interpreta-tions similarly complicate matters, especially as the U.S. becomes multilingual, and sub-cultural slang is sometimes indecipherable. How might police handle a Serbian immigrant knifing a Croatian while demeaning his heritage using Rus-sian colloquial speech lacking precise English equivalents?[4] What if Asians are harassed and called "FOBs"? Must police recognize that "FOBs" is an acronym for "Fresh Off the Boat" and is *sometimes* derogatory. Recall from our discussion of offensive words that many insults derive their meaning from who utters the phrase, not the word itself (i.e., groups themselves, but not outsiders, are often "permitted" to use nasty ethnic invectives).

Many states expressly add "mental disability" to the hate crime list, yet this is not only inherently vague but it might be unrealistic to expect criminals to play instant psychiatrist in selecting victims. Similarly, group-based hatefulness may only be evident after an attack thanks to relentless probing. A generic bar fight thus becomes a hate crime if an industrious detective discovered afterwards that the victim was Hispanic thanks to a Spanish-sounding last name and one or two minor "Hispanic" physical traits (and again recall the ambiguities of this and other ethnic labels). This may appear to be splitting hairs, but the consequences are real—uttering an ethnic slur shouted during the crime, or if the victim was wearing a religious symbol, can in the hands of an aggressive prosecutor extend prison sentences by *years*. It is arguable that miscreants should enjoy a reasonable opportunity *not* to commit hate crimes, but this "opportunity" nearly vanishes as indistinct categories multiply.

The upshot of these complexities can be a field day for clever prosecutors, and while this may occasionally benefit law enforcement, outsiders see capri-cious justice. Consider a few examples. The first was the 1990 New York City "dart man" case. Here an African-American man wandered about Manhattan shooting darts in women's posteriors, and all of the dozen plus victims were white women save two light-skinned Hispanics. Despite the near infinitesimal odds of uniform skin color choice in a highly racially diverse city, the police insisted that the attacks were not racially motivated (cited in Wilcox, 1994, 17). Closer in time is the New York City robbery in which three culprits from Pakistan and Afghanistan yelled "Get the white m*******er before robbing and fatally beating a white male. The culprits were arraigned for murder and robbery but no hate crime was charged since, according to the police, the racial slur was used only to establish the victim's intoxication level (Burke, Fenner, and Gendar 2006).

On the other side of this bizarre divide was the case of Jozef Mlot-Mroz, a notorious anti-Semite living in Salem, Massachusetts. When anti-Semitic graffiti was painted on a local synagogue, he attempted to *paint over* the graffiti since, in his opinion it gave a false impression of anti-Semitism. For his "helpfulness" Mlot-Mroz was charged with malicious destruction of property and the violation of civil rights, both felonies under Massachusetts law (cited in Wilcox 1994, 28).

These inescapable complexities are hardly hypothetical quibbles to be leisurely resolved by scholars. The concrete implementation of anti-hate statutes are *legally imposed* on police officers, investigators, prosecutors, defense lawyers, judges, and juries, who must, often quickly, tackle these tribulations. Resolution typically occurs with incomplete evidence, conflicting reports (e.g., did the drunk assailant really mumble, "Kill all blacks" when staggering from the crime scene?), all within a trial where proving guilt or innocence is sufficiently demanding. That these statutes usually included perceived victim traits, even if inaccurate, can add a surrealistic element. Conceivably, defendants might now under oath be interrogated regarding their beliefs about what, for example, a gay person looks like, how a beard worn by a devout Muslims differs from one grown by a hippie and so on to convince a jury that the mugging was "really" a hate crime. In some instances searching the perpetrator's home to find racist or other inflammatory literature can establish hatefulness. Owning "hateful" paraphernalia such as a Nazi Iron Cross, even a copy of Hitler's *Mein Kampf,* might, then, add years to a prison sentence.

It is hardly surprising that the menu so favored by educators generally infuses legislation though the sheer number of jurisdictions enacting anti-hate laws insures an almost incoherent jumble. The 1994 federal Hate Crime Sentencing Enhancement Act (HCSEA) defines a hate crime as one in which "the defendant intentionally selected any victim or property as the object of the offense because of the actual or perceived race, color, religion, national origin, ethnicity, gender, disability or the sexual orientation of any person." Omitted in this particular listing are other possible candidates, namely age, immigrant status, appearances (so-called "lookism"), veteran status, illness (such as HIV or AIDS), or ideology, though some of these routinely surface in anti-discrimination regulations. This act also specified eight types (later raised to eleven) of crime, from murder to property vandalism, subject to prosecution as hate crimes. Some of the less popular categories include marital status, political affiliation, and involvement in the civil or human rights movement. Obviously, prudent criminals should monitor state and local statutory revisions so as to avoid needlessly raising the costs of their criminality.

Significantly, as we noted, the term "perceived" is included in these statutes, so attacking someone who appeared to be black or homosexual could increase a convicted person's sentence though the assailant was mistaken. Ironically, the "appearance" element can contradict what tolerance-minded educators warn about "dangerous stereotypes." Somebody indicted for beating an exceptionally effeminate man could plausibly defend himself by saying that this person did not appear to be "homosexual" since effeminacy is "only a false stereotype" of gays. Going one step further, is a prosecutor using the effeminate trait as hate crime evidence "guilty" of stereotyping, and should he or she then be punished, too? A devious university-educated white mugger might plausibly insist that stabbing a black man was not "racially motivated" since "race" does not scientifically exist and, for good measure, black skin is just "socially constructed."

Deeply embedded in this quest is a potentially dangerous prescription that rarely surfaces but has paradoxical implications for cooling group-based animosities. If, as champions of this enterprise insist, criminalizing hate aims to eradicate hate against those at risk, *it is absolutely essential* that criminal acts receive front page attention featuring the victim's animus-attracting traits. Again, this is the modern-day equivalent of public hangings though authorities need not worry over ample space for spectators or other conveniences. The educative aim means that treating the crime as routine, even if a conviction results, defeats the very purpose of the legislation. Hate crimes cannot be just another crime statistic. That is, if a homophobe kills a gay person because of his or her sexuality, nobody will be "educated" by a terrible act *unless* it receives the widest possible publicity.

This sensationalism component was illustrated when in October of 1998 Matthew Shepard, a Wyoming teenager, was brutally murdered supposedly because he was gay (though some argue that this was just a bungled robbery). This horrible event brought a media circus and inspired congressional hearings to ponder additional hate crime legislation. An even more publicized incident was the June 7, 1998 killing of James Byrd, a forty-nine-year-old Texas black man who was brutally beaten and dragged behind a pick-up truck until he died. That the perpetrators were whites belonging to a white supremacist group instigated a chorus of calls for yet more federal anti-hate legislation. During the 2000 presidential election the NAACP even sponsored TV commercials nationwide about the despicable incident in which it was intimated that then governor George W. Bush was somehow responsible for the crime since as governor he had failed to enact state-level hate crime legislation. Though these commercials were eventually withdrawn as too partisan (thus endangering the

NAACP's tax exempt status), such notoriety is essential, even justifiable, given the need to educate the public.

This proclivity—commendable or questionable—was illustrated in Jeannine Bell's (2002, 102-6) insightful ethnographic account of hate crime coverage in a medium-sized city. She found that one local newspaper went on a feeding frenzy with inflammatory tales when one city neighborhood was undergoing painful racial integration. Though incidents did occur, many of them relatively minor, the parade of bad news gave the misleading impression of a racial war. Almost forgotten antagonistic encounters were endlessly rehashed, and even upbeat news of progress were given negative spins. In her estimation, local editors found these tales "good stories" though often inaccurate and misleading. No doubt, such exaggeration, no matter how benign, will only add fuel to the fire as group champions seize free media exposure for personal and organizational advancement.

The need to publicize attacks on legally protected groups may also bring factual distortions, a situation akin to how teachers sanitized reality to show that "all cultures are equally valid and useful." To wit, if weaning the public from hatefulness toward at-risk minorities is the aim, media accounts *must* disproportionately feature attacks by whites on blacks, gays, the disabled, and the like. This "education" is typically mis-education insofar the pattern of violence is just the opposite—attacks by black perpetrators on whites far outnumber the reverse, but well-meaning journalists who view hate crime reporting as a means of promoting tolerance may well hide this awkward fact.[5] As was true for students exposed to obvious distortions regarding cultural equality, the outcome of these compassionate intentions may breed cynicism, not a new-found awareness of rampant bigotry.

Does this hyper-publicity help? An answer cannot be deduced logically or commanded from statutory intent. Assertions may also be highly contentious given varied perspectives on what constitute "grievous threats" and what specific events signify. This empirical question, let alone the complexities inherent in resolving it, sad to say, draws slight scrutiny. It is just assumed that criminalization of despicable acts must be progress. Indifference to outcomes is a far cry from the endless studies regarding, say, the impact of capital punishment on the murder rate. Perhaps following the Matthew Sheppard incident many gays felt *less* safe, more vulnerable to homophobia while deranged homophobes were inspired to pursue "copy cat" assaults. Or, as hate crime advocates would expect, gays felt reassured that the police would exercise greater vigilance and that homophobes would now resist loathsome urges. On the other hand, did African Americans feel even more vulnerable since the James Byrd incident failed elicit fresh federal intervention, and alleged hatemonger George W. Bush was elected president?

But, it certainly is true that if gruesome stories do boost circulation, the mass media will generate a steady diet of them, and the result will be that "hatefulness" appears to be a burgeoning epidemic though exceedingly rare compared to other crimes. And the more the good-intentioned publicity, the "worse" matters may become, at least psychologically. The irony, then, is that what endeavors to eradicate a defect conceivably creates the false impression that society abounds with this malady.

A further ambiguity concerns calibrating "hatefulness." This is comparable to the problem of measuring "tolerance" that chapter 2 explored when educators reduce this inherently finely grained term to black and white categories. The law generally speaks of hatefulness as a dichotomous motive—one does or does not hate gays, for example. While black/white usage may make legal sense (akin to non-divisible liability in many state laws), it fails to capture the normal gradations of human emotions, separating, for example, virulent hatred from mild aversion. That a thesaurus lists multiple synonyms—detest, loathe, abhor, disdain, dislike, scorn, among many others—all with different nuances attests to this gradation. As we now have misdemeanors and felonies, should the law stipulate First and Second Class Hate Crimes, often for similar behaviors. Should we amend the statutes so as to provide both "dislike" and "hate" offenses? This certainly applies to killing—from involuntary manslaughter to premeditated murder, so why not here?

It is equally obvious that, as with all human emotions, aversions ebb and flow as situations change. Humans are moody and excitable, and laws traditionally recognize extenuating circumstances such as intoxication or drug use to mitigate punishment. How, then, are we to deal with a heterosexual who normally feels only vague discomfort about gays but gets worked up into a lather when confronting an aggressively obnoxious, intoxicated homosexual? If this heterosexual pushes the gay and calls him a faggot, does this become a hate crime given his or her momentary fury? Given that this behavior does not originate from someone normally classified as homophobic, would punishment—let alone therapeutic counseling—for "hateful homophobia" be warranted? Might other forms of retribution, say, just a friendly warning to control one's temper, be more useful? Though such calibrations appear quite reasonable, these provisions can only complicate trials and make them longer and more expensive.

Perhaps the most worrisome element in certifying hatefulness as a criminal motive concerns the possibility of uncovering widespread unconscious repugnance. The pressures here point in divergent directions. Frederick Lawrence (1999, 67-70) from a strictly legal perspective argues *against* unwitting bias as grounds for punishment. Hate crime perpetrators, he insists, deserve punishment for what they do voluntarily, and even when disentangling such motives, documenting below-the-surface drives can be a Pandora's Box. Avoiding subconscious intent is captured by the honored legal principle of *mens rea*—criminal intent. The classic legal exemplar of the *mens rea* is finding innocent the sleepwalker who committed an unrecollected crime.

Nevertheless, at least some proponents justify expansive visions of hate crime legislation since racism, homophobia, sexism, and similar pathologies are deeply, perhaps even permanently, culturally ingrained in American society. Thus, every white person is a racist, every heterosexual a homophobe, and so on though guilty parties typically cannot recognize their flaws. Scientific studies have recently joined this bandwagon though this evidence remains fairly inconclusive. MRI studies of the brain, for example, report that the area called the amygdala, which normally reacts to fear, responds when whites see pictures of blacks and vice versa.

Perhaps the most ambitious though still under-the-radar test for uncovering hidden, unconscious biases is something called the Implicit Association Test (IAT). This device is promoted by the evidently well-heeled Millennium Foundation in conjunction with Harvard University faculty. Basically, the IAT presents pictures of different people of different races, sex, age, sexuality, religions, even U.S. presidents and solicits visceral reactions. "Odd" and "unpleasant" reactions are interpreted as intolerance and prejudice, which, according to these Harvard-based researchers is akin to "viruses and bacteria [that] can be the source of ill health…" The test is now web-based (implicit.harvard.edu) and has been taken by some 4.5 million visitors. The project has also spawned several multi-disciplinary research papers. Significantly, the instrument and its results have garnered extensive mass media coverage, everything from the *New York Times* and the *Wall Street Journal* to numerous TV network shows plus scores of local papers. This test, together with other Millennium-sponsored, Harvard-based projects is clearly a major effort to expand intolerance's meaning to include absolutely normal, reality-based reactions to people without different outward traits. Now, thanks to what Harvard researchers have discovered, almost everyone is "mentally ill" and requires tolerance instruction (see http://spreadtolerance.org for a fuller account of this industrious project).

Should this "subconscious-hate-everywhere" perspective replace *mens rea,* the consequences would be momentous. Almost any hostile act toward subordinated minorities would now qualify as a hate crime regardless of protestations to the contrary. Even black-on-black crime could qualify if, for example, parties were of different skin hues, economic background, or sexual inclination. The tone of one's voice could reflect unrecognized disgust. A hate crime "explosion" would be the upshot and even more resources might be committed to combating hate crimes.[6] To repeat yet one more time, an effort to quell discord paradoxically leads to its expansion, at least in name though not in actual behavior.

The Rise of the Hate Crime

Locke and Voltaire, among other tolerance champions of that era, made their pleas in reaction to the horrific religion-inspired carnage then plaguing Europe. By comparison, occasionally overheated rhetoric aside, the last several decades have witnessed an incredibly peaceful United States. Government and ecclesiastical prosecution of heretics has been replaced by occasional personal harassment and, on exceedingly rare occasion, criminality. How, then, might the recent rush to criminalize hate be explained? Why is it that 1985 saw only eleven newspaper articles mentioning "hate crime" while five years later this number exceeded 1,000? Articles in law journals similarly rose during this period (Jacobs and Potter 1998, 4-5). Surely today's race-related riot is not the equivalent of government lynching African Americans by the thousands. If anything, today's violent outburst attract notoriety given their rarity and, most critically, this lawlessness is nearly universally government and popularly condemned. Something else besides burgeoning racial/ethnic mayhem must lie behind this sudden infatuation.

The explanation, we submit, has to do with the current emergence of organizations dedicated to advancing group-centered agendas. Jacob and Potter (1998, chapter 5) characterize this mobilization as "identity politics," and one of its defining features is the claim of being victimized, and the hate crime is ideally suited for this purpose. A past record of harm can now justify present-day special preferences and privileges. Of the utmost importance, this mission was (and is) greatly assisted by a multitude of academics, often but not exclusively located in entire group-focused departments (e.g., black studies, women's studies) where uncovering suffering past and present is fêted. Hate crime aficionados are often ingenious in pressuring public officials to assist their cause, for example, the 2005 Higher Education Security Act mandates colleges and universities to collect data on campus hate crimes.

What is paradoxical about this phenomenon is that it occurs *after* centuries of far more serious race/ethnic persecutions. That is, organizations to protect dissident Protestants during the colonial era (some of whom were executed while others were banished into the wilderness), nineteenth-century Chinese immigrants who lacked *any* legal protection against criminal acts, Native Americans who were massacred with legal impunity, violent intimidation of blacks under Jim Crow, and other tormented groups, never existed when the need was greatest. Now, with harm largely reduced to verbal slurs and miniscule serious crime, these protective alliances have, like mushrooms after the rain, exploded. To invoke an old cliché, with great fanfare the barn door is closed after the cows have escaped.

This group-protection movement began in the first half of the twentieth century with the 1910 founding of the NAACP and soon thereafter various Jewish groups monitoring anti-Semitism. Gay equivalents, notably the Mattachine Society and Daughters of Bilitis emerged in the 1950s. But, explosive growth had to wait until the early 1960s when the black civil rights movement spawned a plethora of organizations dedicated to pressuring government for group-centered benefits. The significance of these advocates and their remarkable legislative and private sector successes cannot be exaggerated. Organizations like CORE, SNCC, the Urban League and their countless locally based chapters perfected an easy-to-imitate formula in which establishing a grievance, the more attention-getting the better, and then extracting government benefits could be endlessly adapted to almost any constituency, from ethnic groups to those suffering from a humdrum debility (Jennes and Grattet 2004, 21-27, 32-39 details this diffusion).

Politics was central, and legislative enactments often became the primary measure of success. Burgeoning public awareness of new-found group needs was virtually guaranteed by innovative, technologically dependent tactics, notably dramatic public events to garner free publicity supplemented by mass mailings to potential sympathizers nationwide. Outrages were critical in this menu, and calls for government action to intervene soon became an incessantly loud chorus. Within an historical nanosecond, so to speak, dozens upon dozens of protective organizations sprouted to represents gays, the disabled, women, countless ethnic and racial minorities, and just about any interest that could make a claim to being at risk.

The very nature of the campaign for protection against hate helped immeasurably. First, from the outset the quest was effectively defined as being "anti-violence," and it is nearly impossible to imagine defending brutality, particularly when those seeking protection could otherwise claim victim status resulting from historical mistreatment (e.g., African Americans) or marginal current status (e.g., gays). Indeed, a long and honored legal tradition already exists in which the vulnerable, e.g., children, the disabled, the elderly, financially dependent women, receive extra protection, so this battle resonated well with traditional American values. Ambitious politicians enjoyed a feeding frenzy denouncing hate and bigotry with almost zero downside. That advocacy groups could easily supply the media with shocking examples of victims who suffered due to their race, ethnicity, or other trait yielded a public relations bonanza. What newspaper editor could resist a tale of innocent black children humiliated by a gang of white hoodlums? The obvious rejoinder to the call for "more laws" was that dozens of statutes already protect those at risk but this had, apparently, little influence.

Secondly, anti-hate nostrums appeared inexpensive and hardly clashed with the demands of potential rivals. Appending sexual preference to the hate crime list did not mean that others already included, or those who might apply tomorrow, would surrender anything of value. Rather than the pursuit for hate crime protection being a zero-sum game (e.g., government contract quotas), it could be construed as truly positive sum—*everyone* would benefit from the ensuing tranquility. Interests that might resist, say, affirmative action or ethnic-centered school curriculums were unlikely to mobilize against shielding gays from baseball bat-wielding rowdies. Nor was any moral issue involved—reducing gay-bashing is hardly endorsing same sex unions.

Moreover, enforcement mechanisms were already in place or could be easily adapted. No costly "hate crime police" units were necessary nor would police departments require expensive retraining or equipment. Adding new statutory language posed few legal predicaments, especially since many states could just copy from others while advocacy groups conveniently supplied well-crafted "model legislation" gratis. Admittedly, local police might allocate a few extra hours for paperwork or ask some additional questions when investigating crimes, but this was, obviously, a seemingly trivial price to pay for allegedly huge benefits.

Jennes and Grattet (2004, chapter 4) detail the rapid growth of anti-hate legislation so that within a mere two decades, nearly all states took the plunge. It soon became comparable to championing apple pie and motherhood. Washington and Oregon led the way in the early 1980s, and nearly every state soon followed (Jennes and Grattet 2004, 74). Not surprisingly, given American federalism plus special circumstances, these enactments occasionally incorporated provisions rarely found more generally, for example, bans on paramilitary training, shielding military veterans from hate attacks, prohibiting the wearing of hoods and masks (except for events like Halloween), and compensating victims. As would be expected from the pressures exerted by advocacy groups ever on the lookout for innovative opportunities to demonstrate their clout, states have generally expanded these laws to cover new categories and offenses.

A new legal vocabulary and classes of crimes now emerged. One could be guilty of "ethnic intimidation" or "malicious harassment," while, as in the case of Montana's new legislation, *annoying* somebody due to his or her ethnicity became an actionable offense. West Virginia, perhaps attuned to academic fashions, included "oppress" in its statutory language while Oregon, perhaps more sensitive to everyday tribulations, spoke of "substantial inconvenience." Louisiana's 1997 law specified some forty-one specific offenses potentially treatable as hate crimes, including "oral sexual battery" and purse snatching. To add further confusion, some statutes, technically addressed "hate crimes" while others spoke of "bias crimes" (see Jennes and Grattet 2004, 88-90 for additional variations in legal language).

Many of these laws eventually found their way into complicated court challenges. One compilation identified some eighty-three court cases in which the challenges rested on included vagueness, free speech (including criminalizing only selected ideas), and legislative overreach (Jennes and Grattet 2004, 107). Critically, while laws were occasionally struck down or narrowed, the legal movement to criminalize hate has generally withstood judicial scrutiny. Among the few examples of invalidated law was the early case of *R.A.V. v. City of St. Paul* (1992) in which the U.S. Supreme Court unanimously invalidated a St. Paul ordinance prohibiting cross burning and similar acts that would cause "anger, alarm or resentment in others on the basis of race, color, creed, religion or gender." An unanimous Court (though two groups of justices differed on key details) found that this ordinance impinged upon freedom of speech since, among other things, it was exclusively directed at certain types of speech, that is, racist speech, not all types of inflammatory speech (Lawrence 1999, 31-33, 86).

Vagueness so as to make virtually anything an act of "hatefulness" has also brought judicial rebuke. After all, even the most despicable, dim-witted criminal has to know what can bring additional punishment. For example, in October 2004 the Georgia Supreme Court unanimously declared a state law as unconstitutional on grounds of vagueness and overreach. Its statute had increased criminal penalties if the crime victim was singled out on the grounds of "any bias or prejudice." This unacceptable statutory language had replaced earlier wording that referred to a crime motivated by race, religion, gender, national origin, or sexual orientation (Associated Press 2004).

More typical have been judges upholding these statutes. The case of *Wisconsin v. Mitchell* (1993) was particularly significant since it legitimized harsher sentences for hateful motivation. Here a newly enacted Wisconsin hate crime law was employed to prosecute several blacks who had attacked a white teenager. The leader of the assailants, a nineteen-year-old named Mitchell, was convicted of aggravated battery and, as per hate crime law provisions, the usual sentence of two years of prison was augmented to a four-year term. Of the utmost importance, evidence presented at the trial showed that Mitchell had previously made remarks displaying a strong anti-white animus and that the victim was selected solely on the basis of his (white) race. Mitchell's attorney appealed the judgment to the state's Appellate Court where it was upheld. But, Wisconsin's Supreme Court overturned Mitchell's additional penalty on the grounds that the law, with its focus on inner thoughts, constrained Mitchell's right to think whatever thoughts he wanted, and thus violated Mitchell's First Amendment rights. The U.S. Supreme Court upheld the Wisconsin anti-hate legislation, a crucial decision insofar as it sanctioned the punishment of motivation.

All in all, then, between the early 1980s and the first decade of the twenty-first century the expression of hate went from something that might prove criminality but was not itself an offense to being a crime itself if accompanied by detailed unlawful behaviors. This was not merely a traditional "anti-crime" strategy of making new things illegal. Nor did these laws commit fresh resources to fighting crime. Their purpose was to alter people's *thinking* not just curb reprehensible behavior. Today's mugger may still prowl the street in search of victims, but woe to the miscreant who selected marks on the basis of race, ethnicity, or some other statutory-specified category. Now, it might be said, even criminals would be tolerant.

The Alleged Hate Crime Epidemic

The principle underlying a hate crime is straightforward. But, that acknowledged, cataloguing this malevolence accurately and reliability remains an exceptionally daunting task given countless ambiguities and practical tribulations. Nevertheless, this mission is of the utmost *political* importance. Without a precise, agreed-upon yardstick we are vulnerable to never-ending claims and counter-claims from all sides of the ideological spectrum. Everything, conceivably, from high-profile riots to minor quarrels over gambling, can become hate crimes. Surely it is unwise to make public policy based upon a few ambiguous, lurid newspaper headlines or TV specials, especially since these may reflect a hidden agenda. Equally relevant, without a yardstick it is impossible to assess progress. Monitoring media accounts might usefully alert us to riveting outrages, but their absence might just as readily reflect public boredom with yet another beating of a gay person.

As the hate or bias crime concept emerged during the second half of the twentieth century, private, advocacy-based organizations, notably the Anti-Defamation League of the B'nai B'rith, the National Institute Against Prejudice and Violence voluntarily handled data collection. Feminist groups have similarly gathered information about wife beating, sexual exploitation, plus other sex-related offenses that often went unreported or lay at the criminal code's edge. Limited resources and untrained personnel often resulted in sloppy reporting while categories frequently lacked legal precision. Organizations also focused narrowly on what was relevant to members, for example, the NAACP just tracked the lynching of blacks.

These unsystematic efforts typically exaggerated incidents to advance a "we are victimized" agenda. For example, gay organization in the early 1980s casually distributed questionnaires at openly gay gatherings soliciting information about varied unpleasant encounters, everything from verbal abuse to actual violence. Questionnaire design coupled with one-sided interpretation virtually guaranteed grim tales galore. Some questions asked about disagreeable encounters over an entire lifetime; others included spats with parents. Even the subjective "worried over personal safety" could enter the unofficial hatefulness record. Anything that vaguely appeared homophobic became anti-gay violence, for example, mugging a lesbian. Organizations gladly supplied press releases to "document" that gays were constantly besieged by homophobia. As was commonplace in such early make-it-up-as-you-go-along endeavors, personal tales went unchallenged and lacked independent verification. Truthfulness was just assumed (early compilations are described in Weissberg 1998, 156-65).

This changed dramatically in 1990 with the passage of the federal Hate Crime Statistics Act (HCSA) that directed the attorney general to collect data on crimes that showed "manifest prejudice" based upon specific victim traits. The act did not criminalize anything, it merely provided for information collection, and thus drew upon states and localities to supply data. Though twelve states (and several non-government advocacy organizations) already collected these data, this legislation was supposed to provide a clear, authoritative national picture for journalists and concerned citizens. The act assigned the Justice Department authority to devise methods for assembling information, and the responsibility was then consigned to the FBI which, in turn, passed it on to its Uniform Crime Reporting (UCR) Section.

The HCSA seemingly substantially improved matters. Local police now completed a "Hate Crime Incident Report" after every alleged incident which was then periodically submitted to the FBI. It is relatively detailed, including crime location (for example, a bar/night club, a school), the number of perpetrators and spells out alleged motivation (for example, anti-Catholic). Listed are the victim's relevant traits, and besides the obvious one of "individual person," it also includes "society."

Though a major step forward, as is true for collecting any potentially sensitive information across thousands of political jurisdictions, each with their own resources and cultures, the HCSA suffered technical problems when actually applied. Jacobs and Potter (1998, 40-2) note several, and many are nearly inescapable. The FBI itself in its preliminary statement regarding UCR data, of which hate crime data are a subsection, explicitly warns users about attributing too much precision to the information while assuring users that those providing information make "a good faith" effort to satisfy the guidelines. Nor are collection formulae always crystal clear or consistent, and remember that this compilation reflects countless state and local laws, all with their own quirks and provincial vagaries.

Limits also exist to what supplementary written instructions can accomplish, especially given the varied officials daily navigating inherently imprecise terms. The official *Training Guide* designed to help here would, accidentally or even intentionally, permit myriad humdrum offenses to be construed as hate crimes, for example, assaulting a gay in the belief that gays are promiscuous or hating a Jew because Jews "are greedy" (Bureau of Justice Assistance 2000). This *Training Guide* also, perchance inadvertently, opens the door to an overly generous categorization standard since it permits the hate crime label to be pinned on a crime if there is "some evidence" that the offender was "partly" motivated by hatefulness. That almost any human being has some, however slight, aversion to those who differ, and tumultuous situations can momentarily exacerbate these emotions, relentless psychological probing can convert any incident into a hate crime. Particularly troublesome has been gaining state and local cooperation, no small matter since, at least in 2004, some 12,499 jurisdictions were—or are supposed to be—reporting, and this can be voluntary or mandatory depending upon jurisdiction.

Early reports (as is true today) showed that hate crimes were very rare, typically associated with lesser offenses. Ironically, several groups that had ardently lobbied for this legislation now *denounced* the entire FBI-led project! It was if the cult of victimization was now itself under attack via government compiled statistics. For some "everybody knew that hate was rampant" so the statistics must be lies. A 1992 *USA Today* story even proclaimed, "no one needs a government report to know such [hate crime] offenses are rising" (cited in Jacobs and Potter 1998, 57). With time, the number of forwarded reports grew, and accounts of incidents likewise multiplied, but the HCSA has hardly ended debate over the hatefulness of American society.

Complexities and statistical uncertainties aside, then, how commonplace are hate crimes? Overall, they are but a tiny outcropping of all criminal behavior. According to the 2004 compilation, some 2,046 agencies report a total of 7,649 hate-related incidents that totaled 9,035 offenses (U.S. Department of Justice 2005, 5). The majority were racially motivated (52.9 percent), followed by religious bias[7] (18.0 percent), sexual orientation (15.7 percent), ethnicity or national origin (12.7 percent)[8] and disability bias (0.7 percent). Predictably, most (62.4 percent) were against people, the rest largely property related (crimes against "society" came in at 0.7 percent). Equally telling, offenses were overwhelmingly at the minor end of the criminality continuum. Outrages that typically draw intense media coverage (e.g., the Sheppard and Byrd killings) are *exceedingly* rare. A total of five hate-related murders were reported in 2004, and three of these were racially motivated, two anti-white, one anti-black. The most common offense (31 percent) was intimidation. Of all reported crimes, a mere 6.0 percent involved what the FBI classifies as serious—murder, forcible rape (a total of four, three against whites, one against blacks), arson, motor vehicle theft, and the like.

Further undermining alarmism are attacker characteristics. Legislation proponents, and especially those representing "underdogs," characteristically depict an epidemic directed against racial and ethnic minorities. This relationship certainly holds for sexuality, disability, and perhaps other traits, that is, few homosexuals purposely rob heterosexuals nor do the disabled prey on the able-bodied. When it comes to race, the *ne plus ultra* of hate crimes, however, the story is entirely different and, as we shall argue below, these data probably minimize black-on-white hate crimes. According to the 2004 FBI hate crime data (7), among known offenders 60.6 percent were white and 19.7 were black. If hate crimes were roughly proportional to population, white perpetrators should outnumber African American by a ratio of about eight to one; in fact, the ratio is closer to three to one, and this roughly applies to all hate-related crimes with substantial numbers, for example, aggravated assault, robbery and vandalism. Put frankly, whites, not "at-risk" minorities, are bearing the brunt of hatefulness.[9] These ratios should come as no surprise given that blacks in general are more criminally prone than whites, so hate crimes just reflect a larger pattern.

Viewing these data over time fails to alter this picture. Admittedly, while comparisons with the earliest reports (see Jennes and Grattet 2004, 46-47) does show a modest percentage increase, at least some of that undoubtedly results from early imperfect reporting. Overall, incidents have remained fairly steady since the mid-1990s. In absolute terms, the number of offenses still remains small given population size and opportunities for contentious incidents. Nor is there any notable shift from minor incidents (e.g., intimidation) to far more serious offenses such as arson or murder.

Perhaps the best case against those insisting upon soaring hatefulness is to compare these figures with crime more generally. In this context, hate crimes are an insignificant blip on the misdeed landscape. In 2004, there were approximately 1.4 *million* violent crimes reported, including 16,137 murders, 94,635 forcible rapes, 401,326 robberies, and over ten million property crimes. Compare these statistics to the 7,649 documented incidents of hatefulness (FBI 2004).

Government-compiled data need not necessarily end discussion, however. Those still insisting that America is awash with hatefulness look past these "deceptive" numbers and offer several contrary arguments. One is that hate crimes are endemic but most of them go unreported. Many feminists long expressed a similar view regarding domestic violence— harm is real, but almost always silenced by those preferring to look the other way. Typical of this "silent epidemic" view is a Massachusetts report that found that some 10 percent of public school students from thirty schools across the state had experienced some form of hatefulness but a mere 3 percent of the victims reported it to the police. One response to this problem was to revamp the state's website—www.stopthehate. org—to educate students about hate crime (Rosenwalt 2002).

Explanations for the hush typically include distrust of the police, language obstacles, fear of unwanted attention, and trepidation about perpetrator retaliation. Certainly no illegal immigrant would report an ethnic insult to the police. Further alleged is that at least some of the victims construe the offense as "minor" and thus refuse to bother the police so as to avoid all the paperwork and other disruptions, including a possible trial (Lawrence 1999, 23 reviews these arguments). Totally absent from this rejoinder is the possibility most offenses are minor and have more to do with daily life in a multicultural society than bitter racial/ethnic antagonisms.

A different tack stresses cumbersome reporting mechanisms, notably the extra labor required to arrive at a hate crime judgment, and this effort unnecessarily complicates already demanding police work. In many instances, the detailed nature of the statutes (dense "legalese"), a necessity given punitive consequences, requires investigators to play mind-readers, even linguists. For example, the Montana hate crime statute requires that the act be motivated by an "intent to terrify, intimidate, threaten, harass, annoy or offend" and the precise nature of the emotions at the time of the crime do matter legally (this illustration comes from Jenness and Gratett 2004, 87). One can only imagine the battling attorneys, let alone jurors, trying to divine the perpetrator's exact mental condition during a mugging. Was the comment about the victim's Canadian ancestry really an "ethnic slur" when "Canadian" is generally not considered an ethnic identity? Better to let sleeping dogs lie.

Enforcement can reflect values, especially where law enforcement officials are popularly elected. This can, of course cut both ways in terms of accuracy. An ambitious prosecuting attorney up for reelection can manipulate hate crime prosecutions for electoral advantage depending on which way the political winds are blowing. A New York City situation in 2006 well illustrates how local political sensitivities might shape what comprises a "hate crime." The facts are fairly straightforward. A white college student—Broderick Hehman—was in a black neighborhood when attacked by five black teenagers, apparently to rob him. He fled into traffic and was hit by a passing car and died a few days later. Several witnesses heard at least one of the blacks yell, "Get whitey" or "Get the white boy" prior to the attack. Though initially investigated as a hate crime, this angle quickly vanished. The investigator insisted that the motive was "substantially" economic and the racial remark "gratuitous." Moreover, the police continued, his slight build, not his white skin, made him an attractive target.

This was in sharp contrast to a previous but parallel New York City case in which a white assailant, Nicholas Minucci, aged nineteen, was charged with a hate crime and spent a year in jail, unable to post $500,000 bail, for attacking three black teenagers. The alleged proof of the racial hatefulness was, supposedly, the utterance of the phrase, "What's up N***er." The accused white insisted that this was purely a robbery, and he used the phrase, "What's up nigga," not "What's up N***er " and the former phrase was an inoffensive "hip hop" greeting in the overwhelming black community in which the assailant grew up. In short, the "a" at the end of "Nigg" was a conventional, inoffensive greeting, the "er" a vile slur. A more plausible explanation is that local politics intervened—it was just easier to accuse a person of Italian ancestry of a hate crime than black teenagers (Gelinas 2006).

During Minucci's trial in June of 2006 for the robbery and beating of one of the blacks (who had admitted that he was in the defendant's neighborhood to steal a car) considerable expertise was brought to bear on just, exactly, how "N***er" and "N**a" differed. New York newspapers covered the trial in often lurid detail black hip hop record producer Gary Jenkins expertly explained that he would require additional information about the accused's cultural milieu before he could say, precisely, what word Minucci uttered (Goldstein 2006). Noted Harvard professor, Randall Kennedy, who has authored an entire scholarly book on the "N" word and is an authority on "race linguistics" testified that the "N-word" does not necessarily imply racial animus, and may even be a term of endearment (Weintraub 2006). One can only recall arcane medieval scholastic disputations but here the term is a vulgarity. In the end, after a jury deliberated for two days he was convicted of first- and second-degree robbery as a hate crime.

Jeannine Bell (2002, especially chapter 5) has closely investigated police discretion in reporting hate crimes and catalogues several pressures to underreport incidents that could, conceivably, be classified as hate motivated. Particularly relevant here are her observations about resident cooperation in a section of a large city in the throes of contentious racial integration. In her estimation, hate crimes, particular by white residents against black newcomers (but the reverse, too) were commonplace but were almost entirely unreported. White residents absolutely refused to assist police regarding incidents, even alerting culprits of the impending arrival of police. Officers were also prevented from gathering vital evidence. Local arrested teenagers further received free legal help to impede police interrogation. Public interracial fights in broad daylight, amazingly, had no witnesses! Community leaders even made non-cooperation with investigations unofficial community policy.

Yet a third "more than it seems" argument concerns victim classification. This is less an argument about an alternative reality than wordplay to accomplish a political aim. Recall that categories are statute-specified, and typically reflect today's understanding of who is at risk, that is, racial/ethnic minorities etc. This relatively specific approach, some argue, is too restrictive. Levin and McDevitt (nd), for example, would substitute a far more open-ended definition, notably "...any group difference that separates the victim from the offender in the offender's mind" (1). This view, needless to say, opens the door to endless idiosyncratic hate crimes. Conceivably, a hate crime could now involve attacks on people who are short, smelly, vegetarian, talk loudly, wear backwards-facing baseball caps in restaurants, display noxious political buttons, have weird hair styles, and so on and so on. Most (if not all) rapes would now be transformed into hate crimes if juries agreed that it was misogyny driven.

Less ambitious, and more reasonable, are those who would adjust offenses to local conditions. In a city that had union-related strife, it might be a hate crime to attack union organizers solely because he or she was associated with a union. In some university towns the conflict would be between town and gown, and thus mugging college students *qua* college students would be a hate offense. Needless to say, though this more modest definition of expansion would undoubtedly boost hate crimes numbers, it would also generate immense political wrangling in thousands of localities as each interest sought its own special protection.

A final argument regarding understatement is totally future oriented: FBI-collected figures may be miniscule today, but insofar as they reflect shifting economic conditions, they will undoubted soar as globalization decimates middle-class prosperity. Lawrence (1999, 25-26) harkens back to various nineteenth-century depressions and links these to attacks on immigrants, especially Roman Catholics, as a harbinger of bad things to come. That is, as the children of today's middle class lose their comfortable lifestyle thanks to outsourcing and automation, they will scapegoat those who differ as (allegedly) responsible for their plight. The Klan may be moribund, but the urge that created it in the first place can reappear at any moment. Increasingly familiar phrases such as "low-wage immigrants took my job" or "affirmative action gives blacks an unfair advantage" will ultimately be translated into overt, sometimes violent hostility. Implied is that enforcement mechanisms must be strengthened while time remains.

The under-count objections hardly end disputes and altering reporting protocols cannot close debates. On the other side of the ledger are serious claims that legal accounts exaggerate, not minimize, burgeoning hatefulness.

From this perspective even these puny numbers are uncertain indicators of hate, and closer inspection of instances drawing public notoriety suggest that the gap between what is publicly portrayed and hard reality is probably exaggerated.

The place to begin is that FBI statistics are reports of a *suspected* crime, not the result of a trial. It is difficult to say how many reported incidents eventually resulted in a confession or guilty verdict ("clearance" in police terms), but one can safely assume that many failed to survive courtroom scrutiny. Verdicts of "not guilty" do not, of course, mean that the crime never occurred. The "not guilty" outcomes may only reflect insufficient evidence or even inept prosecution. Moreover, charges could have been dropped as part of a plea bargain. Still, when all is said and done, FBI figures might be best interpreted as the largest estimate of hate crimes, not their true Platonic, federal government certified number.

To be sure, surveys asking about victimization often substitute for FBI data, and almost always report a higher incidence of these crimes. Still, as we observed before, these data can be even more troubling given the vagueness surrounding offences and, critically, the accompanying ideological agenda. Also recall that past victimization studies failed to heed strict legal definitions and events are often unverifiable, a situation totally unlike a trial, let alone a formal police report. To appreciate this potential distortion, consider one recent investigation of anti-gay incidents in Sacramento, California. Here more than half the men report verbal threats and harassment during the previous year (APA, 2006). If this were extrapolated into "hard" crime statistics, and assuming approximately 4 million adult gays nationwide (about 2 percent of the adult population), this would bring the incidence of anti-gay hate crimes to 2 million, a far cry from the less than 8,000 of all offenses reported that year.

Powerful organizational pressures also exist to overstate hatefulness. "Setbacks" become rallying cries to boost membership, extract special treatment from government and, most critically, collect donations necessary to pay executive salaries. The energetic exposure of once-hidden hatefulness parallels creative efforts to depict once-hidden dangerous racism. The conflict of interest between success and failure is probably endemic and, as we saw, appetite for publicity practically requires lobbying for even broader hate crime definitions and law enforcement diligence. The situation becomes circular: tales must be ever more lurid, and investigations ever more diligent, to overcome public indifference. Cross burnings, Nazi graffiti, and racial epithets may harm their immediate victims, but they are valuable for organizations dedicated to eradicating these behaviors. Hate and anti-hate are now in a symbiotic relationship.

Our final point regarding exaggeration concerns hoaxes—the falsification, or the conscious misleading interpretation, of a claim not its mere rejection by the police or courts as unproven. This is a topic that scarcely draws any scholarly attention, perhaps a result of the academy's sympathy with victimized groups.

Nevertheless, hoaxes do exist despite the one-sidedness of academic scholarship. Newspapers periodically expose fictitious claims though these rarely appear in headline grabbing stories.[10] Typing "hate crime hoax" in Google (as of May 14, 2006) gets some 80,000 "hits" and this may reflect the by now familiar disjunction between the academy and the larger world.

As for the question about the proportion of claims that are outright hoaxes, an answer is exceedingly tricky. Nor are data available regarding who is disproportionately inclined to make such false charges though anecdotal evidence reveals that almost all groups avail themselves of this tactic. The FBI lacks a "hoax" category in its hate crime reporting forms, and if a hoax is uncovered, the reported incident simply disappears from the compilation. And while falsely reporting a crime is an actionable offense, and occasionally prosecuted as such, there is no distinct legal category for such falsehoods.

In addition, perpetrators are often minors and these culprits escape prosecution while adults often receive mandatory mental health counseling instead of criminal sanctions. The extent to which prosecutors will bend over backwards to avoid punishment was illustrated in a Virginia case in which a black apartment complex dweller distributed Ku Klux Klan fliers so as to "shock" young African Americans. Despite complaints to the police and emotional distress among many tenants, authorities were inclined to treat the incident as a case of "free speech" and not press charges (*Daily Press* 2006). The most likely prosecutions are for insurance fraud and thus not recorded as a hate crime hoax. Laird Wilcox (1994) based on years of extensive interviews with law enforcement officials and newspaper accounts, nevertheless suggests a ballpark figure of 25 percent. But, debatable numbers aside, hoaxes often draw immense publicity, and can have major impacts, even when exposed as frauds.

No doubt, part of the reason for crying wolf is that in today's ever-sensitive world they are so easy to accomplish and relatively risk free, to boot. Powerful incentives exist in a society that seemingly venerates victimization, particularly if a racial minority is the injured party, and one might even profit financially from the hoax thanks to an outpouring of community help. It hardly takes much brainpower for a Jewish person to claim that Nazi skinheads vandalized his car in the middle of the night if he wants insurance money to repair his jalopy. Apprehended perpetrators sometimes justify their actions for "good" reason, for example, sensitize people to underlying racism, homophobia, anti-Semitism, or other collective malignancy. The lure of free publicity similarly entices many. A rational element may be present if miscreants assume that the cry of "hate crime" in today's political climate will insulate them from unwelcome police inquiry that would uncover their own misdeeds.

An almost generic illustration was the case of an interracial Georgia couple whose home burned to the ground who then filed a $301,000 insurance claim. The husband and wife emotionally told police of hate calls and spray-painted swastikas, and immediately received an outpouring of public sympathy. According to the tearful white wife, the arson was punishment for loving a black man. Unfortunately for the couple, the FBI discovered that this arson was self-inflicted, a verdict assisted by the fact that supposedly incinerated expensive computer equipment eventually reappeared in a rented locker (Carter 1997).

A more serious offense occurred in St. Paul, Minnesota when a black woman sent twenty-eight pieces of mail to herself and two members of Congress, each one scrawled with racial insults on the outside. She then attempted to extort $150,000 from UPS since in her opinion "white supremacists" had vandalized these insured packages. During the trial she insisted that this was all part of a "racist conspiracy" but the jury remained unconvinced (AP 1998). In another case, a San Francisco man claimed that four "neo-Nazi" types abducted him and then carved a swastika on his chest. After an investigation, including a police trip to Oregon to find these alleged culprits, the man confessed that he had done the carving himself for "personal reasons" (Delgado 1999).

Publicizing questionable hate crimes also promotes a political agenda, especially given media aversion to challenge stories that portray Americans shamefully. Several occurred post 9/11 when American Muslim groups sought to represent themselves as innocent victims of American intolerance, not terrorists. When in July 9, 2004 a Muslim-owned grocery store in Everett, Washington burned to the ground, its owner claimed to be victimized by hatefulness. Investigators soon discovered that its owner was the culprit who was facing a missed payment and needed the insurance money. A similar insurance fraud occurred in Texas. Still, in both instances, the nationally prominent Council on American-Islamic Relations (CAIR) cried, "hate crime." CAIR further reported a bombing of a mosque outside of Houston, Texas, supposedly by "two white men." The local sheriff's department had never heard of this alleged incident (Pipes and Chadha 2005).

In other instances, supposed anti-Muslim incidents were construed as hate crimes only by stretching the term's meaning to the limit, not according to a legal determination. In some instances alleged outrages were actually criminal prosecutions of Islamic terrorists! Tiny increases were also opportunistically converted into to huge percentage increases (Pipes and Chada 2005). A lack of close scrutiny—intentional or otherwise—can readily permit ideological spin. When a burnt copy of the Koran was left in a shopping bag outside a Virginia mosque, countless Muslim leaders were outraged, lambasting the police and Americans for their ignorance of Islam. In reality, a Muslim student who was leaving the country and hoped that the mosque would give the damaged book a "respectful disposal" had left the charred Koran (Malkin 2005). Nevertheless, despite contrary evidence, Muslim organizations did achieve a modicum of success—an October 9, 2001 *Chicago Tribune* story announced "Hate Crime Reports Reach Record Levels" and blithely went on to report just what the Muslim organizations asserted (Coen 2001).

Universities are particularly vulnerable since aggrieved group members can manipulate incidents to extract ethnic centers, special programs, even additional scholarships and faculty appointments. Universities also seem to cherish their reputation for tolerance and thus will go to extraordinary lengths to remediate claimed offenses, even accepting tales at face value despite contrary evidence. At the University of Mississippi's fortieth anniversary of racial integration, two black students encountered racial epitaphs scrawled on their dorm room doors. Black students soon organized a "Say No to Racism" march while the director of minority affairs demanded a litany of racial sensitivity and black pride programs. High-profile meetings followed and the national news media lamented that Old Miss race relations had not changed in forty years. Eventually the graffiti was discovered to be the work of black students, and despite $600 worth of damages, no charges were filed (Kanengiser 2002).

An especially well-publicized hoax occurred when a professor of psychology at California's Claremont McKenna College reported that her car was vandalized with painted anti-Semitic slurs and slashed tires, apparently, as retribution for her campus tolerance pleas. The college responded with rallies on her behalf, cancelled classes, sponsored anti-racist speeches plus a $10,000 reward for information on the culprits. The outrage seemingly vindicated her appeal for more tolerance and diversity. Regrettably for the professor, witnesses saw her defacing her own car. Investigators also soon traced purchase of the color and brand of paint to her. She was eventually convicted of a misdemeanor for filing a false police report and two felony counts for attempted insurance fraud (AP Daily Bulletin 2004).

In another campus case, crude racist drawings appeared in Ohio at Miami University's Center for Black Culture and Learning. As per a by now familiar script, black demonstrators stopped traffic and the university's president promised to recruit more black student and professors. Fingerprint evidence showed that the head of the Black Center and a friend perpetrated the outrage. The chief culprit nevertheless was rewarded with an hour-long meeting with the university's president (McNutt 1999).

Without doubt the most serious, well-publicized, and consequential hate crime hoax concerned the wave of arson of black-owned Southern churches.[11] For two months this became a national hysteria, appearing on prominent magazine covers and drawing over-the-top accusations from several public figures. Hillary Clinton compared these fires (in which nobody died) to the Holocaust (in which 6 million perished) while her husband, the president, spoke of sharing the pain of those victimized. An organized assault on blacks appeared imminent, and the national government's full power was mobilized. The president beseeched Congress to spend some $6 million for extra security patrols, extra lighting and other steps to end the hatred. Two hundred federal agents and 800 state and local officers joined the investigation. President Clinton personally visited a burned-out church and prayed with a local pastor. Christian churches nationwide meanwhile organized "Sabbaths of support," offered to pay for rebuilding, and often apologized for being white. The National Council of Churches promised $4 million for rebuilding, of which $275,000 was to fight racism. Major foundations—Ford, Rockefeller, and others—similarly promised lavish funding. On July 10, 1996 the president signed the Church Arson Prevention Act that made this church arson a federal offense, doubled prison terms, and offered loan guarantees to help congregations rebuild.

The reality was dramatically different. As is true for all older wooden, often isolated structures, accidental destructive fires (e.g., lightning) are commonplace, and in the case of black churches, the incidence had been *falling* for years. Insurance industry calculations held that this "outbreak" was within the normal range given circumstances. Indeed, figures from the past were significantly larger and barely anybody noticed. Investigations, despite thousands of hours of probing, uncovered zero evidence of a vast racist conspiracy, and of the few miscreants apprehended who set fires, eight were blacks themselves, twelve were white. In only three cases was a white caught who seemed to be racially motivated. The arsons were in fact typically set by teenage "copy-cats" who were probably out for cheap thrills. In fact, in 1996 a black woman, thanks to DNA analysis of saliva on an envelope was arrested for mailing hate-filled letters threatening to kill blacks and burn more churches. The real winners in this fraud were various anti-hate organizations, principally the Center for Democratic Renewal, which received money to rebuild churches but instead kept much of it to "fight racism." Not surprisingly, these organizations were also active in publicizing the "hate epidemic."

What was significant about this church burning hoax, and almost certainly applied to most other frauds, is that subsequent retractions seldom draw as much publicity as the initial outrageous story. Exposés of the church burnings did appear in the *Wall Street Journal* and varied local papers, but this coverage paled in comparison to months of frantic national publicity stressing an impending American racial holocaust. Much of this, no doubt, reflects today's incentives—victimization can pay handsomely. Save insurance companies in a small proportion of these incidents plus a few skeptical reporters, fewer benefits derive from careful scrutiny of possible fraud. Doubters are even likely to be castigated as unsympathetic racists, homophobes, or worse. The upshot, then, is that it is all too easy to believe that hatefulness is a modern plague.

Conclusions

As was true of "appreciate differences" classroom tolerance instruction, this coercive solution is a troubled pathway to social tranquility. Confusions and ambiguities abound though here they are far more serious than what plagues the classroom since alternative interpretations can bring prison sentences. It is easier said than done to certify complicated motives as "hateful," decide, exactly, what crime victims deserve extra protection, and how the law's didactic function can be performed short of irresponsible sensationalism. Further, add administrative

costs like cumbersome police procedures and time-consuming trials where simply establishing guilt or innocence is taxing enough. In a world in which scarce
resources must combat terrorism and ample humdrum criminality, appending
hate crimes to our law enforcement agenda caries serious opportunity costs.

Nevertheless, leaving these philosophical and economic tribulations aside,
the bottom line must be whether this nearly two-decade-old investment has
paid sufficient dividends. Has hatefulness diminished versus decades before
these laws? Are those "who differ," especially African Americans and homosexuals, any safer, more comfortable thanks to intimidated hate mongers? The
most straightforward answer is that hatefulness, judged by the crime reports,
is relatively minor matter compared to ordinary crime, and it hardly seems to
be skyrocketing. Percentage increases (or decreases) must also be taken with a
grain of salt given the low initial base and vagaries in reporting.

Hate crimes also rarely involve the most grievous offenses and their pattern
fails to suggest organized conspiracies, something akin to the Catholic monarch
ordering all Protestants to be burnt. Typical miscreants are youngsters choosing
victims for multiple "practical" reasons (e.g., victims appear vulnerable, rich
looking, or intoxicated) and "being different" is only one of those traits. Even
if every hate crime vanished tomorrow, the total decline of criminal violations
would be barely noticeable. If enforcement were doubled or tripled, prudent
perpetrators would probably adapt by suppressing racial slurs during a mugging
or prowl middle-class bars for white drunks to roll.

Still, the hard data scarcely quiet discussions about this pathway to tranquility and, as we saw, serious quibbles remain regarding some Platonic reality.
Unfortunately, a firm answer regarding the "true" incidence of such crimes is
impossible, and even more significant, such a conclusive answer may be *forever* beyond reach. The entire enterprise, regardless of intentions or diligence,
does not lend itself to exact calibrations, and so we might be improving, getting
worse, and going nowhere, but statistics are unlikely to confirm a judgment.
Attempting to suppress hatefulness by criminalizing it is, to be frank, far more
an exercise in symbolism than traditional crime control though it is customary
to argue otherwise.

To understand this gloomy assessment, consider how combating hatefulness differs from conventional policing. While terms like "murder" or "arson"
naturally evolve, and legislatures periodically tinker with criminal statutes, they
generally possess enduring historic definitions carefully spelled out in everything
from police manuals to court decisions. Ambiguities reside largely at the edges
(e.g., rules for admissible evidence) or are resolved by juries or via negotiation
(plea bargaining). It is also unthinkable that private advocacy groups would
collect their own data using vague categorizations so as to supply "more accurate" authoritative pictures. Moreover, most people generally grasp what these
traditional legal categories signify. Of the utmost importance, politics seldom
intrudes to redefine these understandings. Abortion foes wanting to prosecute

as "murderers" doctors terminating unwanted pregnancies face an exceedingly arduous task. Ditto for those who would eliminate penalties of abused spouses who kill their tormentors. Shifts of this magnitude typically move at glacial speed, if at all.

The contrast with hate crimes is immense. This entire campaign, from initial definitions to countless enforcement-related choices is *continuously* politically driven, and given the enterprise's very controversial nature, fluidity is endemic. Commentators are seldom disinterested bystanders, and as we saw, they occasionally falsify accounts to advance ideological agendas. Recall how grievance groups lobby, often successfully, for hate crime victim status and wider legal categories so as to boost claims for special benefits. Lurid tales of ethnic harassment might receive front-page treatment if this assists the media's veiled political agenda. Meanwhile a thriving academic cottage industry exists to reformulate hate crime boundaries and provide "creative" interpretations to seemingly firm but "disappointing" FBI statistics. Yesterday's prosaic rape, then, may be a "hate crime" tomorrow.

On the ideological divide's other side, ample discretion permits an overworked conservative district attorney facing an upsurge in murders to drop hate crime charges where provision for harsh punishments already exist. It is also likely that police operating in certain conservative settings might find it too troublesome to gain public cooperation in prosecuting rowdies who shouted "queer" at local gay bar patrons. This is light years distant from enforcing the regular criminal code. To be sure, law itself ultimately mirrors the political environment but these strictures, as we suggest, are virtually written in stone compared to what transpires with hate crimes. Today's lawmakers do not debate whether burglary committed by the poor should be excused since all property results from "capitalist exploitation."

These tribulations understood, how are we to interpret shifting statistics? What if next year's FBI report found that hate crime doubled? Would this confirm, as some group champions insist, that American grows ever more mean-spirited towards outsiders? Or, credibly, does an upsurge merely reflect greater diligence in reporting and record keeping or, even more plausibly, a shift in definition of a hate crime, for example, reclassifying rumor mongering about alleged homosexuality from plain-Jane libel to one that draws added punishment as a bona fide hate offense. To exaggerate only slightly, it would be as if climatologists debated global warming with idiosyncratic, constantly recalibrated homemade thermometers with readings taken at different altitudes so as to get ideologically comforting best results.

As was true for classroom tolerance instruction, champions disappointed in achieving classroom and schoolyard bliss, the effortless rejoinder is, "Can't hurt." Our rebuttal is, "yes it can, and in ways that produce far more harm than good." A potential totalitarian "thought crime" offense lurks here. This assessment assumes that as the current hate crime strategy fails to produce desired results, that is, ending *all* hatefulness, anti-hate prescriptions will become more draconian. Failure is particularly likely since the message's intended targets—criminals or thrill-seeking juvenile—are unlikely to heed these strictures, let alone decipher the bewildering legalese.[12] If attuned to such warnings they would not be criminals in the first place. It is, moreover, hard to imagine how this legislation will reduce criminality; anti-hate crime laws merely suggest that malefactor choose their victims with greater care.

This pattern is commonplace as classroom failures mount: if a few tolerance admonitions come up short, expand the lessons and, if that does not yield the correct outcome, make "appreciating differences" part of the graduation requirement via mandatory diversity training. If the end result (ending hate) is deemed achievable, and many "experts" affirm the malleability of human nature, it is just a matter of finding the proper recipe, and this will surely bring more vigorous state intervention. This sadly resembles the central economic planning script: if people refuse to cooperate voluntarily, compel them. If they still refuse, kill them.

One way of compelling results is via Soviet-style police state tactics. This is not as far fetched as it might initially seem. In Boulder, Colorado which is well-known for its progressive politics, the City Council is considering establishing a "hate hotline" so residents can confidentially report neighbors partial to tactless language (Harsanyi 2006). This approach resembles the familiar "hot lines" to report child abuse but here the "offense" is not (yet) a crime and, critically, "offensiveness," a term clouded in endless ambiguity absent a precise legal definition. Where does "ethnic humor" fall? Is *any* joke about ethnic traits inherently offensive? Imagine government administered data bases of "bad" jokes, slurs, derogatory national characterizations, all periodically adjusted to who says what to whom, with what tone of voice and accent. Ease of reporting is only one step removed from East Germany's infamous Stasi network of police informers, and an inviting opportunity to settle scores while ruining careers. Though this police-state approach remains hypothetical, it already occurs in schools where ideologically minded censors scrutinize textbooks to banish anything that might, in some form or shape, offend the most sensitive soul (Ravitch 2003 depicts this in great detail).

More foreboding is the escalating push to redefine hate crimes as stand-alone offenses. Recall that the presence of hatefulness currently counts *only if* another crime were committed; ethnic slurs and the like are not themselves currently punishable. This principle seems to be gaining momentum, and is undoubtedly welcomed by many frustrated anti-hate champions as the "next step" in a thus far inadequate crusade.

Legally, this is less a reach than it may first appear. Courts have traditionally accepted the constitutionality of laws punishing language ("fighting words") inciting violence. The well-known prohibition against "shouting fire in a crowded theater" has become an unchallenged cliché. Recent interpretations of laws against sexual harassment permit penalizing those whose utterances (e.g., demeaning language, lewd humor) create hostile environments. The First Amendment still protects speech, and judges still check ambitious assaults on this freedom, but a legalistic argument may be scant comfort during media inspired hysterias that accompanied the burning of black churches, especially if academics have cleared a path via ideologically inspired "theorizing."

Signs of this shift are already visible. Recently, members of a Christian group were arrested for preaching at a Philadelphia homosexual street festival. Prosecution occurred under a newly enacted state hate law, and the most serious of the charges could have drawn a forty-seven-year prison sentence. The presiding judge, however, dismissed all charges (Knight 2005). From this sweeping perspective, even a Bible reading could be construed as instigating "hate" if hypersensitive gays or Muslims hear certain "inflammatory" passages.

Advocacy groups are already formulating "hate" strictly as words, even insisting that constitutionally protected activities might constitute "hate." The organization civilright.org. has recently characterized opposition to immigration as "hateful" with opponents using such perfectly lawful tactics as joining anti-immigration groups, distributing anti-immigrant propaganda, and holding anti-immigration rallies and protests. According to this group, immigration opponents are neo-Nazis, hardcore white supremacists, skinheads and, of course, right-wing extremists, all labels conjuring up impending violence (cited in Anti-Defamation League 2006). Another organization announcement calls for the "termination" of divisive rhetoric based on race, ethnicity, or religion, a view sharply at odds with traditional First Amendment protections (Lewis 2006). Though such distorted alarmism remains at the edge of public debate, the aim is unambiguous: make the expression of "divisive" ideas tantamount to shouting fire in a theater.

European laws have already shifted sharply in this direction, a fact hardly irrelevant given the occasional proclivity of U.S. judges to import foreign rulings. The distinguished American scholar Bernard Lewis faced both civil and criminal charges in France for merely *suggesting* that the killing of Armenians by Turks fell short of a full-blown genocide. Politicians in both France and Belgium have been taken to court for demeaning Muslim immigrants (Alexander 2006). Many nations have criminalized Holocaust denial, and Austria recently sentenced the British writer David Irving to jail for this offense. Prosecutors in England have even sought criminal penalties against professors who publish scientific books and articles about unflattering racial differences. Though innocent verdicts were returned in most instances, the cost of defending oneself can be substantial, and this in of itself punishes "bad thoughts."

Examples can be multiplied endlessly, but the common thread is that, at least for these tolerance devotees, criminal prosecutions are necessary to quell hatreds *apart from any overt criminal behavior*. Ironically, this new rush

to impose tranquility occurs at a time when peacefulness—even including violent terrorism—may have reached its apogee judged by historical
standards. As is often true with crime, enthralling misdeeds often draw the
greatest media attention when incidents are relatively rare. Lawmakers apparently assume that while hatred has existed for eons, the modern state possesses
the means to eliminate group strife once and for all. Though undoubtedly well
intentioned, this impulse is bound to fail and will only make matters worse for
those who cherish a free society. One might argue that government would have
better luck abolishing the desire for private property.

Notes

1. One of the exceedingly rare cautionary analyses of hate crime is offered by Jacobs
   and Potter (1998, 145). After an extensive review of these laws and their impact,
   they suggest that all of them warrant repeal, and policing should return to the
   enforcement of generic criminal code.
2. Lawrence (1999, 11-12) further argues that the aversion must be widely shared
   to warrant this designation. He illustrates this with someone who abhors blue-
   eyed people and thus only attacks those with this trait. Though eye color is the
   motivator, Lawrence would reject "eye color" from the protected list since it is
   idiosyncratic. He counsels choosing only attributes that deeply divide society.
3. The FBI issued 2004 Hate Crime Report says that race for hate-related crimes
   is the same as for other reported crimes, and is "…the minimally accepted des-
   ignations for race and ethnicity as established by the Office of Management and
   Budget (OMB) and published in the *Federal Register* (3)." Keep in mind that the
   constantly updated *Federal Register* runs for tens of thousands of pages.
4. The translation problem is hardly hypothetical. Recollect the famous January 13,
   1993 incident when Eden Jacobowitz, a student at the University of Pennsylvania,
   called a black woman a "water buffalo." He was soon charged with racial harassment. University officials interpreted "water buffalo" as primitive dark animals
   living in Africa and thus, by implication, a racial insult. As this case marched
   forward, Eden's defenders pointed out that water buffaloes were native to Asia,
   not Africa, and Eden, who was from Israel, was probably using a rough translation
   of *Behema,* Hebrew slang for a rowdy person that lacks any racial connotations.
   Even zoologists testified in this controversy. This circus-like incident is described
   in Kors and Silverglate (1998, chapter 1).
5. Twisting reality so as to protect certain groups is, to some degree, officially
   sanctioned. The U.S. Department's video tape and accompanying training books
   ("Responding to Hate Crimes: A Police Officer's Guide to Investigation and
   Prevention, Bureau of Justice Assistance," 2000) overwhelmingly depict whites
   committing hate crimes. The two instances of black criminal behavior involve
   blacks attacking Asian shopkeepers. No hate crime victim is white, a peculiar
   depiction given both the number of whites in America and the Justice Department's
   own data on interracial crime. In some sense, then, a convoluted reality is public
   policy.
6. Discussions here occasionally draw distinctions of malfeasance based upon
   unequal power. From this perspective those in socio-economically inferior positions (e.g., African Americans, gays) cannot be hate crime perpetrators since they
   are subordinated to their oppressors. Those of higher status, by definition, must
   be the oppressors. Thus, a black who beats a white solely because the person is

white is not committing a hate crime but is, instead, striking back at his or her subjugation. Only whites, males and other in commanding power positions, then, are subject to prosecution for hatefulness regardless of what may appear to be contrary evidence.

7.   As in the Soviet Union where religion and atheism were legally given equal protected status, current standards of reporting include crimes motivated by aversion toward atheists and agnostics. How a miscreant could possibly identify an atheist save one actively engaged in atheistic activities is an interesting question, as is the one regarding how police would separate the militant atheist from the wavering agnostic.

8.   The ethnic category requires caution given the murkiness of ethnicity. One special problem is categorizing Hispanics. In the case of perpetrators, Hispanics are deemed whites though the same person is "Hispanic" if the victim. Hence, at least some fraction of crimes committed by whites are actually inflicted by Hispanics.

9.   The black economist Walter Williams suggests that the "controversial" nature of these data prevent their public dissemination, a situation reversed for white-on-black crimes. Writing in 2001 he tells of a press conference at Washington's National Press Club to publicize a report about this pattern. Some 400 representatives of the major news and electronic media were invited but among the handful who arrived, only fourteen stayed until the end and media coverage was miniscule. One reporter averred that while he would like to write a story about these statistics, his editor would kill it (Williams 2001).

10.   One possible explanation for inattention is that the reporting of hoaxes is often conducted by "controversial" organizations with an allegedly "racist" agenda. The best example is American Renaissance (www.amrn.com) which simply assembles countless local newspaper accounts of hoaxes and occasionally offers larger analyses (e.g., http://www.amren.com/hoaxartcile/hoax.htm). These are culled by readers and reprinted verbatim. The Laird Wilcox (1994) book similarly offers a compendium of tales though it is dated. Since both those volunteers compiling the tales and newspaper reporters are non-academics, such unwelcome evidence can easily be dismissed by scholars perusing ideological agendas.

11.   This tale is reported in several places and our account relies on the overall summary and analysis reported in http://amren.com/hoaxarticle/hoax.htm.

12.   The comic potential here is immense. One could imagine savvy muggers stalking victims to determine the mark's race/ ethnicity and then "interviewing" the potential target regarding his or her religion, sexuality, mental and physical well-being and other legally relevant traits. Perhaps the victim would then have to sign a legal release verifying that they are not members of any "protected" group before the mugging could proceed. Meanwhile, those wandering through bad neighborhoods might want to carry signs with "Warning—I am physically disabled, gay, and a member of a protected ethnic group" so as to discourage assault.

6

Summing Up and a Disconcerting Alert

"Nothing is more important for the public weal than to inform and train up youth in wisdom and virtue."—Benjamin Franklin, Letter to Samuel Johnson, first president of Columbia University, August 23, 1750

"When there is a gap between one's real and one's declared aims, one turns as it were instinctively to long words and exhausted idioms, like a cuttlefish squirting out ink."—George Orwell, "Shooting an Elephant" (1950)

The preceding chapters depict an apparent paradox regarding today's educator-led quest for the "appreciate differences" brand of tolerance. On the one hand, this is a huge, uphill effort to solve tribulations that, arguably, scarcely exist or, if such quandaries admittedly bedevil us, far better ameliorations reside elsewhere. Contemporary America is hardly awash in the violent antagonisms historically associated with the emergence of tolerance theorizing. Threats to tranquility originate overwhelmingly outside our borders, not from domestic discord. Even if turmoil does occasionally arise from within, it is largely addressable via the criminal code, and is far different from what concerned Locke or Voltaire. Periodic friction is, moreover, endemic to any multiethnic, multiracial society and cannot be banished altogether short of imposing a draconian police state. It would be bizarre, as some educators imply, to equate offhand ethnic slurs with ethnic cleansing.

Critically, discord *never* flows from state-sanctioned repression as when monarchs burned heretics at the stake or official churches converted disbelievers on the pain of death. Our hate crime legislation tour revealed the reverse—quelling animosities is now public policy. Amidst Islamic-inspired terrorism, political and religious leaders plead for tolerance towards Islam, not revenge. To suggest that early classroom instruction must somehow push to transform a troubled contemporary America into an idyllic paradise where everybody respects everybody else, where nobody is stigmatized, or no group feels inadequate is utopian. This enterprise is a total misreading of human beings' inherently quarrelsome, contentious nature.

Nevertheless, upbeat characterizations aside, today's champions of "new and improved" tolerance soldier on, ever more determined. This is an odd cosmology in which heretofore barely noticed personal slights become "serious" threats to civil tranquility. Judged by the rhetoric surrounding these alarms, an extraterrestrial visitor might surmise that contemporary America has scarcely progressed beyond sixteenth- or seventeenth-century Europe in stamping out heresies.

More than gratuitous speechmaking is involved here; the monetary and time costs are substantial. That a proven remedy, namely classic tolerance—bearing the objectionable—has been blithely replaced by the far more demanding (and futile) "venerate the objectionable" version only compounds this wastefulness. That these calls, definitional substitution and perceptions of debilitating turmoil seem so heartfelt only deepens this paradox: A guaranteed futile war against reality, so to speak, is afoot. It is no exaggeration to say that educators have created an entire crying-wolf industry when wolves have virtually gone extinct while further demanding allocations of prodigious resources to guard against ever-lurking wolves.

American society has always been intoxicated with idealistic nostrums so the lure of this contemporary "we need still more tolerance" is, true to form, irresistible. Even hard-headed skeptics seem seduced by facile historical parallels: society has, after all, advanced from killing homosexuals to criminalizing homosexuality to treating it as a psychological disorder to just accepting it as a repugnant condition, so the next "logical" step would seem to be, at last, embracing it as perfectly normal. This upbeat progression seems equally applicable for the treatment accorded innumerable once disdained ethnic/racial groups (e.g., African Americans, Jews) and women. At least for some tolerance champions, then, pleas for yet more "respect" versus suffering the less-than-perfect merely reflect a commendable natural evolution.

That proponents of this view cleverly surround their appeals with glittering rhetoric, phrases like "being inclusive" or "protecting the vulnerable" while labeling opponents as "hateful bigots" makes outward resistance nearly unspeakable. How could any well-meaning parent rebuke school administrators who insist that their latest expert-certified tolerance curriculum will quell schoolyard fights and assist their children to prosper in today's multicultural global village? Who can countenance assaulting blacks just for being black? At most, parents disturbed by this embrace of nearly blank check acceptance of myriad differences may disregard these messages at home or, in extreme cases, withdraw their offspring from school, but flight hardly shields those left behind. Where resistance to unqualified appreciation emerges, it emanates largely from a handful of Christian-oriented scholars residing far beyond today's educational mainstream. Elsewhere the reaction is largely silence.

The potential damage from this doomed quest far exceeds just misspent resources. It is also a duplicitous campaign promoting an artfully disguised radical political agenda. A "soft totalitarianism" also infuses what appears to be naïve if not harmless idealism. Viewed from this disdainful angle, the paradox of pushing a doomed-to-fail nostrum against all obstacles is not really a paradox at all. It is not misguided romanticism or the "natural" evolution of "fairness," though its defenders insist otherwise. A more truthful characterization is that it is an ideologically constructed Trojan horse though, we happily concede, scarcely any of the teachers preaching this gospel consciously intend harm. What is innocuously presented as "making a better status quo" should properly be construed as "making a *different* status quo" and this allegedly new and improved world will only insure destruction despite the glittering contrary assurances.

Why Teach "Appreciate Differences" Tolerance?

It might be useful to recapitulate several previous qualms regarding "new" tolerance before moving on to its hidden agenda. The most elementary starting point is the economic concept of opportunity costs—the pursuit of one aim necessarily means neglecting others. Opportunity costs ineluctably apply to education though those wanting to enlist schools to "cure" whatever ails American society easily brush them aside. This price is especially disproportionately burdensome on underachieving racial and ethnic minorities who can ill afford classroom time squandered on "feel-good" exhortations. It is not that education is exempt for being recruited to cure maladies *du jour;* rather, inserting new tasks, short of extending the school day or year, must crowd out what has already been certified as necessary. Admonitions, then, requires explicit justification over and above the vacuous "it might help," and for educators to ignore this obvious requirement is professional irresponsibility.

That youngsters must welcome a virtually endless parade of "differences" chosen from some multicultural smorgasbord is hardly a national priority. It almost certainly ranks near the bottom of any legislative agenda. Policymakers usually stress inadequacies in basic subjects such as reading, mathematics, and writing. If the subject of race and ethnicity arise, the focus is overwhelmingly on gaps in academic achievement, not whether Hispanics suitably appreciate African-American classmates and all the rest. Cries to add this tolerance mission arise from only a handful of publicly unaccountable though exceedingly vocal educators and non-academic advocacy organizations.

When inadequacies regarding non-academic topics occur, a long litany of qualms surface—lack of discipline, drug use, among others—and inadequate tolerance instruction seldom (if ever) draws attention. A 2006 poll of parents reported that 73 percent reported that the most important problem facing our schools was misbehaving children. A prior 2002 survey found that 73 percent of low-income parents worried a lot about protecting their children from drugs and alcohol; 65 percent also were anxious about their physical safety, including being kidnapped. High-income parents also expressed apprehension regarding drugs and security though in lesser proportions (cited in McCluskey 2006). When the topic of "appreciating differences" is forced into the public agenda, and ordinary citizens do speak, more often than not, parents *oppose* this addendum.

Absent popular groundswell for this instruction, how might pedagogues themselves justify these opportunity costs and, critically, can these assertions about impending strife withstand scrutiny? Our overview illustrated that well-crafted rationalization are conspicuously absent in this sprawling literature. Even if we momentarily assume that this disaster-is-everywhere mentality has some validity (surely a debatable assumption, as is plain to see), the next question is, or at least ought to be, is teaching today's version of tolerance the most efficacious solution vis-à-vis alternatives? To return to the medicine analogy, a doctor always asks if the prescribed drug or procedure is demonstrably the *best* remedy, not if the advice just sounds plausible. Prescriptions are always drawn from a menu of alternatives, so justification implies comparisons. Expert admonitions that imparting tolerance is necessary to calm ethnic hostilities tacitly argues that this nostrum outshines rivals in terms of cost, ease of implementation, speed of results and all other criteria by which purported cures *must* to be evaluated.

Chapter 2's overview strongly suggests that among all possible remedies for civil strife, imparting an appreciation of the loathed must rank near the *bottom* of any list. Reversing a tenacious biological impulse is not easy, and if inhibiting aversion is the elected pathway to this goal, a traditional *modus vivendi* notion of tolerance—accepting the odious despite the odium—is a far superior option. Instructing youngsters in self-restraint, anger control, and obedience to conflict-quelling rules surely offers proven options far more in keeping with human nature. Etiquette and good manors—cultivating young ladies and gentlemen—have historically served to cool hostilities. More important, innumerable alternatives to psychological solutions abound and these have proven themselves highly effective, so reinventing the wheel is wasteful.

That this newly fashioned tolerance attempts to cure self-imposed turmoil only compounds wastefulness. It would be as if doctors first infected patients so as to heal them with dubious untested drugs. Why labor to heighten group identities if these are likely to spur hostilities? Schoolyard ethnic/racial mayhem would surely decline if the mixing of students from diverse socio-economic backgrounds were not court imposed. If educators fear rampant homophobia among grade schoolers, it may be wiser to avoid the subject altogether versus inviting gays activists into the classroom to urge greater respect. Appreciating outsiders is always easier if one never personally encounters them. Similarly, today's trendy cultural relativism squanders precious classroom time manufacturing a convoluted reality that even third-graders will likely reject.

The obligation to justify this enterprise also extends to what, exactly, is singled out as worthy of appreciation (or tolerance). Without some *raison d'être* instruction will surely be ad hoc and this is a surefire recipe for confusion if not political strife as sensibilities might be accidentally bruised. Chapter 2 highlighted that this task's futility given limitless candidates for inclusion. These selections, moreover, will surely bring disruptive quarrels over whose deserves curriculum recognition, hardly what tolerance devotees fantasize. Further, add all the tribulations of precisely defining just who belongs to groups (and the groups' sanitized defining traits) needing heightened admiration and how can these admirable traits best be taught. Clearly, this conflict-inspiring venture requires serious justification prior to launch.

Such intellectual sloppiness can only breed confusion and thereby undermine clear thinking, the very purpose of education. Proffered examples routinely imply that revulsion in and of itself is inherently mistaken, so the worse the odium, the greater the need for appreciation-laden tolerance. Students might recall school dieticians hectoring them to eat cauliflower, not cheeseburgers, but here the consequences may be far worse. Pasamonik (2004), in an otherwise thoughtful essay, begins by warning about the dangers of political correctness in tolerance instruction, but nevertheless suggests classroom exercises for upping appreciation for the homeless, panhandlers, drug abusers, the obese, and women wearing veils, among others. Why these people require "more appreciation" is hardly self-evident. Pasamonik, as is typical in such glib sermonizing, seems oblivious to how panhandlers and drugs addicts can render cities virtually unlivable, a condition hardly beneficial to the urban poor, while obesity is a serious health hazard. Nor is there any recognition that veiled Muslim women may privately reject veils, and that outsiders "appreciating" this custom may undermine the wearer's desire for personal autonomy.

If a compelling case exists for inserting "appreciate differences" tolerance in to today's schools, we fail to see it. To be frank, it cannot be justified short of bogus alarmism. Judged by historical standards the sky is not about to fall nor are we so mired in violent repression that re-socializing Americans is the only, desperate way out. The cavalier "can't hurt" defense tacitly assumes zero costs and that contemporary schools are already so proficient in fulfilling state-mandated responsibilities that this pedagogical luxury is affordable. Evidently, as we shall consider below, something else is going on here well beyond quelling discord.

The Awaiting Failure

Even if advocates of "appreciate difference" tolerance could sway skeptics, the preceding analysis strongly suggests failure no matter how fervent the application. Most plainly, the entire enterprise rests on sloppy social science research, and to exacerbate matters, its champions typically disdain the very notion of rigorous inquiry. Ad hoc inquiry means that there can be no learning curve despite repeated failures. There is also a degree of misrepresentation as when "positive results" have zero to do with calming troubled waters (the nominal purpose of instruction) and everything to do with "improved" thinking about others, as if a momentarily altered mental state solves everything. To repeat, this is totally unlike what transpires in medical campaigns to cure serious illnesses. Unwelcome messengers are not shot since nobody volunteers to be the bearer of bad news.

In lieu of precise measures and rigorous experimental studies, we witness a steady parade of unverifiable grandiloquent slogans ("diversity is our national strength"). These are more akin to religious tenets, and contribute zero to progress. Going one step further, given the campaign's very nature of implicitly denigrating scientific inquiry, one suspects that these "researchers" lack any idea what constitutes scientific verification. One can spend days navigating entreatments and *never* see, for example, a precise definition of "homophobia" though we are endlessly told that it is somehow "dangerous." Words like "minority" and "culture" are tossed about as if their meaning were crystal clear.

Plain-to-see theoretical contradictions and convolutions abound. Our qualms are not about shoddy ivory tower philosophy; real-world advancement requires their resolution, and to be forthright, progress may be beyond the capacity of today's tolerance-infatuated pedagogues. Recall, for example, how a curious youngster must be baffled when distinguishing a "dangerous stereotype" from a "commendable difference" when even a positive assessment (e.g., Asians excel at math) may be harmful. If all cultures are equally valid, how do students judge female genital mutilation? If tolerance for differences, even practices that initially seem abhorrent, is desirable, why are other things, some of which seem harmless so "bad"? As in grammar, there must be rules for bestowing tolerance, even if boundaries are murky, but, alas, "experts" refuse to supply them.

If this were insufficient, classroom tolerance rhetoric frequently contradicts daily experience, let alone what is visible in the mass media. The carefully managed, tolerance-infused classroom is not the world, and this gap will probably expand as pedagogical shortcoming mount. Energetic pleas about the worth of every ethnic group aside, students will inevitably personally encounter disparities in academics and disorderliness. Hundreds of hours will be spent viewing entertainment built on the very "dangerous" stereotypes teachers deplore. Homilies about "everybody wanting peace" will surely ring hollow for those following the news. Parents and friends can readily refute Pollyannaish entreatments about human beings being the same but different, and this resistance is no small matter given an hour or two a week hearing the opposite.

Confusion and garble will probably render lessons pointless though, as we shall argue later, they are hardly risk-free. It is hard to envision students learning anything of enduring value. To continue with the grammar parallel, it would be as if in every school, every teacher was free to interpret matters idiosyncratically, the equivalent of teaching localized spelling and punctuation. In one classroom students might learn that asserting that girls and boys were different was a "harmful" gender stereotype; down the hallway the teacher admonished pupils to prize girls for their superior empathy and kindness. Elsewhere some students struggle to learn that there is no such thing as "race" while in the next grade they spend months immersed in African-American history. Next year the political winds may have shifted so last year's lessons are now obsolete. Such conflicting, often nonsensical messages are the functional equivalent of learning random numbers and all this well-intentioned effort might, sadly, bring education itself into disrepute.

All in all, *everything* here forecasts failure. If held to the same rigorous standards pharmaceutical companies must meet when seeking FDA drug approval, this bring-tranquility-via-teaching-children-tolerance would be summarily rejected. It fails the most basic scientific standards, and while this literature abounds with assertions of success, closer inspection reveals them to be baseless. In medical parlance, this resembles quackery.

Less Obvious Motives: Easy Solutions

While the ostensible impetus for imposing this new-sprung tolerance is to quell alleged burgeoning discord, less grandiose motives lie below the surface. This is a pedagogically "soft" undertaking insofar as it requires little, if almost any intellectual acumen from either teachers or students. Daunting quandaries become "fun." Academically inept teacher can readily master this cliché-filled curriculum while pupils happily escape painful tasks such as spelling. The absence of exams, let alone mandatory, state-imposed benchmarks, only adds to the allure—everybody passes while no school is embarrassingly left behind. Practitioners can also burnish their teaching resumés since students appeared excited about skits and potluck meals. One can only envision students' (and teachers') pained reaction if told that their multicultural tolerance lesson suddenly required mastering French since cultural appreciation necessitated linguistic proficiency.

So-called education experts also quickly grasp that preaching "appreciation" helps advance a career without the bother of conducting serious scientific research. If there are no tests, no standards, and user satisfaction certifies success, every nostrum is deemed a triumph of pedagogical proficiency. Everybody is now an "expert" at instilling tolerance—"the kids loved it" suffices. For good measure, these lessons openly display one's commitment to today's ideological fashions. Only curmudgeons might complain that wasting time extolling exotic ephemera defrauds taxpayers in light of declining performances in more weighty, legally required subjects.

More than mere sloth is involved. A terrible intellectual example is being set regarding what education is about. These supposed tolerance-related insights are always shallow, and for good measure almost always misrepresent or seriously twist reality. The catalogue of willful misinformation is immense and includes the all-too-familiar claims that diversity makes us strong, that societal conflict flows from unhappy, loveless families, that impolite language inspires great calamities, countless "disadvantaged" groups realistically live in dread of hatemongers, and coerced personal encounters can reduce bitter animosities. Mendacity thus becomes "official" professional policy, and those adroit at articulating it will undoubtedly gain professional standing. Such blatant contradictions of plain-to-see-reality call to mind Marxist functionaries whose tenure required publicly repeating boldfaced lies.

Ambitious advocates may even financially profit from facile prescription for alleged woes. This appreciate difference mantra has evolved into varied commercial ventures (despite a formal non-profit tax status), everything from textbooks to pre-packaged lesson plans to expensive on-site consulting. As our account of hate crimes has shown, racial/ethnic grievance organizations enjoy a symbiotic relationship with bigotry and thus encourage rewarding obsessions with minor "outrage." A cynic might argue that the task's very intractable nature adds to the attraction since it guarantees lifetime employment and marketing opportunities.

A convenient escape from certain awkward education-related tribulations is also present. It is no secret that many American schools *are* bedeviled by crime, violence, and a general lack of the orderliness necessary for learning though, critically, this disorder is never state-sanctioned repression. According to data collected by the federal government, some 88,000 students were victims of serious violent crimes in 2004 and many times that number suffered from physical attacks that were not themselves criminal. Meanwhile, between 1998 and 2002, some 234,000 teachers were crime victims while at school, 90,000 of which were violent (NCES 2004). Statistics do not, of course, reflect all-too-common chaotic school environments of unruliness and student-teacher confrontations.

This is hardly a new problem and any history of American schooling will catalogue comparable tribulations. What makes today's bedlam so troublesome is that disruptions disproportionately involve blacks and Hispanics, and the presence of quick-to-anger, group-based organizations inevitably instigate political trouble if traditional remedies are used.[1] Schools that disproportionately expel African Americans will suffer heavy costs, even if administrative actions are objectively justified. The political fallout might possibly invite Department of Justice-instigated litigation, and grievance groups enjoy a public relations bonanza. The school's legal defense would be exceedingly time consuming and expensive, and a "victory" might be pyrrhic given burdensome future record keeping.

Instituting appreciate differences exercises while simultaneously ignoring almost every disorder short of blatant criminality (which requires a police report) is, by contrast, cost free politically. That students might enjoy escaping harsh discipline only adds to the allure. As applies for impersonal technology-based security "solutions,"for example, metal detectors and security cameras, proving clear-cut disparate impact of such measures is difficult. Parents alarmed about schoolyard mayhem receive an absolutely politically correct and expert-certified response: anti-violence measures are underway, namely mandatory lessons in multicultural awareness and respect for people of varied racial/ethnic backgrounds. This tolerance vision now suffices as the perfect pseudo cure to sustain political peace.

Less Obvious Motives: The Hidden Political Agenda

Over and above these enticing advantages, another and far more serious incentive exists for pursuing a futile quest: advancing an ideological agenda. Politics here differs from conventional campaigns where aims are relatively distinct and visible. This "game" is better understood as a below-the-radar effort to remold Americans culturally and thus, eventually, alter the socio-economic status quo. It is fundamentally about gaining power (eventually) but for the present it is a thinly veiled war of ideas and, to be frank, it often defies accurate cataloguing. Advocates seldom acknowledge their ideological aspirations, no handy name depicts the movement, and no single organization publishes tracts stating objectives. The expression "impulse" may be more apt. It is also largely framed negatively, superficially banishing what everybody deems objectionable, for example, unfair discrimination, and is frustratingly vague about the future.

These ideas disproportionably originate from a relatively small number of university-based intellectuals, and there largely concentrated in the social sciences, the humanities, and, especially, schools of education and social work.[2] These prescriptions in turn filter out into various "do-gooder" organizations like the Southern Anti-Poverty and Law Center and the Museum of Tolerance plus sundry "group protection" organizations. Numerous allies in the mass media also play a proselytizing role. Ultimately, or at least this is the wish, these notions will become a practical, detailed pedagogy distributed to teachers "promoting tolerance" to impressionable youngsters.

For these ideologues, current American society is irrevocably flawed as a result of its sharp unequal distribution of wealth and its dominant ("privileged" in their terminology) white Christian, middle-class culture. Cultural relativism is central so, put colloquially, children must learn that nobody outshines anybody, and all differences are normal and thus worthy of celebration. The campaign's stealthy ingenuity, at least according to Christian conservatives, is often remarkable. The Public Broadcasting System (PBS) once inserted an episode in its popular children's program *Postcards from Buster* in which a cartoon bunny visits children of a Vermont lesbian couple.[3] What makes this stratagem particularly clever, opponents claim, is that few adults are likely to monitor children when watching such a "respected" education channel like PBS, so the idea of lesbianism can just becomes "natural" (Crary 2005).

A strong anti-Christianity theme is also evident. Churches are typically portrayed as wellsprings of hostility-producing bigotry while alleged enemies of tolerance are reflexively described by catch-phrases such as "the Religious Right" or "Christian Conservatives," as if to suggest that there is just something lurking within traditional organized religion that renders it, in contrast to liberalism, inherently mean spirited. New Age religions, spiritualism, paganism, and similar cultish movements on the other hand receive a free pass here. If there is an exception looking askance at major religious groups, it usually concerns Islam which, predictably, is judged as being at risk and therefore in need of greater tolerance regardless of its possible hate-inciting activities. Condescension generally also applies for any celebration of national sovereignty, patriotism, and the military though, predictably, these sentiments are often muted in today's terror-sensitive political climate.

This agenda's tell-tale sign is an infatuation with stamping out homophobia, sexism, racism, discrimination, inequality, patriarchy, oppression, and comparable assumed pathologies connoting the powerful tyrannizing the weak. That human nature is malleable and reshaping people to build a better world is well within the pedagogue's reach is axiomatic. Specific policy demands generally echo what prominent liberal, race/ethnic-based civil rights organizations demand from government: forceful affirmative action, boosted social services spending directed toward the poor, and a general expansion of the welfare state. But such enactments are clearly secondary to a more thoroughgoing transformation of American society via re-socializing youngsters. While these ideologues concede that repression may be nearly invisible to victims, and the downtrodden may superficially live free and materially comfortable lives, astute experts can nevertheless detect the elite-imposed camouflage. In fact, what passes for educational research is often devoted to exposing debilitating repression where none may be immediately visible.

These advocates hope to first secure control of the sources of culture— schooling, books, films, TV programs, even fairy tales, and all else that defines "normal." The current expression "culture wars" accurately reflects the essence of this quest, and no opportunity, no matter how non-political or seemingly inconsequential, is immune to spreading the word. In one case a local, widely circulated North Carolina advertisement-filled "shopper magazine" (*Charlotte Parent*) featured an article called "Parenting A Gay Child," which, in the eyes of religious critics offered a sympathetic account of same-sex attraction while endorsing same sex-marriage as the same as conventional marriage (Archibald 2004).

Reconfiguring ordinary language is central since, according to perspective, vocabulary shapes worldviews and, ultimately, behavior. To alter definitions thus remakes reality, and it is no accident that critics condemn it as Orwellian (as in *1984* "Newspeak"). Chapter 2's account of how "tolerance" has been deviously transformed, and how unpleasant (but true) facts were to be expunged psychologically by labeling them "harmful" illustrates this strategy (a "Thought-crime" in "Newspeak"). Contemporary wrangles over the meaning of "family" and "marriage" likewise exemplify this language-is-reality stratagem. Though "capture the culture to seize power" has traditionally been associated with Marxism with its insertion of political content into the very fabric of society, in principle it is ideological neutral.

In this radical cosmology *all* education is *inherently* political—if not brain-washing—insofar it overtly or tacitly helps to support a *particular* political order. Education is therefore of the utmost importance in sustaining the ruling elite, so classroom instruction and indoctrination are inseparable. Predictably, then, at least some of today's schools of education explicitly require students to demonstrate commitments to "social justice" to graduate. Hidden indoctrination, it is argued, equally applies for the sciences insofar as early lessons highlight the contributions of some (e.g., white males), but excludes others (e.g., women of color), stress some pathways to knowledge (e.g., rationality) above others or praise some outcomes (e.g., high pollution industrialization) over alternatives (e.g., low pollution pastoral societies). That today's schooling generally appears to be "non-political" merely reflects that the pervasiveness of the embedded ideological content. The cliché "a fish has no concept of water" captures this argument about invisible but very consequential bias.

The real debate, then, at least for these ideologues, is not whether to politicize the classroom, even at the earliest grades, but *whose* politics will be permitted to dominate instruction. Yet again: the defense of non-political education by traditional educators is but a ruse to sustain elite power. For devotees of newly fashioned appreciate difference tolerance, their mission is identical in form to what conservative capitalist rivals accomplished decades back when they "captured" the schools to impose economic unfairness and social hierarchy. From this vantage point, today's textbooks and all else infusing the classroom is a running summary of ideological battles, and surreptitiously inserting ideological messages is legitimate politics.

As currently fought, ground zero is the quest for equal recognition, if not veneration, of currently marginalized groups centered on common racial/ethnic or sexual identities. Diversity and inclusion are the two words that most fully capture this spirit. Ultimately, everybody will be, hopefully, co-equals in power and legitimacy (see, for example, Macedo and Bartolomé 1999). Specifically, Christian males will cease enjoying their "privileged" position and the contributions and talents of all races, heterosexuals and homosexuals, men and women, the physically able and disabled, are heralded as uniformly valid. Derogatory labels undergirding today's nefarious hierarchy, words like "underachiever" or "unassimilated" will vanish from peoples' vocabulary. Today's disdained groups will no longer feel stigmatized. Economically, victory means income transfers from the rich to the poor ("economic justice"). Teachers will not demand blacks act "white" nor will they portray heterosexual marriages as the gold standard.

The alter-the-culture-on-the-installment-plan approach has its advantages. For one, it is often unnoticed by those who otherwise reject the underlying radical ideological message and thus may even be unconsciously absorbed. Proposals appear strongly idealistic and hardly evil, and this smokescreen expediently shields the below-the-surface message from closer scrutiny. An educator who defends Hispanics against being stigmatized for speaking broken English is more likely to be condemned for misguided "bleeding heart" compassion than as an ideologue subverting America's common English-based culture. After all, who wants to excoriate compassion for the downtrodden, even if this compassion is debilitating or culturally destructive?

Taken one item at a time this agenda appears almost inconsequential and thus hardly worth resisting, no small advantage for those believing that "minor" details cumulate to shape reality, fermenting a barely noticed revolution, so to speak. For example, many feminist activists sharing this perspective relentlessly pressure textbook publishers to include pictures of women as doctors, pilots, and similarly "masculine" roles (while men are nurses and caregivers) in grade-school textbooks to chip away at the patriarchy. Now, if the plan succeeds, youngsters will believe that all-encompassing gender equality is "perfectly natural" and wholly unrelated to innate physical traits.

This strategy also exploits an educational system whose very permeability invites guerilla-war politics. Unlike the typical centralized European arrangement controlled by insulated bureaucrats, meddling in U.S. schools occurs at dozens of access points ranging from state legislative committees to local school boards. Organizations by the hundreds, from proponents of sex education, civil rights groups, church-based advocates to ethnic groups obsessed with historical grievances, meddle in the curriculum, and of the utmost relevance, this ideological intrusion is judged legitimate, if not First Amendment protected. Permeability also applies for textbook publishers who will modify content to satisfy annoying complainers.

Schools also welcome inexpensive or gratis pedagogical materials to stretch their budgets, and groups advancing ideological agendas are always willing to help. Child-oriented media firms can also slip in ideological messages via freely distributed auxiliary materials. In one notable incident, a cooperative effort by Nickelodeon, the Disney Channel, and the Public Broadcasting Service (PBS) sent copies of the DVD "We Are Family," together with teacher's guides, to some 61,000 elementary schools nationwide (delivered free by Federal Express). The video included over 100 cartoon characters such as Miss Piggy and the Cookie Monster. Nevertheless, despite the seeming innocuousness of the DVD's celebration of diversity message, religious conservatives perceived a veiled "pro-homosexual message," a fear deepened by the fact that the We Are Family Foundation, an openly pro-gay group, had a major hand in this project (Vitagilano 2005).

Finally, this under-the-radar strategy to shift the culture is well suited to an ideological faction that is numerically inconsequential—perhaps not exceeding a few thousand advocates—incapable of prevailing against more numerous adversaries via traditional civic channels. Proponents of this multicultural, morally relativistic agenda are unlikely to ever gain public office, let alone triumph in open debates. Nor, unlike past radical movements can it threaten force or disruption since it disdains fleeting government-supplied material benefits. To prevail, ideologues must concentrate the few resources they possess, notably institutional positions that disproportionably shape culture (e.g., the universities, the mass media) and do so in ways that leave current sensibilities undisturbed, e.g., stress anti-violence or heightened self-esteem. This reflects necessity since, to be frank, the influencing culture card is probably the only card available.

Not all school administrators and teachers celebrating the "appreciate all differences equals tolerance" message are nefarious, radical activists. The overwhelming majority of those echoing these high-sounding messages undoubtedly act in good faith. Ideological content may even be unnoticed given its ubiquity among pedagogues. Others, as we speculated, just heed academic fads to keep their jobs. Still, uncertainty of the proportions acknowledged, political ideologues *are* certainly prominent among the educators who have created a radical pedagogy, packaged it in the glittering rhetoric of tolerance and multiculturalism, and then successfully market it to thousands embracing it as the latest expert-certified tool to insure harmony in a hate-filled world.

Proselytizing

This ideologically laden agenda is rarely straightforward, if even acknowledged. After all, if the anti-status quo mission were boldly stated it might create a firestorm of public opposition. Consider an early-grade classroom exercise offered by the Teaching Tolerance Project (1991) designed for children about to enter school. The lesson begins by announcing its indisputably high-minded purpose of inculcating a sense of fairness among youngsters so children learn how to balance their own needs with those of others. Thus far everything is perfectly commendable if not prosaic, points that might be preached prior to a team-based athletic competition—don't cheat, be a good sport, and compete as a team

The next step is the tip-off that something more is required than old-fashioned fairness: "encourage dialogue to identify social issues important to children" (48). These "social issues" are never explicit here since the emphasis so far is about discussions—taking turns speaking and so on. Nevertheless, after exposing children to how to talk about "moral and social dilemmas" (49), the teacher's task becomes "to expand the sense of fairness into a vision of justice…" This, the guide suggests, is achievable by involving youngsters in projects outside the school, for example, a day trip to a nursing home or homeless shelter, perhaps supplemented by collecting food and clothing for the homeless. Other learning possibilities include having social service professionals talk to children or constructing a bulletin board depicting "social/moral" topics.

Everything still looks absolutely harmless, even commendable, though critics might ask if these children have first mastered academic skills before having their social awareness boosted. To ideological outsiders, however, something is amiss. Most plainly, can grade-schoolers even dimly comprehend such "moral issues" as homelessness other than as deplorable conditions needing amelioration? Nor will children possess a full understanding of the inevitable imperfect settings under which today's impoverished elderly often live. A sophisticated appreciation—not just empathizing with "bad things"—of these quandaries may, moreover, exceed their age-related intellectual ability. Try imagining second graders wrestling with self-induced chronic alcoholism or dementia as "social issues."

It is equally improbable that teachers—let alone professionals formulating the instruction—can navigate solutions to thorny "moral issues." This is dumbed-down teaching and only acknowledges that life is imperfect. Discussions can only exhibit insipid feelings of cost-free compassion. How many teachers, for example, can relate homelessness to complicated zoning laws, laws protecting the mentally ill who refuse intervention, or community resistance to homeless shelters in their neighborhoods? Or the financial impossibility of providing resort-like facilities for the elderly poor? It exaggerates only slightly that when it comes to teachers and third-graders "discussing" these complicated policy issues, the well-meaning blind lead the inexperienced blind.

These "dialogues" will probably convince children that untold Americans suffer deplorable neglect, a conclusion that is indisputably correct. That at least some human misery is inevitable, and today's assistance may be all that is affordable given competing demands of equally worthy causes will, however, probably go unmentioned. Everything will be one-sided so what began as fuzzy "tolerance" eventually becomes a message that only federal bountifulness can (and must) reduce misery. Such is the nature of "fairness" and "tolerance" according to this ideological worldview.[4]

This hardly ends these artfully disguised liberal or even radical entreatments. Teaching for tolerance here can also mean promoting identity politics, hardly, one would think, a self-evident cure for cooling racial/ethnic antagonisms. In their "Affirming Identity" chapter, teachers receive hints on strengthening children's racial awareness, including affirming the beauty of varied skin tones. Teachers are further advised to bone up on racial awareness by reading scholarly books, an appeal that probably excludes *The Bell Curve*. Lobbying administrators to hire teachers of diverse backgrounds is to provide positive role models to minority students is likewise advised. How this possibly illegal employment measure assists student achievement goes undocumented, however.

Elsewhere a unit on gender differences (53-54) depicts how to suppress any trace of separate male/female identity. "Tolerance building" measures include having only "non-sexist" learning materials, forbidding any activity where only a single sex participates, replacing sexist terms like "fireman" with "firefighter" and allocating equal time to male and female historical figures. Especially important is combating the "hidden curriculum," ridding all learning of anything, no matter how seemingly minor, connoting clear sexual identity. One suggestion is to invite to the classroom people whose job confounds sexual stereotypes, e.g., female police officers. Needless to say, "policing" the classroom to stamp out sexism is a full-time job given natural sex-based behavior, including children's self-imposed segregation and conventional English, and may overwhelm even a competent teacher.

Another popular stealth gambit stresses reversing the "root causes" of intolerance, hate, and bigotry. The argument is absolutely simple-minded and remarkably sweeping in its implication, a trait that makes it especially alluring for those alarmed over intractable hostilities and inequality. In this cosmology hatefulness (intolerance) arises from a litany of deplorable (though, assumingly,

reversible) socio-economic conditions, so achieving tranquility-producing tolerance requires virtually remaking society. Now, almost any deplorable condition, real or imagined, is connectable to "hate" so bereft of any scientifically
demonstrated causal links, ideologues now enjoy carte blanche in selecting
crusades though, as one might anticipate, "root cause" menu choices are highly
selective ideologically.

One typical missive (Hurwitt nd) identified these "root causes" as urban decay
and overcrowding, unemployment, competition between groups and the loss
of economic status. As commonplace in this vacuous literature, just how these
conditions engender hatreds is never explicated—they just do! A more subtle
version occurred in a high school course dealing with, among other topics, the
consequences of intolerance (Fleming and Gilmore 2000). Here students discuss
African economic conditions with African poverty being a black condition, while
U.S. affluence is white. One of the suggested discussion questions was why
the U.S. ignored this deplorable war-engendering poverty. The lesson is vague
regarding whether the hundreds of billions of ineffectual U.S. aid to Africa was
considered or, indeed, whether (as some experts aver), this aid exacerbates strife?
Yet one more time, then, promoting tolerance becomes expanding government
ameliorative spending.

A clever variant of this "root cause" pathway is the everything-is-con-
nected-to-everything-else model, so we need to change *everything* to achieve
tolerance. Now, constant personal intervention, no matter how inconsequential
begets tranquility. As theocracies demand total 24/7 religious obedience, these
tolerance advocates demand a full-time dedication to respecting each and every
daily encountered difference as the price for harmony. After all, a haphazard
schoolyard insult or stereotype remark could, conceivably, instigate the next
urban riot, so better to expel every "bad thought" as a precaution.

Sara Bullard (1996, chapter 9) nicely illustrates the alleged interconnectivity
when she argues—citing an Indian poet—that, as in the physical world, even
the slightest personal act, even a private unvoiced opinion, brings worldwide
ramifications. Tellingly, the place to begin the conquest of world violence is via
self-transformation, a tactic oddly reminiscent of thirteenth-century Europeans
who believed that self-purification, possibly self-flagellation, would rescue them
from the Black Death. As she put it, "…by changing ourselves, we are doing the
only thing we can do to change the world. To say that this is not enough is a lack
of will, a lack of faith. It must be enough, for it is everything" (172). Identifying
"bad thoughts" as the root of all evil suggests an almost mystical (and danger-
ously one-sided) prescription for today's woes—just keep purging hatefulness
to achieve self-purification and one's adversaries will become friends.

There is also a penchant for ideologically lopsided examples. Commemorating
the contemporary civil rights agenda is, as we have repeatedly seen, the most
commonplace illustration of this tactic.[5] This instruction is not merely combating racial antagonisms or recounting historical events; recruiting adherents for

today's battles may be a more apt description. Students lacking any comprehension of contemporary civil right debates are subtly indoctrinated to believe that the entire civil rights agenda advances "tolerance." Reservations about racial preferences or the debilitating impact of white racism, then becomes, at least here, signs of intolerance. Recall how hiring more African-American teachers plus heightened sensitivity to black culture, sans any empirical evidence, are repeatedly heralded as solutions to race-based school strife. Elsewhere, sanitized, one-sided accounts of African-American political triumphs becomes "tolerance instruction" though it is a stretch to see how, for example, oft-violent police confrontations and boycotts promote racial "appreciation." Perhaps it is just administratively easier for partisans to avoid attention-getting, quarrelsome terms such as "black civil rights" when promoting curriculum revision.

The twisting necessary to conflate the official civil rights agenda to quelling strife can be amazing. Few unsophisticated parents, let along youngsters, will recognize the hidden ideological baggage. According to an account in the widely distributed *Teaching Tolerance* magazine, the absence of black students in one high school's advanced placement courses just reflects the low expectations of blacks coupled with white administrator bias. Moreover, this imbalance contradicts the school's otherwise noble commitment to diversity, which suggests that administrators were disingenuous. Nothing is mentioned, however, regarding study habits, motivation, or cognitive talent, let alone the logical disconnect between advanced placement and tolerance. And what might be the solution to this intolerance-signifying imbalance? Answers, true to form, include raising academic expectations, enrolling African Americans in these classes regardless of inadequate test scores, hiring more black teachers and counselors plus greater sensitivity training of whites (Walker 2004). Only the "intolerant" might suggest that AP enrollment imbalances might be tolerable as a necessary cost for having an achievement-driven society.

In other instances ideologues manipulate tolerance to condemn their political rivals not just for their ill-advised policy preferences, but for the far worse sin of undermining the very attribute—tolerance—sustaining our constitutional order. A masterful wordplay example occurs in *The Religious Right: The Assault on Tolerance and Pluralism in America* (1994) published by the generally well-regarded Anti-Defamation League. The book's foreword, written by Abraham H. Foxman, begins by praising religion's contribution to American life but, that briefly acknowledged, much of what follows links today's fundamental Christian views with a hateful, paranoid often underhanded assault on American political traditions. These fundamentalists, according to Foxman, want to replace our open, pluralist society with a Christian theocracy, not just roll back abortion or return prayers to the classroom.

How is this possible? Foxman contends that for many on today's religious right, tolerance and pluralism have been "…invested with sinister meaning amid the besiegements of modern life…" (iii), an assertion that is certainly accurate given, as we have observed, how tolerance has been manipulated to normalize homosexuality and other non-traditional values. But, of the utmost importance, what might "tolerance" or "intolerance" mean to Foxman? Could it be that Christian conservatives want to prosecute all deviants? Are Christian fundamentalists so mired in hate that they are unfit for democratic politics?

Since fundamentalists are generally innocent of harming anybody or even wanting to harm anybody (though they certainly disapprove of much), their intolerance "guilt" must be established by other means. The guilty verdict arrives by distorting the meaning of tolerance. To accomplish this goal, Foxman glibly defines tolerance as striving for equality (iv), and so, by implications, those who opposed leveling are not only intolerant but, as he makes explicit, they are attacking our traditional values, one of which is, ironically, religious freedom.

This is blatant sophistry in which tolerance is given an idiosyncratic (if not bizarre) definition so as to turn the tables on traditionalists who claim to be the true victims of a newly manufactured "cherish differences" conception of tolerance. With this "tolerance means equality" understanding in place, it is easy to characterize those who prioritize some values as "intolerant" threats to political freedom. In a nifty bit of banter, refuting one's enemy policy-by-policy is unnecessary. A person's view is *automatically* wrong if it rejects the equal legitimacy of all views. It is almost as if the Constitution now affirms "anything goes" (save, of course, hate) as our Supreme Political Principle. Thus, an opponent of gay marriage is not just ignorant of its benefits or irrationally homophobic; he or she hopes to subvert the constitutional order by insisting that some things—heterosexual unions—are better than others.

Finally, and plausibly of even greater significance is the quest to undermine the very legitimacy of rendering cultural and moral judgments. We have already observed how tolerance, combined with multiculturalism, condemns being "judgmental" as the most grievous "Thoughtcrime." Now everything is "different," not better or worse, good or evil, so one's sexuality, work habits, or speech pattern are just a matter of choice as one might select hamburgers over a salad.

This equality of everything assertion is obviously nonsensical; *all* societies hold some values as superior and, one might convincingly argue, preference ordering is hardwired into human nature. A society lacking common cement is oxymoronic; this is the essence of anarchy. Admittedly, much of what we prefer does result from learning and may fluctuate with passing fads. But, to suggest that deeply rooted practices, for example, family structure, erotic attraction, sexual roles, a proclivity for economic competition among other dispositions are "arbitrary," and thus any choice is no better than any alternative, and thus easily interchangeable, is nonsensical and certainly lacks empirical foundation.

If "equality of everything" is so out-of-touch with reality, what, then, do these proclamations intend? Will browbeating youngsters that no race is any "better" than any other quell interracial strife? Or close gaps in learning? Unlikely. A more credible (though unarticulated) motive is to undermine *existing* cultural foundations. Telling youngsters that "nothing is better than anything else, only different" defeats inculcating *any* culture, since acculturation *must* be about priorities. In a world where all values are inherently equal, and a proclaimed hierarchy only reflects power, not demonstrable worth, why should one embrace capitalism over socialism or heterosexuality over homosexuality? Why hold attachments to *anything* since nothing is better than anything else? This is a world of indifference where nothing is worth defending.

To the extent that a society built upon these relativistic foundations is unworkable, and probably Hobbesian to boot, given the lack of a common culture, why chase fantasies? The reason, we suggest, has zero to do with this alleged paradise; rather, the corrosive aim is to build a world with a *new* hierarchy. This is bait and switch of the grandest type though what this paradise promises is unimaginable, especially since a forthright blueprint would contravene the very idea of equality of everything. Still, a rough guess suggests the mirror opposite of today's world. There would be zero guidelines regarding sexual orientation, no sex-specific employment or family roles and, imaginably, no stigmatization of those craving unproductive leisure. People would, to invoke an old 1960s expression, "just do their own thing" and live peacefully ever after though, as in any society, not everything thing would be permitted. Who knows the punishment awaiting a parent who, for example, told his son not to be a sissy or counseled a Calvinist work ethic (would this be "parental abuse"?). A harsher description might be that this is a Marxist fairy tale, the communist end of history supposedly accomplishable *sans* harsh violence.

Teaching Tolerance for Homosexuality

The preceding analyses have focused on conscripting classroom lessons that generally pass unnoticed by the public and parents. Matters differ dramatically where "respect" for homosexuality is demanded. This is an exceedingly "hot button" issues when young children are targeted. Make no mistake, this is not just telling youngsters to ignore "odd" classmates, the traditional tolerance-based solution. Nor is this intrusion particularly pressing concern given that few youngsters can personally harass homosexuals. Rather, this is a drive to legitimize homosexuality, swathed in the rhetoric of tolerance, by portraying this sexual predilection as "normal" at a time when youngsters barely grasp sexuality of any variety. This quarrel is hardly an academic one: confrontations are real, and, ironically as so often is the case, their tumultuousness undermines the very social tranquility tolerance instruction is supposed to bring. Oscar Wilde once called homosexuality the love that dare not speak its name; today a more apt description is a love unable to keep quiet.

Presenting sexually explicit material to grade-schoolers predates today's infatuation with tolerance as respect. The Sexuality and Information and Education Council of the United States (or SIECUS) has made sex education almost commonplace, even state-mandated, in K-12 classrooms. Depending on grade level, topics routinely included birth control, masturbation, abortion, puberty, and ever so delicately, the "birds and the bees." The 1980s HIV-AIDS epidemic energized the mission, and youngsters soon graphically learned about "safe sex" complete with hands-on condom demonstrations. The instruction's key public rationale was health—preventing sexually transmitted diseases (STDs), unwanted pregnancies, even guilt, via the earliest possible intervention. Some states even required "safe sex" education to start in kindergarten. A public consensus on combating burgeoning STDs and teen pregnancy greatly mitigated controversy, at least momentarily.

Matters quickly evolved as leading liberal educational theorists took charge, and the upshot has brought ideological skirmishes galore. This new openness partly reflects society's growing sexual explicitness plus past failures to reverse STDs and teen pregnancies. For example, a recent SIECUS guidelines advise that by the time children reach the age of *five* they should be told that "it feels good to touch parts of the body." Also advised was that five year olds should be acquainted with same-sex physical attraction and that a "sexually healthy adult" will "affirm his or her own sexual orientation." Political counseling is also present—SIECUS hopes that their guidance will encourage citizens to exercise their democratic responsibility on matters dealing with sexuality, that is, support candidates endorsing this liberationist view of human sexuality (cited in Shalit 2001, 80).

Broaching the once "unspeakable" to captive grade-schoolers has pushed the envelop regarding classroom discussions and, predictably, this has opened the door for the homosexual agenda.[6] When it comes to advancing the gay agenda via the schools, the Gay, Lesbian, Straight Educational Network (GLSEN) is the vanguard. Founded by gay teachers in 1990, it rapidly expanded to a national volunteer group to protect gays (including teachers) in K-12. This loose alliance became a formal national organization in 1995 with a paid director and a sizable professional staff. Its explosive growth and triumphs have been remarkable by any standards. It boasts of partnerships with the powerful National Education Association and the National Middle Schools Association. GLSEN now holds national conferences while organizing some 2,500 Gay Student Association (GSA) chapters. Its high-profile activities included the well-publicized National Day of Silence in which some 2 million students and teachers in some 3,029 schools recently participated to alert educators of the presence of gay students. By 2006 there had been ten national Days of Silence. A similar notable "No Name Calling Week" is now underway to rid schools of taunting and bullying gays.

Many of GLSEN's activities resemble the tactics of countless racial/ethnic protective organizations. In recent years, for example, several localities and states have attempted to ban any supportive teaching about homosexuality (so called "No Promo Homo" policies) or prohibiting referring homosexual student to pro-gay groups for counseling. GLSEN has advised local sympathizers on how to challenge these measures (e.g., refute misinformation about gays and AIDS) and, occasionally sued to protect threatened school-based student chapters. Advocacy often entails protecting gay-friendly school materials by invoking First Amendment free speech guarantees or, occasionally, defending classroom discussions about homosexuality in terms of state-mandated "educate for life's experiences" statutes.

But, far more is involved here than just warding off alleged homophobic public officials. On the contrary, GLSEN's campaign stresses the incorporation of flattering views of homosexuality into the schools, a tactic reminiscent of the early civil right movement's "Black Pride" message (an explicit parallel). This strategy is light years from, say, defending students expelled simply due to their private off-school grounds sexuality. In 2001, for example, GLSEN commenced a campaign for an October Lesbian, Gay, Bisexual, and Transgendered (LGBT) history month, a time expressly chosen since this celebration would always occur during the school year. The latest GLSEN quest is to get school celebration of a "Transgender Day of Remembrances' (November 28) to acknowledge trans-gendered people's contribution so as to quell violence against this sexual minor-ity. (On this date a Boston transgendered woman, Rita Hester, was, allegedly, murdered due to prejudice.) Already students in New York, Colorado, Illinois, and Vermont have organized events to honor this day. Hopefully, according to Kevin Jennings, the GLSEN director, teachers can highlight the contribution of LGBTs to the history of Greece, the Roman Empire, China, and virtually every other civilization. Featured will be Alexander Hamilton, Eleanor Roosevelt, and other supposedly notable (though currently little-known) contributors to American history.

In principle, and this is undoubtedly intentional, this easy-to-satisfy stan-dard regarding who is gay (Alexander Hamilton?), and the modest size of a contribution needed to enter this Parthenon, guaranteed endless talking about homosexuality. Certainly there must be some gay mathematician (e.g., Allen Turing, a founder of modern computing, who was driven to suicide as a result of being prosecuted for his homosexuality), so his or her contribution can be heralded in algebra. More might be involved than perfunctory announcements. To insure success of the latest group appreciation month, sympathizers are ad-vised to pressure school libraries and local bookstores to create special displays, encourage public officials to issue official proclamations and donate gay-themed books to libraries. Ultimately, Jennings hopes, homophobia and heterosexism will become mere history thanks to new-found awareness of gays.

Legitimizing homosexuality under the guise of tolerance promotion has been remarkably adroit.[7] A critical first step is encouraging the publishing of books for children and young adults with explicit gay-friendly themes, and then promoting their classroom adoption. Those far removed from today's early education can scarcely imagine the published cornucopia. A recent GLSEN compilation, for example, listed some fifty-three gay-themed fiction books suitable for young-sters, most published by respectable firms such as Simon & Schuster, Random

House, Harpers, Henry Holt, and Houghton Mifflin. In addition were several non-fictional books, personal memoirs, novels, and picture books. One twelve-book series—the "Pinky and Rex" collection—is particularly noteworthy since it is directed at children just starting to read. The "gender bending" books tell about the adventures of two seven-year-old friends—a boy named Pinky (whose favorite color is pink) and a girl named Rex who likes dinosaurs. Pinky and Rex are clearly a long way from hyper-conventional Dick and Jane.

Like black civil rights organizations that have used litigation (or its threat), gay groups are increasingly turning to judges to impose their agenda.[8] In Kentucky's Boyd County Middle and High School both staff and students are now, thanks to a consent decree by the U.S. District Court, legally required to take sensitivity training "…on the subject of preventing harassment and discrimination on the basis of actual or *perceived* sexual or gender orientation" (italics added). Students who refuse to comply will receive an unexcused absence. A written research alternative (500 words, legibly handwritten and with footnotes) documenting the negative impact of sexual identity-related bullying may be substituted for skipping the training. A court created "Compliance Coordinator" oversees training sessions or research papers and will report on progress by Affidavit (*U.S. District Court v. Board of Education of Boyd County, Kentucky et al.,* 2006). This propagation of this gay-friendly agenda is, of course, exactly what GLSEN intends and while this Kentucky case is only a single item, this legal precedent can be universally applied given that some *perceived* homophobia is probably ubiquitous. More likely, the threat of possible GLSEN-inspired lawsuits will encourage preemptive training to avoid future legal bills.

Much of this agenda appears anchored in solid social science research, complete with handsome statistical presentations supplemented by numerous references to scholarly journals. As one might expect, the entire project basks in high-sounding rhetorical appeals unrelated to sexual behavior. That some of this to-be-accepted behavior may be illegal—even deadly given AIDS—and the age of the participants naturally goes unnoticed. Everything is upbeat and celebratory; a naïve person would have no idea from this documentation of inflicted harm what gays actually did to inspire ire; being a homosexual might even strike some youngsters as no different than, say, being a Methodist.

The GLSEN website's report on a survey of public attitudes regarding gay students is called "Talking About Respect" and includes the term "safe schools" in its subtitle. Instead of defending what might outrage many parents (e.g., endorsing underage same-sex experimentation), the agenda, we are told, is one of promoting mutual respect among all students, a vision consistent with the core American values of justice and equal opportunity for all. In fact, an uninformed outsider might get the impression from this report that GLSEN was nothing more than a school safety champion, not a group devoted to promoting certain illegal (given the statutory age of consent) or life-threatening sexual practices currently enjoying less than 100 percent public support.

The report's aim is to establish beyond any doubt that gay students are *seriously* at risk, and then by implication, that schools currently fail in protecting them. The National Education Association's "Task Force on Sexual Orientation" featured in the GLSEN's website speaks of creating a "safe and hospitable environment" for gays, and then explicitly defines this environment as one without physical, mental, or emotional threats and, critically, an environment that is welcoming, where gays are treated fairly. Harm, according this understanding, can come from stereotyping, bullying, verbal and physical threats and abuse, lack of acceptance and discrimination. This sweeping definition is reminiscent of how gay organizations sometimes define hate crimes, especially prior to a federal law enforcement standard—*anything* upsetting, including petty annoyances far beyond the criminal code, qualified as hatefulness.

This is a quixotic mission, if only because such allegedly grievous incidents indisputably occur, sometime, in some shape, to *everyone* who has ever attended school. Just growing up guarantees tribulations; not even the most authoritarian setting can insure perfect harmony. In at least thirteen years of schooling, everyone might been teased for fashion ineptness, body shape, brown-nosing, athletic clumsiness, complexion, accent, ethnic background, or hundreds of other ire-inspiring traits and, assuredly, returned the favor to teasers as part of normal verbal give-and-take. We are *all* both victims and culpable as evildoers. If this NEA manifesto were fully implemented every student should spend years in detention (or worse) for chronic hatefulness.

But, leaving unrealistic standards aside, are gay students so endangered, so threatened by rampant heterosexism, and school administrators so indifferent to their plight that such interventions as Gay History Month are indispensable? According to the NEA report, the answer is decidedly "yes," and the organization now sponsors a once every two year national survey to expose tribulations. The poll-created news is always bad: anti-gay antagonism in today's schools has reached epidemic proportions, schools themselves often instigated some discrimination and this traumatizes gays. According to GLSEN's statistics, in 2000 some two-thirds of lesbian gay bisexual transgendered (LGBT) students were at some point made uncomfortable due to their sexuality, 41.9 percent reported more serious harassment (21.1 percent of which entailed physical contact such as kicking). The 2005 update confirmed the bad news. Now three-quarters had encountered derogatory remarks such as "faggot," nearly 90 percent had overheard slang phrases like "you're so gay." Meanwhile, over a third had experienced sexual identity-related harassment and nearly a fifth had been physically abused (Snorton 2006),

This animosity, it is asserted, often leads to mental illness, self-endangerment, low self-esteem, self-injury, and poor academic achievement. The 2005 survey documented that harassed LGBT students had significantly lower grade point averages. Overall, most gay, bisexual, and transgendered students felt unsafe in their schools, especially compared to non-gay white students. Given that, according to GLSEN estimates, there are between 2.25 and 2.75 million gay students in American schools, the number of those at-risk is sizable and thus cannot be ignored.

Meanwhile the schools themselves stand by idly. The GLSEN 2000 survey found that 81 percent of at-risk students reported either zero or minimal teacher intervention to protect them from harm. Most alarmingly, a quarter of the LGBT students heard teachers or other staff members make derogatory remarks about their sexuality. Paralleling this hostility is discrimination against LGBT teachers. Though GLSEN cannot offer any firm statistics (a result of the murky nature of the issue, such as the fear of being publicly outed), it is nevertheless claimed that such employment discrimination is both severe and rampant.

On the surface, the evidence appears absolutely professional, particularly since the well-established Harris organization conducted the survey. The numbers of students interviewed only add gravitas to the indictment. The 2005 version involved some 3,450 students in a password-protected on-line survey; these anonymous "interviews" took about fifteen minutes. A separate on-line survey of teachers was also conducted and this "interview" lasted ten minutes. To the naïve, all the charts and footnotes suggest solid science.

The aura of neutral professionalism is a bit illusory, however. As was true when advocacy groups voluntarily compiled hate crime statistics, the instrument's very design, especially the sweeping definition of "hatefulness," virtually guarantees a troubling "the-sky-is-falling" picture. Every recollection of anything unpleasant becomes hatefulness data, no matter how fleeting or incidental. Put into technical social science jargon, these surveys make it difficult to reject the null hypothesis—insignificant antagonism. GLSEN, the study's sponsor, is, moreover, hardly a disinterested party since fund raising (which pays for the survey) depends on documenting crises. A more accurate description of the project is "advocacy research."

GLSEN's picture certainly does not square with what apparently agitates Americans regarding deplorable disciplinary conditions in many schools. Federal government data collected in 2003 regarding students hearing "hate-related" words over the previous six months found that "sexual orientation" slurs were exceedingly rare—a mere 1.3 percent of all students report encountering such affronts (NCES, 2004, table 14.2). Though these data are not categorized by respondent sexual preference, so gay students might, conceivably, still be inundated by abuse, but it would be odd if homophobic remarks overwhelmingly occurred totally out of earshot of non-gay students. One might speculate that the federal government has no ax to grind regarding antagonisms toward gays and is far more attentive to race and ethnic animosities.

Further add zero verification, even a (seeming) willingness to probe the possibility that antagonisms were avoidable or partially self-inflicted, let alone misinterpretations by the overly sensitive.[9] Keep in mind that the "defendants" in these accusations never receive their day in court and gays are almost by definition innocent victims. Plausibly, a rude though heavy-handed wisecrack might be construed as threatening belligerence though that was not the intent. Moreover, gays are not above "inviting trouble." LGBT students can readily flaunt their sexuality, wear "Gay Pride" buttons and similar provocative emblems. A more thorough investigation might reveal that much of what is catalogued as "homophobia" merely reflects the highly charged sexuality (especially vulgar insults) that colors today youth culture. A better account is that these offenses are almost inevitable when undisciplined, rowdy youngsters assemble.

The more telling case against this gay agenda does not, however, have anything to do with calibration incidents. Assessment flaws are really a sideshow though their existence helps highlight the devious nature of this battle. The primary question is, or should be, whether promoting this brand of tolerance represents the superior cure for these disorders. Even if we assume that society generally scorns gays, and that ill-will periodically erupts, and youngsters are really harmed by verbal slights, *will teaching students about famous gays, or holding a National Coming Out Day quell the petty insults or more serious taunting?* Is this remedy the cure for the homophobic disease?

Logic, even common sense, seemingly *recommend the very opposite.*[10] A dispassionate inventory of all possible cures would probably have "teaching respect" for a once hidden proclivity as nearly useless, a nostrum far inferior to such proven remedies as instilling decent manners. GLSEN's own survey data certainly fail to show an upbeat trend thanks to ameliorative interventions, and every reason exists to believe that matters will only deteriorate as gays purposely draw attention to themselves. GLSEN conceivably has it backwards—invisibility promotes tolerance. Specifically, as students increasingly "come out," targets for abuse only proliferate while the greater the number of students making a "big thing" of their gayness (gay pride), the more enticing they become for mocking. Going one step further, gratuitously inserting gay history and gay personalities at every classroom opportunity, regardless of relevance, would indubitably strike many students as convoluted and, possibly, an opportunity for ridicule, not the desired respect. Snickers (if not worse) are to be expected when an American history instructor announces, "Alexander Hamilton was bisexual."[11] Will LGBT students feel safer if their straight classmates know that the once-famous Jane Addams was, possibly, a lesbian? Will transgendered students complain if history books lack role models for them?

That this "cure" for homophobia is worse than the disease is hardly hypothetical. In countless communities organized efforts to mitigate alleged aversion to gays by upping "respect" has, as we would predict, produced the opposite effect—a divisiveness inflaming hostility towards gays. A June 9, 2005 *New York Times* with the "Gay Rights Battlefields Spread to Public Schools" headline summarized several "unexpected" conflicts. Partisans on both sides of the divide admitted that passions were at an all-time high, and sometimes resembled bitter election campaigns. The conservative Alliance Defense Fund has counter-attacked with its "Day of Truth" to oppose the pro-gay "National Day of Silence" (340 schools participated). In Montgomery Country, MD, the school board under pressure abolished the required eighth-and tenth-grade health courses since both openly discussed homosexuality. This was only six months after unanimously approving these courses.

As anticipated, the strife quickly spilled over into litigation and legislatures are now considering laws regulating teaching about "homosexual lifestyles." The Southern Baptist Convention implored its members to investigate whether pro-gay instruction has filtered into local schools, a call to action that can only bring lurid exposes and yet more controversy. In Cleveland, Georgia, school officials said that if a gay and lesbian club in their schools were legally required, they would abolish *all* school organizations rather than comply with this law (Janofsky 2005). The fire trucks seem to be rushing gasoline to the fire.

Nowhere has this battle been fiercer than in Lexington, Massachusetts where parental opposition to the teaching about homosexuality has escalated beyond what anybody initially imagined. It is a complicated and evolving tale, but the facts are fairly straightforward.[12] The place to begin is that the local school's diversity efforts include several books explicitly touching on homosexuality. In the "Diversity Book Bag" given to five year olds are titles like *Who's in a Family?* showing that "families" can comprise varied human combinations, including same-sex couples. Stories tell of these nontraditional families engaged in pursuits as ordinary as bathing a poodle named Daisy. Another book designed for first graders recounts two lesbian mothers helping their son choose the best color (there is none, he is told). By fifth grade, students encounter a heart-wrenching account of a family with "two uncles."

The trouble began when Allen Parker's kindergarten son brought home *Who's in a Family?* and Parker believed that this book endorsed homosexuality. As per Massachusetts law stipulating parental right to withdraw their children from sexually explicit instruction, Parker requested that his six-year-old son be excused from class. The interim superintendent denied this request on the grounds that these lessons were not about sexuality, but instead described varied family structures, though he acknowledged that a few of these arrangements were homosexual. After Parker personally confronted school administrators who refused to grant a release, the local police arrested Parker and charged him with trespassing since he had refused to go home until his son received an exemption from the lessons. He was eventually released on $1,000 bond and barred from school grounds. The newly appointed superintendent then made this ban permanent so, for example, Parker cannot see his son play sports or talk to teachers.

On the other side of the divide are various gay activists who, together with local clergy, organized a demonstration to support Parker's exclusion from the school. After a rally near the school, a block-long line of these pro-gay activists marched to Parker's house, many carrying signs with messages such as "Anyone

Can Go to School" and "Support ALL Our Children." Local gay newspapers and mass media have also fervently defended school policy, often accusing Parker of being opposed to families, children, and schools.

This divisive saga continued onward. The following year other parents—Rob and Robin Wirthlin—met with the principal of their second grader son's school over the book, *King & King*. In their eyes the book's message contravened their Christian religious beliefs and, like Parker, requested their son to be excused during discussion about the book. The story's homosexual element is hardly subtle. In a royal "romance" Prince Bertie, who is supposed to marry a woman instead falls in love with Prince Lee, also a male. The chronicle ends happily with the two marrying and sharing a kiss. According to the publisher, *King & King* affords parents an opportunity to "discuss differences in modern society" and how wonderful it is to start a family. Publisher accounts aside, the Wirthlins and others are suing the school since they were not properly notified, as Massachusetts requires, of their son's exposure to sexually explicit instruction.

The lengths to which school officials, not just agitated bystanders, are willing to justify gay-infused instruction are remarkable. The teacher who presented *King & King* actually claimed that the children themselves requested the book, which was not on the official curriculum, be read, an unlikely event in second grade. The school superintendent insisted that sexual orientations and homosexual relationships do not constitute "human sexual" issues as defined under Massachusetts law. He contended that the law (which he misquoted in his written explanation) only covered teaching about sex, and since this formally began only in the fifth grade, kindergarten discussions of same-sex relationships fell outside the statute. A few teachers explained that since gay marriage was now legal in Massachusetts, same-sex marriages were a settled controversy, and thus beyond debate, perhaps a akin to arguing about 2+2=4. Meanwhile the School Committee chairwoman insisted that since several same-sex couples resided in Lexington, schools had an obligation to affirm homosexuality for the sake of their children.[13]

The pot continues to boil. Several conservative-minded parents have departed Lexington and organized resistance has mushroomed. Traditionalists created MassResistance to carry on the battle and a lively website (massresistance.com) provides nationally syndicated columnists access to this drama. Opponents have countered with their website—www.lexingtoncares.org. Litigation has meanwhile attracted the liberal ACLU plus prominent lawyers from conservative-oriented foundations. Boston media and out-of-state radio stations have enjoyed a feeding frenzy with seemingly uninterrupted theater (including allegations that the children of adult participants were drawn into fisticuffs as a result of parental disputes). A delegation from the Westboro Baptist Church of Topeka, KS traveled to Lexington to picket the school to buoy up Parker and his co-resisters while the beleaguered principal now receives nasty out-of-state emails. Since many conservative religious parents are still probably oblivious to assigned sexually tinged books, yet more polarizing confrontations, litigation and ill-will are on the horizon. Local homosexuals may now, ironically, feel even *more* threatened as they become recognizable to outraged parents. This is, naturally, a far cry from the promised tranquility if schools only celebrate differences and behaved more inclusively.

Conclusions

Collateral damage is endemic to war, including wars of ideas. In today's skirmishes over tolerance defined as unambiguous acceptance of differences, particularly serious collateral damage concerns what we have labeled classic tolerance—bearing the loathed despite its odium. What Locke and Voltaire carefully explicated at great personal risk has been replaced by a glittering mish-mash of "theory" offered by devotees suffering zero consequences for flawed put-gasoline-on-the-fire admonitions. To exaggerate only slightly, tolerance has been expropriated to denote something virtually useless save as a rhetorical ploy. That the older, more constrained version performed so admirably to mitigate harm while the new rendering remains unproven further compounds the damage. It is impossible to calibrate harm, but it must be immense judging by its obvious failure and its knack for instigating the very pathologies it claims to heal.

This substitution is as unnecessary as it is deplorable. Though we clearly reject the radical egalitarian agenda with all of its ill-advised group identity in-fatuation and repudiation of merit, we can hardly demand expelling its advocacy from democratic politics. Linguistic thievery is a time-honored practice—"War is Peace," "Freedom is Slavery" as *1984* put it—but the tactic's commonplace nature scarcely justifies it. Nobody ultimately benefits from public discourse bereft of a clear, common vocabulary. If fans of normalizing homosexuality or relentless multiculturalism want to advance their agenda, they certainly can, but to insist that those who resist are "intolerant" borders on the illegitimate, a ploy akin to labeling a tax increase a tax cut. This deceptive cat can, and should, be belled. The outraged citizens of Lexington, Massachusetts have a huge battle awaiting them, and one element should be recovering "tolerance" from those who have hijacked it.

This is an arduous task that for good measure may appear an "academic" sideshow. After all, who desires to challenge adversaries over "mere" defini-tions? Will those urging impressionable kindergarteners to appreciate gay sex fold their tents and retreat if classic tolerance returns as the standard? Hardly, but that's not the point. It is more useful to see definitions as part of a "home field" advantage across multiple conflicts. Fans of legitimizing homosexuality, proponents of abolishing "white privilege" and others sharing this broad political cosmology, now force opponents to play politics within their own, radical con-ceptual framework. This is a battleground where, for example, those upholding merit can feel guilty when chastising the slothful about ignoring homework. Why should teachers see the inevitable self-segregation of boys and girls to be "a problem" needing a "solution"? Such are the rewards of having armies of academic theorist allies remanufacturing the English language while propagating an alluring vision of worldly perfection. Even before the mêlée begins, then, those upholding time-honored values shared by tens of millions face an uphill fight, and now must struggle to voice "old-fashioned" beliefs without being characterized as wicked Neanderthals. In sum, recovering tolerance and countless other once honored concepts from the meanings bestowed by today's pedagogues is hardly a trivial mission.

Notes

1.   Criminality and disruptive behavior among African-American and Hispanic students is highly sensitive politically and, not surprisingly, difficult to document precisely. The federal government's own data are circumspect, offering only the slightest hints of this problem. For example, while schools are subdivided by geographic location, there is nothing about the racial composition of schools and disorder levels. Nor, unlike criminal statistics for adults, are there data on race/ethnicity of perpetrator and victim. Nevertheless, patterns common for adults plus copious anecdotal data regarding the problems of largely black urban schools strongly suggest that school mayhem has a strong racial/ethnic component.

2.   Sol Stern (2006) offers an excellent though unsympathetic overview of the "social justice" ideology currently permeating education schools plus thumbnail sketches of the leading theorists (e.g., Paolo Freire, Bill Ayers, Maxine Greene, among others). The movement's popularity seems greatly enhanced by its overt anti-business agenda and total disregard for traditional learning though this learning, coupled with capitalist economics has long benefited the downtrodden. Jonathan Burack (2004) incisively depicts the movement's more general assault on western values, particularly its infatuation with "global education," one-sided accounts of the Third World, and the inherently oppressive nature of the West.

3.   The divisive antagonisms instigated by a seemingly innocuous program about a mild-mannered bunny and his friend, Arthur the aardvark, is ironic given the entire rationale of this programming is to promote "inclusiveness." At one point the secretary of education (Margaret Spelling) even intervened when she requested that the episode not be broadcast. In a column for the *Seattle Post-Intelligencer*, an openly liberal writer actually compared religious conservatives seeing a gay theme here as "...the same people who blamed gays and pro-choice advocates for the terrorist attack of 9/11." This statement equates the opinions of two fundamentalists—Jerry Falwell and Pat Robertson—with a large and heterogeneous movement and intends to ridicule as "kooks" those objecting to pro-gay classroom material.

4.   Picture an alternative universe in which alarmed educators decided that America had grown too anti-business. To build tolerance experts created lesson plans in which third-graders discussed the importance of profit and free markets, invited entrepreneurs to class to talk about crushing taxes and counter-productive regulations. Meanwhile, visits to factories were arranged so students could see how employment assisted the once destitute. Everything would engender tolerance for capitalism. Needless to say, this is unlikely to occur in today's ideological climate.

5.   Paralleling this infatuation with black civil rights as the very embodiment of "tolerance" is a near obsession with the evil perpetrated by whites. One noteworthy example supplied by Tolerance.org (http://tolerance.org/news/article_hate.jsp?id=403) lists some 350 dangerous "white power" bands worldwide. Given the fluidity of the music business and the obscurity of many of bands, this investigation represents prodigious labor to document white-based hate. Significantly, the website makes no mention of "hateful" black-oriented rap and hip hop music though this music probably outsells the white version and its anti-gay, anti-white, and anti-women themes are well-known, even deplored by prominent blacks. Finally, there is no mention of Islamic hatefulness though this, too, is well-documented elsewhere.

6.   The envelop surrounding the pro-gay agenda seems almost limitless. TCRecord, the online voice of the prestigious Columbia University's College of Education recently published, "Breaking the Gender Dichotomy: The Case of Transgender Education in Schools" (McQueen 2006). Though conceding that transgendered students were uncommon, the author still strongly pleads for including this category in the curriculum so as "…to remove the mystery, and as a result, the stigmatization of transgendered individuals." This would, purportedly, both boost the self-esteem of transgendered students while helping to break down strict gender adherence of those not transgendered. No instructions were provided, however, on accomplishing this task or how complicated physical or hormonal issues might usefully be explained to adolescents.

7.   A key tactic though not directly relevant to classroom instruction is awarding scholarly respectability to "gay positive" instruction. A sympathetic journal— *Journal of Gay & Lesbian Issues in Education*—is published by the academically reputable Haworth Press. Journal editors and advisors typically teach at mainstream universities, so published advocacy adds both academic propriety to inserting gay sensitive pedagogy while burnishing individual scholarly reputation. The latter creates instant experts available to testify in court cases or advise schools. Few upset parents, by contrast, will have comparable "expert standing," no small matter as judges increasingly rely on credentialed specialists to settle litigation.

8.   Litigation by gays may skyrocket as states increasingly award gays legal protection similar to that enjoyed by racial/ethnic minorities, the disabled and the like. One California gay student received a $130,000 settlement awarded under the state's Student Safety and Violence Protection Act when he demonstrated that students called him names about his homosexuality and teachers failed to protect him (Vang 2006). As is true for protecting schools against similar lawsuits, legal prudence dictates proactive measures such as enhanced sensitivity training, a costly tactic that will undoubtedly create an entire new industry. In fact, the student receiving the settlement has now become a professional counselor in this field.

9.   The popular stereotype of gay adolescents as frail, timid creatures may be, like all stereotypes, exaggerated. In 2003 New York City opened an all-gay high school, the Harvey Milk School, for supposedly vulnerable gays. The facilities were top-of-the-line, if not lavish and everything was done to help students feel comfortable. Unfortunately, students went on a crime rampage in the area's upscale boutiques and terrorized local residents (including stabbing local Starbucks patrons) until a new principal restored law and order. This is not to suggest that gay students are disproportionately crime-prone; rather, like all other teenagers, they are fully capable of mayhem and illegal behavior (Colapinto 2005).

10.   Consider, as a possible alternative, teaching gay students self-defense or, going one step further, hiring toughs to protect them. Now, fearing retribution, aggressors might be reluctant to harm gays. Though this strategy makes sense, it is obviously politically unacceptable since "everybody knows" that violence never solved anything and, more to the point, self-defense fails to advance the ideological agenda.

11.   Reducing leading historical figures to people identifiable only by their sex, sexuality, race or ethnicity will undoubtedly exacerbate already deplorable historical knowledge. It is easy to envision how, for example, teaching about Hamilton's alleged sexuality "crowds out" absolutely vital information on his contribution to the economy. Time better spent on his secretary of the treasury accomplishments now becomes wasted on "was or wasn't he?" A few students might unfortunately dismiss him entirely on the grounds that he, along with countless other "important" figures, appears in the textbook only because of suspected sexuality. Cynicism, especially among more perceptive students, is the likely outcome while many teachers involuntarily teach what they know to be false or unproven.

12.   Our account of these travails are drawn from several websites, most notably www.massresistance.com. as well as the site of the Boston Globe, www.boston.com. The local gay-oriented newspaper, Bay Online Window (www.baywindows.com) also supplied information.

13.   This rationale—celebrating gay family life is vital worldly knowledge—is professionally endorsed. Nancy Carisson-Page, an education professor at the nearby Lesley University in Cambridge, Massachusetts, said that perceiving gay families positively is necessary since youngsters might denigrate gay families when they encountered them unless first receiving contrary messages. She evidently assumes that believing in a hierarchy of family structure, not just holding gay families as inferior though acceptable, is wrong and, moreover, the ranking process is, in and of itself, harmful (see Crary 2005). Again, everything is just "different," not better or worse and rejecting moral relativism sets the stage for harm.

An Epilogue

The Man and His Two Wives

In the old days, when men were allowed to have many wives, a middle-aged Man had one wife that was old and one that was young; each loved him very much, and desired to see him like herself. Now the Man's hair was turning grey, which the young Wife did not like, as it made him look too old for her husband. So every night she used to comb his hair and pick out the white ones. But the elder Wife saw her husband growing grey with great pleasure, for she did not like to be mistaken for his mother. So every morning she used to arrange his hair and pick out as many of the black ones as she could. The consequence was the Man soon found himself entirely bald.
Moral of the story: Yield to all and you will soon have nothing to yield.
—From Aesop's Fables, translated by G. F. Townsend

It might be tempting to dismiss our critique of how educators have replaced "classic tolerance" with a seemingly more generous though ineffectual "appreciate differences" version. After all, this novel interpretation only adds yet another dubious item to an already overflowing national cabinet of injurious educational curiosities, so why fret over yet one more addendum. Skeptics will also note imperfect documentation regarding lasting impact so, conceivably, we—like those we condemn—are guilty of needless alarmism. And, as is true for countless modern-day pedagogical crazes, upbeat claims to the contrary aside, it may all come to naught as mystified students sleep through inane admonitions. Even opportunity costs may be trivial since wasted time cannot be better allocated to genuine learning given institutional ineptitude. In other words, might this damning appraisal be much ado about nothing?

These calming words contain grains of truth but much still counsels unease. The potential for catastrophe is immense and it is irresponsible to remain silent. This quest for "appreciate differences" tolerance is *not* your run-of-the-mill Ed School folly, and while the exact stages of this recklessness cannot be specified, the impulse indisputably gathers momentum. Devotees even sporadically convert otherwise hard-headed legislators. A 1991 Florida statute, for example, forbade teaching that any culture was superior while a 2006 California legislative approved measure would have banned any negative portray of gays in textbooks and other instruction material (Governor Schwarzenegger vetoed it on the grounds that adequate anti-discrimination measures already existed). Its seductive "feel good" therapeutic nature favors proliferation unless a concerted effort forces it back in the bottle and, as we sadly note, resistance has been anesthetized save few outraged parents disturbed over propagating homosexuality. There certainly seems to be no backlash, even misgivings, among professional educators.

To understand the almost insatiable quality surrounding this quest, consider more closely the campaign's core aim—achieving equality of respect. This is unlike typical tangible group-based demands, e.g., hiring more African American teachers, that can be concretely satisfied. It is a vague, inherently open-ended plea eternally beyond reach. Sensitivity, respect, appreciation, and all the rest are without limit, and may be purely psychological, so accomplishments are *always* temporary. Gays, African Americans, Hispanics, the disabled, the doltish, the obese, the HIV-positive, the ugly, the sexually unorthodox, and all others perceiving themselves as castigated outsiders can eternally plead for equal legitimacy, and the academic chorus can second the motion until Hell freezes over, but leveling is a daydream. No amount of classroom distortion can alter disconcerting plain-to-see facts while at least some of this craving may be closer to mental illness than a concrete political agenda.[1]

Nor can well-intentioned cordial politeness always satisfy voracious appetites. Minefields lurk everywhere and are often beyond anticipation, so the long-sought tranquil paradise will always be just over the horizon. Calling an easily upset person of color a colored person may, conceivably, trigger debilitating injury and lawsuits ("hostile environment"). And the list of budding claimants demanding "equal respect" is virtually infinite if officialdom (especially courts) rewards alleged hurt. The columnist John Leo once called this the victimization Olympics. To appreciate just how minor these "hurtful" slights can be, consider the following illustrations making their way to the news media:

In 2005 a Chicago parent of Hispanic ancestry came of the city's Board of Education to complain of the harassment faced by her children at New Lenox's Lincoln Way Central High School. Alleged persecution consisted of the children being called Puerto Ricans or Mexicans and being asked, "How's the landscaping business is going" (landscaping is dominated by Hispanics in the Chicago area). The superintendent assured her that the district had just instituted a new diversity training program (Brautigam 2005).

A Dallas, Texas parent complained to the director of a pre-school program in which her children were enrolled that the logo symbolizing the district's program was racist. The logo depicts a white child doing a cartwheel in front of the earth. The upset parent said that this portrayal was exclusionary. Though t-shirts, book bags and other items with the logo were already printed, the program's director said she would consider making the logo more inclusive (Stoler 2005).

Daniel Burke, the owner of the minor league baseball team, the Portland Maine Seadogs, commissioned a statue of a family to rest outside the stadium. The statue consisted of a father, mother and two children going off to watch the game. Nevertheless, despite Burke's effort to avoid controversy, the statue was denounced by the city's Public Art Committee as failing to reflect Portland's diversity—it was too white, "white folk on pedestals," in their estimation (Farah 2006).

In a Eureka, California newspaper column a lesbian mother complained of rampant hurtful homophobia and heterosexism. This even occured from people sympathetic to gays. As an example she offered an incident in which a well-meaning man incorrectly assumed that she was the grandmother of her daughter and the mother of her gay partner. The man, in her opinion, was guilty of heterosexism (Tharp 2004).

The U.S. Air Force Academy had been accused of fostering an intolerant environment, and this has been document in something called a "climate survey." Among the incidents of religious insensitivity were complaints from non-Christians that they were exposed to too many posters advertising Mel Gibson's *The Passion of the Christ*. A religious sensitivity program has been launched to combat this intolerance (Perry 2005).

Further imagine that applicable standard of "harm" are the feelings of the most sensitive person, even if paranoid or opportunistically motivated. Life becomes akin to a giant Rorschach ink blot in which "protecting" those perceiving disrespect or dangerous stereotyping everywhere must be shielded by a hyper-alert, full-time "tolerance police." Pity those teachers anxious to "make everyone feel good" navigating a possible link between terrorism and Islam in a school with thin-skinned Muslim students. The most incidental blameless remark, truth aside, can ruin one's career if a single Muslim objects. Or bring embarrassing demonstrations complete with "helpful" visits by outside agitators. This is a strife-generating nightmare, not paradise. No wonder potluck dinners supplant American history—no teacher is fired for serving maize and yam salad but the same cannot be said about inadvertently insulting Native Americans by mentioning their problems with alcohol.

The campaign's futility is not in and of itself the chief culprit. Pie-in-the-sky schemes always bedevil education and learning still, miraculously, continues onward. What is critical is that this pursuit may instigate ever sterner "soft" totalitarian measures, a sort of gambler's fallacy applied to social engineering: if a speech code cannot stop petty affronts, install high-tech surveillance equipment and if that, too fails, recruit spies. If victims still claim unhappiness, glib administrative edicts can "send the right message" by banning everything "harmful" though this edict may be window dressing. Recall how federal judges have now forcefully entered this quagmire to shield gays from insults. Eventually, education evolves into therapy while concocting behavior codes brings endless politicization. And, rest assured, only politically vulnerable culprits will be reprimanded.[2] Other failed, though far more violent, efforts to remold human nature to build a grand Workers Paradise immediately come to mind.

A More Serious Danger

Previous chapters catalogued a litany of costs flowing from this misguided campaign: corrupting the English language, conflating therapeutic mendacity with "education," engendering cynicism towards learning, exacerbating racial/ethnic tensions, substituting polemics for scientific research, fermenting needless civic quarrels, and, for good measure, squandering opportunities for students desperate for genuine learning. And let us not forget how some of these devotees attempt to normalize sexual predilections better kept away from children. This sweeping condemnation should be sufficient to doom this project, but, as is often shouted on late-night TV "infomercials," wait, there is more, and this extends far beyond graduating mis-educated youngsters. A truly dreadful paradox lies here, and tolerance proponents may abet the very Hobbesian world they think they are fleeing. In a nutshell, the erstwhile "tolerance" crusade is part of a multi-front campaign aiming to subvert national identity and the likely outcome will be dreadful.

The place to begin is to recognize that the United States' sense of political community grows more contentious by the day though, as the immediate post 9/11 reaction showed, political attachments remain formidable. Attacks are often conscious, ranging from a vocal "grievance industry" characterizing America as the embodiment of racial or ethnic minority exploitation to admirers of contemporary Europe's shallow nationalism. Others may view patriotism as "old-fashioned" if not "simplistic" and welcome a growing globalization so as to create "citizens of the world." A few may even conceive American nationality as little more than a temporary post office address in exile while awaiting repatriation to "home."

In this contest of rival affinities it is easy to overlook what is absolutely central: all political communities have elaborate boundaries, an "us" versus "them" demarcation, and without these lines, America is inconceivable. This is not just taste, as baseball fans might prefer the Yankees over the Mets. Nor is the current self-definition inevitable, as the Civil War demonstrated; a large heterogeneous nation-state is probably the exception in the contemporary world. Nothing is fixed in stone—tomorrow's America will be a very different place if most citizens simultaneously divide their loyalty with other nations (dual citizenship), some of which are anti-American, look to the UN for legal guidance, or reflexively assume that America endangers the world.

Today's efforts to undermine boundaries differ profoundly from the Cold War era when the enemy was Marxism. Contemporary adversaries are not akin to Soviet spies monitored by FBI surveillance or Hollywood film writers slipping in pro-Soviet propaganda; mischief-makers today are respected academics and mass media personalities totally innocent of criminality regardless of inflicted damage. This is a home-grown, self-inflicted war in which adversaries advance a "soft" anti-Americanism. That the targets are impressionable grade-schoolers only makes this crusade all the more insidious.

What is to be safeguarded? Admittedly, no single official compendium of attributes defining "Who we are" exists but certain elements are undeniable. Central are the primacy of national, geographically centered identity (versus, say, transnational religious or ethnic loyalty); the rule of law rooted in Judeo-Christian traditions; limited, decentralized secular government; individual, not group, rights; personal responsibility and autonomy; regulated free markets; pluralist democracy emphasizing public accountability, moderate, accommodating politics together with the right of peaceful dissent; a common English language-defined culture; and separate public and private spheres.[3] Disagreements and nuanced interpretations abound, and many would add or subtract attributes, but imprecision hardly certifies the absence of indisputable core elements. Nobody, at least currently, would argue that America should abandon elections or award self-anointed religious leaders legal authority over congregants. Or that we should surrender sovereignty to the UN. These ideas would, and properly, be dismissed as "un-American" if not "ridiculous."

Believers typically remain oblivious to their tenacious multifaceted identity until traveling abroad or encountering foreigners rejecting these values. Few can even articulate what makes us "us" unless forcefully challenged. Habits of mind, gut reactions, not conscious ideology, better describe attachments. Feel-good clichés aside, we are not all the same, interchangeable humans, all residents of a mythic global village sharing common aspirations and values. Those rejecting the idea of a distinctive American political culture should spend a year in Saudi Arabia or Zimbabwe and behave as if one had never left Kansas.

Prodigious, laboriously collected "baggage" resides in our self-definition, and it does not automatically arrive with birth or residence, and acquiring it is absolutely *subverted* when youngsters are authoritatively told that everything is just as worthy as everything else, and to pronounce some values as superior, is unforgivable (if not dangerous!) hateful intolerance. National pride, a conviction that Florida outshines Haiti as a place to live, is not chauvinism or jingoism though it may become so. Childhood represents a critical window of opportunity to inculcate the political culture, particularly deeper amorphous attachments. To squander it with banalities praising worthless ephemera (e.g., families come in all sizes and shapes) to quell nonexistent strife, while neglecting our own central virtues, far exceeds the costs of inattention to basic skills.

Make no mistake: this enthralling brand of tolerance promotes national suicide on the installment plan. *Soldiers will not die for diversity and inclusiveness.* Most pedagogues (but not all) may not intend corrosive outcomes, but it will happen. Schools are surely not the exclusive vehicle for indoctrination, but American education has historically played an indispensable vital role here and, at a minimum, it should not undermine this fundamental mission (see, for example, Berns 2001, chapter 4). As Stanley Renshon's overview makes clear, the government itself plus key cultural institutions such as museums have long neglected imparting patriotic fever at the expense of highlighting racial/ethnic divisions. Even pressure to master English—a vital conduit for political absorption—lacks government urgency. Indeed, since the 1980 census Americans have been unable to answer "American" when asked their ancestral identity (Renshon 2005, 57). We are plainly living off diminishing patriotic capital accumulated over centuries of conscious Americanization. At some point, unless replenished, this capital may be exhausted. The old adage you don't know what you have until its gone applies here with a vengeance.

A nation of illiterates might survive; enduring is unlikely for people devoid of national identity. Such people will not reject all attachments; that violates human nature. But, bereft of current collective consciousness they are highly unlikely to evolve into the imagined gentle, kind-hearted souls treating everybody, including same-sex bunny couples in Vermont, with equal respect. Rather, they will gravitate toward a hodge-podge of beliefs extracted from a medley of idiosyncratic sources, and the likely upshot will be a civic landscape that may resemble Bosch's horrific "Garden of Earthly Delights," or a "failed nation state" in today's political parlance. To insist otherwise is to deny the lessons of history.

Imparting an "appreciating all differences" tolerance offers a disturbing parallel with laboratory rats bred without any immunities so as to study AIDS. Such rats are "healthy" only to the extent that they subsist in a disease-free artificial environment which must be diligently maintained at great cost. America will not be so fortunate. Why should youngsters defend democratically formulated rule of law (to take just one example) from classmates preferring mullah-run theocracies if these practices are mere preferences akin to blue jean styles? Who wants to stigmatize as "dangerous" immigrant children who tell their classmates that blocking traffic is one way to reverse electoral defeats?

Unlike those who see impending doom from rampant homophobia, sexism, racism, and similar "Made-in-the-Academy" tribulations, our alerts are genuine. It is unnecessary to uncover menaces in textbooks slighting Hamilton's suspected bisexuality. The United States is currently undergoing a huge influx of newcomers, tens of millions, the bulk of whom have minimal affinity for our prevailing political ethos. If anything, most countries of origin embody the antithesis of what America represents, and even securing citizenship need not displace previously absorbed hostile dispositions. Modern technology, especially satellite TV, permits continued immersion in events back home while cheap jet travel can keep "old" national mentalities alive. It is, to invoke a hackneyed label, a "mosaic," but there is no guarantee that it will be a "gorgeous mosaic" if disparate newcomers reject our core civic values. We can quibble endlessly regarding whether this influx is "a threat" or "just a continuing condition" but no sane observer can deny that the situation will automatically solve itself. At a minimum, immigrant children cannot remain partially digested.

There is also a darker side to this influx: conceivably, a few disembark hating America, or become violently disenchanted when residing here, and might recruit "tolerant" natives akin to those "disease free" laboratory rats to execute their destructive intentions. The possibility of native-born converts to Islamic (or any other) terrorism offers a chilling example of what can happen to youngsters finding "soft" national identities insufficient. This is hardly hypothetical as recent terrorist plots in Great Britain plus mayhem in France and the Netherlands demonstrate. Note well: threats from the imperfectly socialized are hardly new or distinctly Islamic—subversive communism once flourished among European immigrants (many of them Jews) arriving during the late nineteenth and early twentieth centuries. Homegrown bomb-throwing Bolsheviks and anarchists did exist. America has *always* had problems, some real, some imagined, with newly arrived outsiders with questionable loyalty (Catholics, for example, were previously judged political subversives). Americans must be able to defend themselves against those bearing troublesome ideological baggage. To welcome immigrant enemies with "Diversity Makes Us Strong" signs at the airport, and happily tell them that their noxious ideologies are just "different" so as not to "cause trouble," concedes defeat. Such pleading may well be taken as a sign of national weakness and inspire yet greater hatred.

Necessary self-confidence to defend ourselves will not come via fleeing "judgmentalism" or refusing to distinguish good from evil. Setting a "good tolerance example" to sway adversaries by unarticulated osmosis is a cheap delusion. Mounting multicultural-flavored classroom skits to convince budding theocrats to embrace religious pluralism hardly comes with a money back guarantee. This quandary is, of course, a familiar one given that we are, correctly, a nation of immigrants, so optimism may be justified. Nevertheless, success did not arrive spontaneously and thanks to misguided educators, today's situation may become a gigantic case of political indigestion. But we can predict that civic absorption will cease if children learn that American stands for "we are all the same but different" and to "privilege" something over something else, e.g., affirming religious loyalty over patriotism, displays "intolerance." The exact opposite is true: a cacophony of rival loyalties only invites civic upheaval. If relativism should arrive under the guise of imparting "tolerance," it may be necessary to resurrect the almost forgotten "live and live despite the odium" pleas of Locke and Voltaire. And recall that these tolerance champions did not live in the best of times; millions were slaughtered, not just made to feel bad about themselves. Educators should be careful what they crave; they might just get it.

Notes

1.   The possible link between mental illness and sensitivity to insults should be important to those hoping to promote tranquility but it is an awkward, easily ignored subject. Conceivably, hostility might cause mental illness or, just as plausibly, the

mentally ill attract hostility. Or the process may be iterative. Serious inquiry is now emerging though causality remains murky. A sampling regarding Muslims is reported by Medved (2006).

2.   According to one recent almost tongue-in-cheek compilation, several cities including Missoula, MT. and Seattle, WA have classified themselves as "hate free zones" (though voters in Santa Cruz, CA rejected this self-designation). Supposedly on the drawing boards are "ridicule free zones" (Leo 2006).

3.   Among the many compilation of key American values, the most insightful is Huntington (2004, especially chapter 3). The classic depiction of what makes America politically distinctive vis-à-vis other nations can be found in Hartz (1955). A third version using modern polling techniques is McClosky and Zaller (1984).

References

Alexander, Gerhard. 2006. "Illiberal Europe: The Long and Growing List of Things You Can't Legally Say." *Weekly Standard.* April 10, 32-6.

American Heritage Dictionary fourth edition 2000. Online version. http://www.bartleby.com/61/31/T0253100.html.

Anti-Defamation League. 2006. "Extremists Declare 'Open Season' on Immigrants: Hispanics Target of Incitement and Violence." April 24. http://www.civilrights.org/tools/printer_friendly.html?id+42877 &prin....

AP. DailyBulletin.com. 2004. "Jury Convicts Claremont Professor in Staged Hate Crime Case." August 18.

APA Press Release. 1998. "Hate Crimes Today: An Age-Old Foe in Modern Dress." The American Psychological Association. Online version. http:// apa.org/release/hate.html.

Archibald, George. 2004. "Support of Gays Pushed in Schools." *Washington Times,* December 1. Online version.

Armor, David J. 1995. *Forced Justice: School Desegregation and the Law.* New York: Oxford.

Aronson, David. 2004. "Best of: No Laughing Matter." *Teaching Tolerance.* 26 (Fall).

Associated Press Release. 1999. "Conviction in Phony Hate Mail Case." November 21.

Associated Press. 2004. "Georgia Court Throws Out Hate Crime Law." October 25. Online at http://www.usatoday.com/news/nation/2004-10-25-ga-hatecrimes_x.htm.

Avery, Patricia. 2006. "Youth, Schooling and the Development of Political Tolerance." In, *Tolerance in the Twenty-First Century: Prospects and Challenges,* edited by Gerson Moreno-Riaño. Lanham, MD: Lexington Books.

Avery, Patricia G. 1992. "Political Tolerance: How Adolescents Deal with Dissenting Groups." *New Directions for Child Development.* 56 (Summer), 39-51.

Avery, Patricia G., Karen Bird, Sandra Johnstone, John L. Sullivan and Kristina Thalhammer. 1992. "Exploring Political Tolerance with Adolescents." *Theory and Research in Social Education* 20 (4), 386-420.

Ayer, A. J. 1987. "Sources of Intolerance." In *On Toleration,* edited by Susan Mendus and David Edwards. Oxford: Clarendon Press.

Bell, Jeannine. 2002. *Policing Hatreds: Law Enforcement, Civil Rights and Hate Crime.* New York: New York University Press.

Bender, Mary. 2005. "Civil rights organization consults shaken school district on tolerance; CORONA-NORCO: Its curricula on diversity will get boost from group's program." *Press Enterprise* (Riverside, CA), October 6. Online version.

Berill, Kevin. 1991. "Anti-Gay Violence: Causes, Consequences and Responses." In *Bias Crime: The Law Enforcement Response,* edited by Nancy Taylor. Chicago: University of Chicago Press.

Berns, Walter. 2001. *Making Patriots.* Chicago: University of Chicago Press.

Bierman, Noah. 2005. "Books for Babies Big on Tolerance." *Miami Herald*, February 23. Online version.

Boghossian, Naush and Lisa Sodders. 2005. "School Hate Crimes Spike." *Los Angeles Daily News*, June 19. Online version.

Brautigam, Charla. 2005. "Voice-Mail Fallout Still Roiling in Lincoln Way." *Daily Southtown* (Chicago), March 11.

Bullard, Sara. 1996. *Teaching Tolerance: Raising Open Minded, Empathetic Children*. New York: Main Street Books/Doubleday.

Burack, Jonathan. 2004. "The Sun Sets on the West." *Education Next*. The Hoover Institution. http://educationnext.org/20042/38.html.

Bureau of Justice Assistance. 2000. "Responding to Hate Crimes: A Police Officer's Guide of Investigation and Prevention." Videotape. Available by calling (800) 851-3420

Burke, Kerry, Austin Fenner, and Alison Gelendar. 2006. "Suspects in Chelsea slay tied to earlier thefts." *New York Daily News*, June 3. Online version.

Burns, Walter. 2001, *Making Patriots*. Chicago: University of Chicago Press.

Carnes, Jim. 1991. "Introduction" in *Starting Small: Teaching Tolerance in Preschool and the Early Grades*. Teaching Tolerance, a Project of the Southern Poverty Law Center.

Carter, Chelsea. 1997. "FBI Probes Georgia Insurance Scam." Associated Press, August 24.

Catalanello, Rebecca. 2005. "Student Event Touts Gay Lifestyle, Pastors Say." *St. Petersburg Times* (FL), April 13. Online version.

Cirone, Bill. 2001. "Moving Beyond Tolerance." *Phil Delta Kappan* 82:8, 635-36.

Civilrights.org. nd. "Hate Crimes: Why You Should Care." http://civilrights.org/issues/hate/care.html.

Clotfelter, Charles T. 2001. "Are Whites Still Fleeing? Racial Patterns and Enrollment Shifts in Urban Public Schools, 1966-1987." *Journal of Policy Analysis* (20), 199-223.

Coen, Jeff. 2001. "Hate Crime Reports Reach Record Levels." *Chicago Tribune*, October 9. Online version.

Colapinto, John. 2005. "The Harvey Milk School Has No Right to Exist. Discuss." *New York Magazine*, February 7. Online version.

Cowling, Maurice. 1990. *Mill and Liberalism*, 2nd ed. Cambridge, UK: Cambridge University Press.

Crary, David. 2005. "Behind the Flaps, Debates Flares Over Teaching Kids Tolerance of Gays." *Associated Press State and Local Wire*, February 2. Online version.

Crary, David. 2005. "Debate Flares Over Teaching Kids Tolerance." *Associated Press, ABC News*. http:abcnews.go.com/US/print?id=465171.

Creppel, Ingrid. 2003. *Toleration and Identity: Foundations in Early Modern Thought*. New York: Routledge.

Crespi, Irving. 1971. "What Kinds of Attitude Measures Are Predictive of Behavior." *Public Opinion Quarterly*. 35:327-334.

Daily Press (Hampton Roads, Va.). 2006. "Black Residents Gave Out KKK Fliers, Police Say." March 3. Online version.

Delgado, Ray. 1999. "Man Admits Inventing Racist Assault in San Francisco," *San Francisco Examiner*, May 8. p. A5.

Deutscher, Irwin. 1975. "Words and Deeds: Social Science and Social Policy." In *The Consistency Controversy*, edited by Allen E. Liska. New York: John Wiley & Sons.

Easton, Mark. 2006. "Does Diversity Make Us Happy?" Story from BBC News, published May 30. http://news.bbc.co.uk/go/pr/fr/-/2/hi/programmes/happiness_formula/5012478.stm.

Ellis-Stoess, Laura. 1996. Tolerating Tolerance in the Classroom. *Journal of Law and Education.* 25: 181-89.

Erikson Kai T. 1968. *Wayward Puritans: A Study in the Sociology of Deviance.* New York: John Wiley.

Farah, Joseph. 2006. "When Tolerance Means Intolerance." *WorldNetDaily.com,* March 13.

Farron, Steven. 2005. *The Affirmative Action Hoax: Diversity, the Importance of Character and Other Lies.* Santa Ana, CA: Seven Locks Press.

FBI. 2004. "Crime in the United States 2004" Available at http://www.fbi.gov/urc/cius_04/offenses_reported/offenses_tablulations/...

Ferrar, Jane W. 1976. "The Dimensions of Tolerance." *Pacific Sociological Review.* 19:63-81.

Finkel, Steven E. 2000. "Can Tolerance be Taught? Adult Civic Education and the Development of Democratic Values," Paper prepared for the conference, "Rethinking Democracy in the New Millennium."

Fish, Stanley. 1994. *There's No Such Thing As Free Speech ... And It's A Good Thing Too.* New York: Oxford University Press.

Fleming, Paul and Barry Gilmore. 2000. "Examine the Origins of Prejudice with Your Students." *Teaching Tolerance,* July. Online version.

Fletcher, George. P. 1996. "The Instability of Tolerance." In *Toleration: An Elusive Virtue,* edited by David Heyd. Princeton, NJ: Princeton University Press.

Foster, Julie. 2000. "California School's New Homosexual Curriculum: 2 Bills Take 'Diversity' to Classroom Effective January 1." *WorldNetDaily,* December 26. (http://www.worldnetdaily.com/news/printerfriendly-asp?ARTICLE_...)

French, David. 2006. "The Unending Hypocrisy of Campus Censorship." *FrontPageMagazine.com,* February 28. http://frontpagemagazine.com/Articles/Printable.asp?ID=21430.

Fryer, Milford. 2003. "Teaching Tolerance in Gonzales: It's a Start." *Sunday Advocate* (Baton Rouge, LA), November 16. Metro Edition. Online version.

Fulbright. Leslie and Heather Knight. 2006. "With More Choice Has Come Resegregation." *San Francisco Chronicle.* May 29. Online version.

Furi-Perry, Ursula. 2004. "Teaching Tolerance: Encourage Kids to be Open-Minded." *Parents and Kids: A Guide to Smart Parenting from Baby to Preteen,* December 17. Online at http://www2.townonline.com/parentsandkids/news/views/.bg?articleid...

Gaede, S. D. 1993. *When Tolerance is No Virtue: Political Correctness, Multiculturalism and the Future of Truth and Justice.* Downers Grove, IL: InterVarsity Press.

Gelinas, Nicole. 2006. "Crimes and Motives: Does it Matter How Violent Criminals Choose Their Victims?" *City Journal.* April 12. Online version.

Gibson, James L. 1992. "The Political Consequences of Intolerance: Cultural Conformity and Political Freedom." *American Political Science Review.* 86: 338-356.

Gibson, James. 1998. "A Second Sober Thought: An Experiment in Persuading Russians to Tolerate." *American Political Science Review* (42) 819-850.

Gibson, James and Amanda Gouws. 2003. *Overcoming Intolerance in South Africa: Experiments in Democratic Persuasion.* Cambridge UK: Cambridge University Press.

Goldstein, Joseph. 2006. "Produce: Youth's Use of Racial Epithet Does Not Mean Racially Motivated Attack." *New York Sun.* June 6. p. 2.

Goodwin, Kenneth, Carrie Ausbrooks, and Valerie Martinez. 2001. "Teaching Tolerance in Public and Private Schools." *Phi Delta Kappan* 82 (7): 542-546.

Gottfried, Paul Edward. 2002. *Multiculturalism and the Politics of Guilt: Toward a Secular Theocracy.* Columbia: University of Missouri Press.

Gray, John. 1992. "The Virtues of Toleration." *National Review,* Oct. 5. XLIV:28, 30, 32, 34-35.

H.R. 1082. 1999. "Hate Crimes Prevention Act of 1999" introduced in the House, 106th Congress, 1st Session, March 11.

Halberstam, Joshua. 1982-1983. "The Paradox of Tolerance." *Philosophical Forum.* 14:190-207.

Harp, Janet M. 2005. "Event Raises Scholarship Money for Gay Students." *San Bernardino Sun,* March 26. Online version.

Harris, Ron. 2004. "Bay Area Groups Seek Tolerance for Transgendered Youth." *Associated Press, State and Local Wire,* October 3. Online version.

Harsanyi, David. 2006. "Hate Hotline Puts Speech on Hold." *Denver Post,* May 15. Online version.

Hartz, Louis. 1955. *The Liberal Tradition in America.* New York: Harcourt Brace.

Heller, Carol and Joseph A. Hawkins. 1994. "Teaching Tolerance: Notes from the Front Line." *Teachers College Record.* 95:337-68.

Her, Luch Y. 2003. "Folks Just not Black or White; The Skin Color Project has a Winning Way of Combating Racism by Teaching Tolerance to Elementary School Kids" *Star Tribune* (Minneapolis, MN), September 20. Online version.

Herring, Hubert B. 2005. "There's No Shortage of Intolerance in the Workplace." *New York Times,* July 24, 2BU.

Holloway, John H. 2003. "What Promotes Racial and Ethnic Tolerance." *Educational Leadership.* 60:6, 85-86. Online version.

Hoosain, Sabina. 2004. "Teaching Tolerance/Forum at Clarence High Celebrates Differences." *Buffalo News,* January 7. Online version.

Horton, John and Peter Nicholson. 1992. "Philosophy and the Practice of Toleration." In *Toleration: Philosophy and Practice,* edited by Horton, John and Peter Nicholson. Aldershot, UK: Avebury.

Hull, Kara. 2005. "Educators Hope to Teach Children to Respect Other Cultures." *Associated Press State and Local Wire.* November 25. Online version.

Huntington, Samuel R. 2004. *Who Are We? The Challenge to America's National Identity.* New York: Simon and Schuster.

Hurwitt, Mara. nd. "Cultural Diversity: Towards a Whole Society." From the CCSF Teaching Tolerance Website. http://www.ccsf.edu/Resources/Tolerance/lessons/div01.html.

Hutter, David. 2005. "Play Puts Diversity Center Stage." *Greenwich Time,* (Greenwich, CT) December 22. Online version.

Jacobs, James B. and Kimberly Potter. 1998. *Hate Crimes: Criminal Law and Identity Politics.* New York: Oxford University Press.

Janofsky, Michael. 2005. "Gay Rights Battlefields Spread to Public Schools." *New York Times,* National Report, June 9, A18.

Jenness, Valerie and Ryken Grattet. 2004. *Making Hate a Crime: From Social Movement to Law Enforcement.* New York: Russell Sage Foundation.

Kanengiser, Andy. 2002. "Black Students Allegedly Behind Racist Graffiti." *Clarion-Ledger* (Jackson, MS), December 12.

King, Preston. 1967. *Toleration.* New York: St. Martin's Press.

Knight, Robert H. 2005. "The Federal Hate Crime Bill: Federalizing Criminal Law While Threatening Civil Liberties." *Concerned Women for America.* www.culture-andfamily.org/articlesdisplay.asp?id=9069&depart...

Kors, Alan Charles. 2000. "Thought Reform 101" *Reasononline. http://reason0003/fe.ak.though.shtml.*

Kors, Alan Charles and Harvey A. Silverglate. 1998. *The Shadow University: The Betrayal of Liberty on America's Campuses.* New York: The Free Press.

Kuklinski, James H., Ellen Riggle, Victor Ottati, Norbert Schwarz, and Robert S. Wyer, Jr. 1991. "The Cognitive and Affective Bases of Political Tolerance Judgments." *American Journal of Political Science* (35) 1-27.

Kurtz, Paul. 1995-96. "The Limits of Tolerance." *Free Inquiry Magazine.* 16:1. Online version at http://www.secularhumanism.org/library/fi/kurtz_16_1.2html.

Lawrence, Frederick M. 1999. *Punishing Hate: Bias Crimes Under American Law.* Cambridge, MA: Harvard University Press.

Leo, John. 2006. "Zoning Challenges Now Extent to Feelings and Belief," column in Townhall.com. Monday, August 7.   http://townhall.com/Common/Print.aspx.

Leslie, Keith. 2004. "Muslims Urged to Allow Teaching Tolerance." *London Free Press* (Ontario, Canada), November 18. Online version.

Levin, Jack and Jack McDevitt. nd. "Hate Crimes" Prepared for *The Encyclopedia of Peace, Violence, and Conflict* (Academic Press, 1999). http://violence.neu.edu/publication4.html.

Lewis, Tyler. 2006. Report: "Hate Violence and Rhetoric on the Rise Against Latinos." civilrights.org. http://www.civilrights.org/tools/printer_friendlycfm?id+43360$print.

Lintner, Timothy. 2005. "World of Difference: Teaching Tolerance through Photographs in Elementary School." *The Social Studies.* 96. (January/February) 34-37.

Liska, Allen E. 1975. "Introduction." In Allen E. Liska, *The Consistency Controversy: Readings on the Impact of Attitude and Behavior.* New York: John Wiley & Sons.

Lloyd, John. 2006. "Study Paints Bleak Picture of Ethnic Diversity." *Financial Times* (London), October 8. Online version.

Locke, John. 1983. *A Letter Concerning Toleration.* Edited by James H. Tully. Indianapolis: Hackett Publishing Company. Originally published 1689.

Losi, Gretchen. 2005. "Junior High Students Examine Intolerance." *Daily Press* (Victorville, CA), November 18. Online version.

Macedo, Donaldo and Kelia I. Bartolomé. 1999. *Dancing with Bigotry: Beyond the Politics of Tolerance.* New York: St. Martin's Press.

Malkin, Michelle. 2004. *In Defense of Internment: The Case for "Racial Profiling" in World War II and the War on Terror.* Washington, DC: Regnery Publishing.

Malkin, Michelle. 2005. "The Muslim Hate Crime That Wasn't." *Townhall Column.* July 6. http://www.townhall.comcolumnist/michellemalkin/printmm20050....

Marcus, George, John L. Sullivan, Elizabeth Theiss-Morse, and Sandra L. Wood. 1995. *With Malice Toward Some: How People Mike Civil Liberties Judgments.* Cambridge, UK: Cambridge University Press.

McClosky, Herbert and John Zaller. 1984. *The American Ethos: Public Attitudes Towards Capitalism and Democracy.* Cambridge, MA: Harvard University Press.

McCluskey, Neal. 2006. "Parents See Bigger Problems than Math and Science." *School Reform News,* 10:5, May 10-11.

McDowell, Josh and Bob Hostetler. 1998. *The New Tolerance: How a Cultural Movement Threatens to Destroy You, Your Faith and Your Children.* Wheaton, IL.: Tyndale House Publishing.

McGrath, Roger D. 2005. "End of the Rainbow." *American Conservative,* December 19. 7-10.

McGreevy, Kate. 2006. "Cyber Bullying on the Rise Among U.S. Teens." *School Reform News,* February, 10.

McNutt, Randy. 1999. "State Investigators Enter Miami." *Cincinnati Inquirer,* November 14.

McQueen, Kand S. 2006. "Breaking the Gender Dichotomy: The Case of Transgender Education in Schools." *TCRecord*. August 14. http://www.tcrecord.org/print-Content.asp?ContentID=12663.

Medved, Michael. 2006. "Does U.S. Bigotry Cause Muslim Madness?" Wednesday, August 16 column in Townhall.com. http://townhall.com/Common/Print.aspx.

Mill, John Stuart. 1947. *On Liberty*, edited by Alburey Castel. Arlington Heights: AHM Publishing.

Moreno-Riaño, Gerson. 2006. *Tolerance in the Twenty-First Century: Prospects and Challenges*. Lanham, MD: Lexington Books.

National Association of School Psychologists. 2001. "A National Tragedy: Promoting Tolerance and Peace in Children Tips for Parents and Schools." Press release September 15. http://www.nasponline.org/NEAT/tolerance.html.

National Center for Education Statistics (NCES). 2004. "Indicators of School Crime and Safety: 2004." Bureau of Justice Statistics. Online version.

Nichols, Sharon L. 1999. "Gay, Lesbian and Bisexual Youth: Understanding Diversity and Promoting Tolerance in Schools." *Elementary School Journal* 99:5, 505-19.

Nie, Norman, Jane Junn and Kenneth Stehlik-Barry. 1996. *Education and Democratic Citizenship in the United States*. Chicago: University of Chicago Press.

Oberdiek, Hans. 2001. *Tolerance: Between Forbearance and Acceptance*. Lanham, MD: Rowman & Littlefield.

Olson, Walter K. 1997. *The Excuse Factory: How Employment Law is Paralyzing the American Workplace*. New York: Martin Kessler Books.

Oskamp, Stuart. 1977. *Attitudes and Opinions*. Englewood Cliffs, NJ: Prentice-Hall.

Paley, Vivian Gussin. 1991. "Forward" in *Starting Small: Teaching Tolerance in Preschool and the Early Grades*. Teaching Tolerance, a Project of the Southern Poverty Law Center.

Pasamonik, Barbara. 2004. "The Paradoxes of *Tolerance*." *The Social Studies*. 95(5), 2006-10.

Paynter, Susan. 2005. "Tolerance is a Casualty of Anti-Gay Crusade." *Seattle Post-Intelligencer,* January 28. Online edition.

Pearl, Jonathan. 2004. "Considering Tolerance and Intolerance." *Record* (Bergen County, NJ). December 7.

Perry, Becky. 2005. "Cries of 'Intolerance' Stifle Legitimate Religious Debate." *Daily Texan,* May 5. Online version via U-Wire.

Perry, Bruce D. 2002. "Tolerance: The Fifth Core Strength." *Scholastic Early Childhood Today.* 16:2 (April), 26-27.

Pipes, Daniel and Sharon Chada. 2005. "CAIR's Hate Crimes Nonsense." *FrontPageMagazine. May 18. http://frontpagemag.com/Articles/Printiable. asp?ID=18108.*

Poussaint, Alvin F. 1996. "Forward" in Sara Bullard, *Teaching Tolerance: Raising Open Minded, Empathetic Children*. New York: Main Street Books/Doubleday.

PR Newswire. "Thousands of Schools Prepare for National Mix It Up Day." November 7, 2003. Online version.

Ravitch, Diane. 2003. *The Language Police: How Pressure Groups Restrict What Students Learn*. New York: Alfred A. Knopf.

Renshon, Stanley. 2005. *The 50% American: Immigration and National Identity in an Age of Terror.* Washington, DC: Georgetown University Press.

Rose, Mike. 2001/02. "United We Stand: Schools Deliver Crucial Message on Tolerance." *American Teacher,* 86:4, 10-14.

Rosenwald, Michael. 2002. "Many Teens Silent on Hate Crimes, Study Finds." *Boston Globe*. January 28. Online version.

Sack, Joetta L. 2002. "Calif. Parents File Suit on Gay-Themed Skits." *Education Week,* 21:25, 10.

Scanlon, T.M. 1996. "The Difficulty of Tolerance." In *Toleration: An Elusive Virtue,* edited by David Heyd. Princeton, NJ: Princeton University Press.

Schmemann, Serge. 2002. "The Nation: Us and Them; Burdens of Tolerance in a World of Division." *New York Times,* December 29. Online version,

Schmidt, Alvin J. 1997. *The Menace of Multiculturalism: Trojan Horse in America.* Westport, CT: Praeger.

Science Daily. 2006. "Young Children Don't Believe Everything They Hear." November 17 Available at http://www.sciencedaily.com/release/2006/11/061116114522.htm.

Shalit, Wendy. 2001. "Sex Ed's Dead End." In *Modern Sex: Liberation and Its Discontents,* edited by Myron Magnet. Chicago: Ivan R. Dee.

Skophammer, Karen. 2004. "Teaching Tolerance through Art: Art Can Make the World More Peaceful." *Arts and Activities.* 135, 16, 50.

Snorton, Riley. 2006. "GLSEN's National School Climate Survey Sheds New Light on Experiences of Lesbian, Gay, Bisexual and Transgender (LGBT) Students. April 26. Available online at http://www.glsen.org/cgi-bin/iowa/all/libary/record/1927.html.

Sommers, Christina Hoff. 2000. *The War Against Boys: How Misguided Feminism is Harming Our Young Men.* New York: Simon & Schuster.

Steinhorn, Leonard and Barbara Diggs-Brown. 1999. *By the Color of Our Skin: The Illusion of Integration and the Reality of Race.* New York: Dutton.

Stern, Sol. 2006. "The Ed Schools' Latest—and Worst—Humbug." *City Journal,* vol. 16, September, 42-53.

Stern-LaRosa, Caryl and Ellen Hoffmeir Bettmann. 2000. *Hate Hurts: How Children Learn and Unlearn Prejudice.* New York: Scholastic.

Stetson, Brad and Joseph G. Conti. 2005. *The Truth About Tolerance: Pluralism, Diversity and the Cultural Wars.* Downers Grove, IL. InterVarsity Press.

Steven, Rebecca and Jim Charles. 2005. "Preparing Teachers to Teach Tolerance." *Multicultural Perspectives* 7 (1) 17-25.

Stoler, Steve. 2005. "McKinney Preschool Logo Causes Flap." WFAA-TV, May 19.

Sullivan, John L., Patricia G. Avery, Kristina Thalhammer, Sandra Wood, and Karen Bird.1994. "Education and Political Tolerance in the United States: The Mediating Role of Cognitive Sophistication, Personality and Democratic Norms." *Review of Education/Pedagogy/Cultural Studies.* 16 (3-4) 315-24.

Tharp, Jamila. 2004. "Homophobia Hurts Everyone, Whether or Not You Are Gay." *Eureka Times Standard,* November 19. Online version.

The Religious Right: The Assault on Tolerance & Pluralism in America. New York: Anti-Defamation League, 1994.

Tinder, Glenn. 1995. *Tolerance and Community.* Columbia: University of Missouri Press.

United States Commission on Civil Rights. 2006. "Media Advisory—USCCR Report Examines Benefits of Diversity in Elementary and Secondary Education," November 28. http://www.usccr.gov/press/2006/0621128PressReleaseK-12.pdf.

United States District Court Eastern District of Kentucky Ashland Division, Boyd County High School Gay Straight Alliance vs. Board of Education of Boyd Country, et al. June 13, 2006.

US Department of Justice. 2000. Federal Bureau of Statistics. Available at http://www.fbi.gov/ucr/hatecm.htm.

Vang, Susie Pakoua. 2006. "Visalia Learns From Case: Gay Student's Suit Against Golden West Led to Changes." *Fresno Bee* (California), August 20, Final Edition. Online version.

Vernon, Richard. 1997. *The Career of Toleration: John Locke, Jonas Proast and After.* Montreal and Kingston: McGill-Queen's University Press.

Vitagiliano, Ed. 2005. "Children's TV Unites to Launch Pro-Homosexual Campaign of 'Tolerance': SpongeBob, Arthur, Pooh, Bob the Builder, Little Mermaid, Many Others Enlisted in Stealth Effort." *AgagePress.* January 10. http://headlines.agagpe-press.org/archieve/1/102005a.asp.

Vogt, W. Paul. 1997. *Tolerance and Education: Learning to Live With Diversity and Difference.* Thousand Oaks, CA: Sage.

Voltaire (François-Marie Arouet). 2000 (originally published in 1763). *Treatise on Tolerance and other Writings,* translated by Brian Master. Cambridge, UK: Cambridge University Press.

Waldron, Jeremy. 2003. "Toleration and Reasonableness." In *The Culture of Toleration in Diverse Societies,* edited by Catriona McKinnon and Dario Castiglione. Manchester and New York: Manchester University Press.

Walker, Tim. 2004. "Best Off: Something is Wrong Here." *Teaching Tolerance,* Fall. http://www.tolerance.org/teach/expand/mag/features.jsp?p+0&is=35&ar=516.

Weintraub, Benjamin. 2006. "Author Testifies in Hate Crime Case Says 'N-Word' Does Not Necessarily Imply Racism." *New York Sun,* June 8, p. 3.

Weisburd, Steven Bennett and Brian Levin. 1994. "On the Basis of Sex, Recognizing Gender Based Crimes." *Stanford Law and Policy Review* 7 (2), 21-47.

Weissberg, Robert. 1998. *Political Tolerance: Balancing Community and Diversity.* Thousand Oaks, CA. Sage Publishing.

Weissberg, Robert. 2005. *The Limits of Civic Activism: Cautionary Tales on the Use of Politics.* New Brunswick, N.J: Transactions Publishers.

Wilcox, Laird. 1994. *Crying Wolf: Hate Crime Hoaxes in America.* Olathe, KS: Editorial Research Service.

Williams, Bernard. 1996. "Toleration: An Impossible Virtue." In *Toleration: An Illusive Virtue,* edited by David Heyd. Princeton, NJ: Princeton University Press.

Williams, Walter. 1999. "What About Hate Crimes by Blacks?" *FrontPageMagazine.com.* August 22. http://frontpagemag.com/Articles/Printable.asp?ID3691.

Winseman, Albert L. 2004 "Values and Social Trends." Gallup Poll Tuesday Briefing, September 28. Online version.

Wise, James Waterman. nd. "Introduction" in *From Bigotry to Brotherhood: A Tolerance Reader,* edited by James Waterman Wise. New York: Council Against Intolerance in America. (Though undated the book is most likely from the early 1940s.)

WorldNetDaily.com 2006. "Illegal Immigration Sparks 'Race War' in Cities, Prisons." August 23. www.WND.com/news/article.asp?/ARTICLE_ID=51644.

Zaller, John R. 1992. *The Nature and Origins of Mass Opinion.* Cambridge, UK: Cambridge University Press.

Index